WHY NOT MODERATION?

Moderation is often presented as a simple virtue for lukewarm and indecisive minds, searching for a fuzzy center between the extremes. Not surprisingly, many politicians do not want to be labeled "moderates" for fear of losing elections. *Why Not Moderation?* challenges this conventional image and shows that moderation is a complex virtue with a rich tradition and unexplored radical sides. Through a series of imaginary letters between a passionate moderate and two young radicals, the book outlines the distinctive political vision undergirding moderation and makes a case for why we need this virtue today in America. Drawing on clearly written and compelling sources, Craiutu offers an opportunity to rethink moderation and participate in the important public debate on what kind of society we want to live in. His book reminds us that we cannot afford to bargain away the liberal civilization and open society we have inherited from our forefathers.

Aurelian Craiutu is Professor of Political Science at Indiana University, Bloomington. His publications include *Liberalism under Siege* (2003), *A Virtue for Courageous Minds* (2012), and *Faces of Moderation* (2017). He has also written book reviews and essays for non-academic publications such as *Los Angeles Review of Books*, *Aeon*, and the *Daily Beast*.

AURELIAN
CRAIUTU

Why Not Moderation?

Letters to Young Radicals

CAMBRIDGE
UNIVERSITY PRESS

Shaftesbury Road, Cambridge CB2 8EA, United Kingdom

One Liberty Plaza, 20th Floor, New York, NY 10006, USA

477 Williamstown Road, Port Melbourne, VIC 3207, Australia

314–321, 3rd Floor, Plot 3, Splendor Forum, Jasola District Centre, New Delhi – 110025, India

103 Penang Road, #05–06/07, Visioncrest Commercial, Singapore 238467

Cambridge University Press is part of Cambridge University Press & Assessment, a department of the University of Cambridge.

We share the University's mission to contribute to society through the pursuit of education, learning and research at the highest international levels of excellence.

www.cambridge.org
Information on this title: www.cambridge.org/9781108494953

DOI: 10.1017/9781108848855

First published 2024

Printed in the United Kingdom by TJ Books Limited, Padstow Cornwall

A catalogue record for this publication is available from the British Library.

A Cataloging-in-Publication data record for this book is available from the Library of Congress

ISBN 978-1-108-49495-3 Hardback

This book follows in no one's train exactly; by writing it I did not mean either to serve or to combat any party; I set about to see, not differently, but farther than parties; and while they are concerned with the next day, I wanted to think about the future.[1]

Alexis de Tocqueville

Contents

Caveat lector!

If you think you already hold moderate views and are happy with them, that's all good and wonderful, but you may still want to read this book. Although it is not addressed directly to you, you might still find in it a few surprising things, some of which might "trigger" you in the good sense of the term.

But if you are a young, passionate, and ambitious radical, this book is especially for you. For here you will find arguments that may challenge almost everything you believe in. These *Letters* invite you to listen to those who hold different opinions than you and are open to talking to – and learning from – you. Here you might also find reasons for rethinking and nuancing your ideas and commitments. You might even come across stronger arguments for criticizing or rejecting the beliefs of your opponents. And, if none of the above holds true, you might still find in these pages a few quotes and suggestions that provide food for thought.

So, open this rather unusual book, read it with a mixture of curiosity and indignation, and be prepared to be captivated and triggered at the same time. If you don't like its tone or ideas, do not close the book immediately; keep on reading and give it a second chance. Do not be outraged! Some day you might return to it with fresh eyes. But if you like something in these pages, if anything catches your attention and stimulates your thought, focus on that and ignore the rest. Whatever benefit you may derive from it, make sure to share it with others. Ideas do have consequences!

Above all, don't forget to reserve a bit of empathy (and mercy) at the end for the author of these pages. In our age of indignation, the publication of the book will (most likely) be regarded by some as an impious act or a bad joke. The author will be seen as too far left (and too "woke") by his ultra-conservative friends, and too far right (and quite "reactionary") by his liberal readers. He will pay a price for praising an unpopular virtue and taking to task young radicals for their illusions and rhetoric.

His moderation will be denounced as cowardice by some or as treason by others. The gentleness with which he treated his opponents and critics will be repaid with harsh insults, undisguised disdain, or sheer indifference. Those generous enough to concede the author's good intentions will claim that although he followed in no one's footsteps and tried (as best as he could) to see farther than all parties, the solutions proposed in this book are misguided, ill-advised, or simply wrong. Others will point out contradictions and exaggerations in his arguments, his loose definitions, and excessive name-dropping. Some will deplore his alleged arrogance and self-assurance, others his chameleonism, verbal pomposity, or lack of "manliness."

Although the author was careful not to draw any false equivalences or misguiding dichotomies, many will take him to task for criticizing the Left at a moment when a good part of the Right is still endorsing the "Big Lie" and promotes a nefarious Manichaeism and cult of personality that threaten the future of our democracy. Others will criticize him for being hard on the Right at a moment when the radical Left pursues a sustained campaign to realize a controversial vision of wokeness in all aspects of politics, culture, and education, and daily interpersonal relationships. The most zealous critics on both sides will warn that we should not try to apply the author's wrong remedies to our discontents because that would make our troubles twice as great.

Whatever the qualities and shortcomings of this book may be, read it as if its author is still searching for the truth. He, too, is a *homo viator*, who has to offer no definitive conclusions or positive discoveries, only hard questions and problems whose solutions must be sought in common. Where will he go from here? Where will he seek refuge? Nobody can tell for sure. All we know is that occasions sometimes appear when it is right to speak the truth and say: This is what I believe, this is where I stand, I cannot do otherwise!

About This Book

Why Not Moderation? Letters to Young Radicals is conceived as an imaginary dialogue with two young radicals – "Lauren" (from the Left) and "Rob" (from the Right) – who, unlike the author of this book, do not believe in moderation. Their voices appear in Parts I, IV, and V. Sometimes, I made them say what real journalists have written about the current state of our politics in various outlets from *The Jacobin*, *n+1*, and *In These Times* (on the Left) to *The American Conservative*, *American Greatness*, and the *American Mind* (on the Right). That is why their interventions occasionally contain quotations from those articles.

There is a close link between moderation and dialogue that must be highlighted from the outset. In a genuine conversation, no one has the monopoly of truth. There are no definitive answers, only tentative ideas and hypotheses, often presented in a playful way meant to keep our imagination and interest engaged. For this book, I have chosen an eclectic genre that combines imaginary letters and short essays with a more dynamic "question-and-answer" format in which the voices of the participants come to life.

A classic example of the first type can be found in Seneca's *Moral Epistles* addressed to Lucilius, Lord Chesterfield's *Letters* addressed to his son, or Rainer Maria Rilke's *Letters to a Young Poet.* Although these wonderful books set the bar very high for anyone trying to emulate them, they do not address political matters. In the past two decades, Basic Books has been publishing a series titled "The Art of Mentoring" that has featured a few books dealing with political issues. Two titles have been particularly useful to my project, although their perspective, focus, and format are different from the present book: Todd Gitlin's *Letters to a Young Activist* (New York: Basic Books, 2003) and Christopher Hitchens' *Letters to a Young Contrarian* (New York: Basic Books, 2001). Another short book might be mentioned here, whose message tailored to young scholars remains surprisingly relevant today: F. M. Cornford's *Microcosmographia academica* (1908).[2]

As for the second category, a good example of a (short) book that addresses political topics and follows a lively imaginary dialogical format is Leo Rosten's *A Trumpet for Reason* (New York: Doubleday, 1970) published two years after the events of 1968. With his characteristic humor and verve, Rosten engaged the ideas of the new Left and Right that, in his view, risked tearing the country apart at that time. The result was a short and witty work that simultaneously challenged the views held by naïve romantics, zealous militants, and shrewd demagogues.

The letters included in the present book start from epigraphs which have been carefully chosen to match the themes of each part. We begin from something that everyone can relate to – the present crisis of liberal democracy – and end with a few rules for "radical moderates" meant to show the reader that, appearances notwithstanding, moderation is a complex and difficult virtue that can helps us deal with some of our present challenges.

PROLOGUE

Why Radical Moderation?

We have now sunk to a depth at which the restatement of the obvious is the first duty of intelligent men.[1]

(George Orwell)

When George Orwell published these words in January 1939, Europe was about to embark on a dangerous and suicidal path. Restating the obvious was then the duty of all intelligent and decent individuals who sought to stop the avalanche of murderous ideologies.

Although written over eighty years ago, Orwell's words still ring true today. Restating the obvious – assuming, of course, we can still agree on what is evident (a big if!) – is again the duty of anyone who cares about the future of our democratic institutions and way of life. If we still believe in liberty, then we have the right – indeed, the duty – to remind the people of the truth they may not want to hear. Yet, telling the truth or admitting that 2+2 equals 4 rather than 5 may sometimes be a risky or revolutionary act.

This point is more relevant than ever in our post-truth age. We suffocate among self-righteous people who think they are always right and are full of fiery zeal for their own tribe and hatred toward outsiders. We gasp for air among individuals who blacklist and excommunicate those whose views they consider impure, dangerous, or unorthodox. Wherever we turn our eyes, we encounter many who are firm and confident in their beliefs and are not shy at voicing them loudly in the public sphere. These self-righteous confidants of Providence do not want dialogue, and dismiss those who embrace moderation as weak, lukewarm, and indecisive. They ignore that the latter may, in fact, be a sign and source of strength and lucidity and is a "radical" virtue suitable only to courageous and non-conformist minds.

But what does it mean to be a "radical" moderate? Can moderates be effective in politics in the present hyper-polarized and fractured political environment? Perhaps, as the *New York Times* columnist David Brooks put it, the greatest challenge is that moderation lacks "a magnetic idea."[2] Some equate moderation with treason, appeasement, and complicity with evil, while others believe that anyone who embraces moderation is condemned to be a loser. Be that as it may, moderation remains a notoriously difficult, complex, and elusive concept that challenges our imagination and is constantly misrepresented and misunderstood in public and political debates.

If you want to read a short book about *political* moderation, you will have a hard time finding one. This lack of attention to – and interest in – political moderation is not accidental; it reveals the scant faith many have in this virtue today. Yet, enlightened minds from the past, from Plato, Aristotle, and Cicero to Montaigne, Montesquieu, Burke, and Tocqueville, held a different view. They saw something valuable in political moderation that its present critics seem to miss. They praised moderation as the "supreme virtue of legislators" and "the silken string that runs through the pearl-chain of all virtues."[3]

It is not easy to recommend political moderation as a fighting virtue to an audience of young and restless radicals. They may want something else that has little to do with this virtue. At the same time, I also want to resist the suggestion that moderation only comes with being older and is suitable exclusively to older people. That is certainly not the case. Moderation has no lower age limit and is a virtue that everyone can practice almost anywhere and anytime.

I hasten to add that the moderation defended in these pages is a strong and muscular virtue which has several faces – epistemological, moral, constitutional, political, religious – and a rich tradition. As an eclectic virtue, it can be found on all sides of the political spectrum and contains both liberal and conservative elements. Properly understood, moderation is much more than the proverbial golden mean between the extremes. It is embedded in a complex institutional framework that includes, among others, balance and separation of powers, bicameralism, judicial review, federalism, polycentricity, and subsidiarity. Moderates are inspired by a few big ideas such as pluralism, solidarity in diversity, and dialogue across political differences. They seek to enlarge public sympathy for the common good and help solve deep disagreements in a civil and peaceful manner.

In what follows, I will emphasize the eclecticism, realism, and radicalism of moderation by resorting to a wide range of sources from philosophy, political science, literature, history, art, journalism, and, of course, real politics. The book makes a case for a bold type of moderation as a *fighting* creed, though not for everyone or for all seasons. We cannot understand what political moderation is unless we study both its synonyms (like prudence, civility, modesty, and compromise) and antonyms (like radicalism, zealotry, fanaticism, and extremism). In other words, it is as important to know what moderates stand *for* as it is essential to figure out what they fight *against*. The critics of moderation can often teach us as much as its friends, if not more.

I agree that merely thinking about moderation will not make us automatically more moderate, though it might help us realize its complexity and difficulty. In my view, moderation is an exotic archipelago for which there are few travel guides and no handbooks. Readers are invited to discover this rough planet on their own and at their own pace. As Montesquieu once put it, "there are certain truths for which it is not enough to be persuaded, but which one must also be made to feel."[4] Such, I believe, is the truth of political moderation.

In writing this book, I did not seek to serve the agenda of any party. Frustrated with the dogmatism, hyper-polarization, and immoderation that dominate our public and political scene, I set out to see "not differently, but farther than parties," to use Tocqueville's words. While parties are concerned with maintaining their influence or gaining power tomorrow, I also wanted to think about the long-term future.[5] The topics discussed in these pages reflect my own priorities and preferences but also take into account objections that may be raised against moderation.

I must emphasize that I use the word *radical* in a broad sense that is *not* meant to be pejorative. Like moderates, radicals – who must *not* be equated with extremists – perform an important role in our democratic society. They hold all of us accountable and keep us focused on our task. Does it mean, however, that we should reclaim political radicalism or utopianism?[6] I don't want to deny that occasional moments of radicalism may be necessary to stave off the decline of liberal democracy and reinvigorate its institutions. But it is essential to acknowledge that there are important nuances and differences between various types of radicalism, as the views of my (imaginary) interlocutors show.

At the core of *Why Not Moderation? Letters to Young Radicals* lie three strong beliefs. *First*, we may not afford to bargain away the liberal civilization and the open society we have inherited from our forefathers; instead, we must be prepared to fight for their values and principles and never give up on them. On fundamental issues such as civil equality, the rule of law, the integrity of elections, and the independence of the judiciary there can be no reasonable compromises with those whose actions endanger our democratic and free way of life.

Second, moderation can be found in many religious and cultural traditions, beyond the confines of what is known as Western civilization. It has a place in Christianity but also in other religions such as Judaism, Confucianism, and Islam. As such, it draws upon a wide range of resources and can have universal appeal across the entire world.

Third, to maintain our free way of life, we should burst out of our bubbles and echo chambers and work hard to rebuild civic bridges. Our task is to rediscover what unites rather than what separates us. To do that, we ought to have the courage to be eclectic and ignore "the arithmetic of easy ideological classifications."[7] That is why we should search for flaws in our own beliefs, not only in the ideas of our adversaries and critics. Only in this way, *sine ira et studio*, may we become aware of the reasonableness (and unreasonableness) of our opponents and grow less dogmatic and cocksure of our own views.

There are many who believe that the distemper of our times and the crisis of liberal democracy are too serious to be healed with gentle remedies like moderation which, in their view, is a mere privilege of the wealthy and the powerful. Young radicals are thirsting today for grand narratives and believe that unbounded enthusiasm and zeal can only lead to good outcomes as long as their intentions are pure. Yet, history invites us to be skeptical. Ardor comes in many flavors – some good, others bad – and excessive enthusiasm applied to political causes can often produce fundamentalism, extremism, and fanaticism.[8]

That's why we (also) need moderation, combined with prudence, courage, and justice, to save us from the zealotry and extremism of those who seek to impose their own views and ideals, no matter the costs. Although moderation does not have all the answers to our social and political problems, it provides a much-needed compass as we anxiously sail stormy and dark seas toward an unknown port.

PART I

THE WORLD WE LIVE IN

The life of the mind has quietly moved out of the way, making room for the terrible and pathetic encounter of the fanatic and the zombie.[1]

Alain Finkielkraut

Interlude

The Interlocutors

I FIRST MET "LAUREN" AND "ROB," two young students, at a lecture on our university campus a few years ago. The topic – challenges to liberal democracy – seemed interesting enough to them to spend a couple of hours reflecting on the trials of liberal democracy. They came with different expectations, agendas, and hopes. "Lauren" is a committed socialist who grew up in a secular family in Brooklyn. She joined the Democratic Socialists of America and was a great fan of the agenda of Bernie Sanders and the (so-called) Squad. As an avid reader of radical left-wing magazines such as *The Jacobin*, *In These Times*, and *n+1*, Lauren has been greatly impressed by the agenda of the Occupy Wall Street and the Black Lives Matter movements. "Rob" could not be more different. He grew up in a Catholic family in the upper Midwest and is entirely committed to traditional family values. He opposes same-sex marriage and is a faithful conservative voter. He, too, is an avid reader, but his preferred magazines are predictably different: *First Things*, *The Claremont Review of Books*, and *The American Mind*, to name only a few.

During the Q&A period, both students displayed a remarkable degree of intellectual maturity and passion for ideas. They asked pertinent questions about the limits of liberal democracy and proposed solutions to the problems we are facing today. After the lecture, we had a chance to chat and get to know each other. One thing deeply impressed me, beyond their interest in politics. It was their meager faith in our liberal institutions which, they believed, no longer hold any real promise for a decent future. The American dream, they argued, is unraveling before our eyes, and so are our hopes for a better world. When I pressed them further on this issue, they told me they never really had the sense of living in a genuine democracy, only in a fake one. Why did they believe that with such certainty and how did they reach that conclusion? What did they mean by "true" democracy? And how representative are they for their generation after all?

I dug into their favorite journals and media outlets so that I could better understand their opinions and perspectives. I was surprised to notice that for a surprisingly high number of young people today, liberal democracy is mostly a thing of the past. In their view, the old types of liberalism and conservatism have failed us, and we should not try to bring them back. What we need instead, they argue, is an entirely new political horizon *beyond* the old liberal democracy.

I share their uneasiness and restlessness even if I reject their solutions. We live in a world in which the fanatics and the zombies dominate the headlines. We all feel like adventurers at sea, sailing into the dark unknown, at the mercy of high winds. Is there any terra firma waiting for us at the end of our journey? To answer this question, I imagined what might happen if I extended an invitation to both students to join me for an extended discussion on the future of liberal democracy. What follows is our imaginary dialogue followed by a series of letters in which I have taken the liberty of developing the line of conversation to advance the purposes of my narrative. My goal has been to tell the backstory of moderation as a *radical* virtue and *fighting* faith very much needed today for the survival of our liberal democracy.

Can Liberal Democracy Be Saved?

Liberalism is the supreme form of generosity; it is the right which the majority concedes to minorities and hence it's the noblest cry that has ever resounded on this planet.[1]

(José Ortega y Gasset)

LAUREN: YOU ASKED WHETHER THERE IS ***any firm land at the end of our journey. That is a good question that also concerns us. For a long time, we have thought that this stable ground may be liberal democracy. Now many are wondering if it can be saved from ruin. Yet all this implies, of course, that the existing liberal democratic values, norms, and institutions are worth saving. This is something we are no longer sure about. Let me explain myself.***

Many of us sincerely believe that our contemporary world is bankrupt and has "the meaningless ring of a hollow drum and the odor of slow death."[2] Liberal democracy has failed to live up to its promises, and in many parts of the world it is retreating before our eyes. How are we to navigate then the troubled waters of our world if we stick to old political and economic dogmas? Isn't it obvious that we need a radically new way of understanding the forces at play? To be sure, there are many unknowns, but we can at least be certain of one thing. We must abandon all illusions and forms of narcissism and self-righteousness if we want to figure out the road ahead. "For only then will the deeper structural changes of a suddenly unfamiliar world come into view."[3]

I suspect that for you, the real culprits are the right-wing movements, parties, and policies that "damage democracies internally through their dismissive attitude toward core civil and political rights," and thereby "weaken the cause of democracy around the world with their unilateralist reflexes."[4] I wonder what your conservative colleague might have to say about the new world disorder and its causes.

***Rob**: We may disagree on the causes of the crisis, but we agree that the latter is real and cannot be ignored. Yet, we have a different view on who is to blame for the current decline of democracy. We are concerned about the extreme woke agenda of the Left that is leading us to ruin. Its politically correct form of identity politics and critical race theory emphasize what separates us instead of what can bring us together. The woke radicals are prepared to call racist anyone who disagrees with their agenda. They seek to dissolve our family and religious bonds and go as far as to call into question the legitimacy of our country. Isn't that obvious?*

I am not surprised that you offer different diagnoses of the present crisis. But I see you both agree that the current predicament did not come from nowhere. It has been in the news for a surprisingly long time.

Lauren: Has the world ever been in worse shape than today?

I wouldn't jump to conclusions so fast if I were you. You might be surprised to learn that the death of liberalism has been announced in the press on a regular basis for some time. Read, for example, an article published in the February 1900 issue of *Blackwood's Edinburgh Magazine* and you will learn that liberalism was already declared dead. The Tory author referred not just to the Liberal Party in Great Britain but had in mind liberalism as a political ideology broadly speaking. For the anonymous author, liberalism had to go because it is a bastard and superfluous philosophy. Three decades later, Mussolini claimed confidently that the liberal state was destined to perish and predicted the future would belong to anti-liberal forces and movements. I am sure that Vladimir Putin agrees with that today. Alas, he is far from being the only one to do so.

Moreover, the eclipse of liberalism was not a phenomenon confined to Europe. Many rushed to declare liberalism dead because it attempts to build a world with "order and justice without violence, a universal dream woven of sympathy, tolerance, a belief in the basic goodness and righteousness of man."[5] The defeat of Nazism in 1945 was a historic victory for liberal democracy and the open society in the West, but let's not forget that obituaries for liberalism continued to be published long after Hitler's disastrous reign became history. Hence, the recent vogue for proclaiming liberalism obsolete or dead is hardly anything new. That should make you think twice before proclaiming liberal democracy extinct.

Lauren: Why do you call it a vogue? Some claims are certainly more rhetorical and provocative than others, yet to dismiss them so casually seems imprudent and unwise. Moreover, how can you deny that the history of liberal nations is the history of systematic acquisitive violence on a large scale? This much is, I hope, uncontroversial, even though it is not easy to talk about it in the open.[6]

If anything, these pronouncements should remind us that the meaning of liberalism has always been ambiguous and contested. Indeed, few words have carried more divergent meanings than liberalism. The latter may have been the dominant intellectual tradition in the Western world, but it does not describe a unified ideology. Liberalism serves as an umbrella for a large family of theories created over the course of several centuries by diverse authors pursuing different agendas.

To give a few examples, the term *liberalism* has been used to describe various systems of governance. The list is quite long and includes doctrines, institutions, and policies as diverse as the laissez-faire of classical liberalism, the libertarians' "nightwatchman state," Franklin Roosevelt's left-leaning "New Deal," the social market economy proposed by the German Ordoliberals on the center-right, or Lyndon Johnson's "Great Society." There are great differences between these agendas that should not go unnoticed.

Rob: Did you say the Great Society? As you know, conservatives oppose liberalism precisely because it makes possible the excesses of the social welfare state, with its encroachments on individual liberty and its state-dependency. Moreover, many on the Right think that liberalism is a doctrine privileged by amoral and callous elites, detached from the real people and their interests. At times, some conservative thinkers have uncritically embraced liberal tropes (like individualism and individual autonomy) and we are paying a high price today for their blindness. That's why we need a novel form of conservatism that goes well beyond liberalism's main tenets and values.

Lauren: I'm afraid you might have the wrong target here. Isn't it obvious that neoliberalism has been the main cause of increasing

inequality and declining social mobility? Shouldn't neoliberalism be denounced as a dogmatic apology for market greed and low taxes? Doesn't it lead to a shallow way of life mired in materialism, hyper-individualism, and consumerism?

I am delighted that my words triggered you in the good sense of the word. It is surprising to see that for all your differences, you seem to share the belief that liberal values and institutions are rotten to the core and cannot be reformed. It also amazes me to note that when it comes to imagining a path beyond liberalism, the alt-Right and the radical Left share surprisingly many ideas in common.

A closer look at what came *before* liberalism might be useful. Think about liberalism's ambitious wager (as described by Ortega y Gasset) in a world dominated by civil wars and absolute governments. At the heart of liberalism, one finds several broad clusters of ideas and themes reflecting the challenges the world had faced in the past.[7] Liberalism presupposes a strong commitment to liberty and civil equality and aims at freeing all of us from coercive authority, superstition, violence, and cruelty. Liberal principles and institutions seek to regulate the ethical and material conflict and disagreement among different groups and interests in society. They rest on the assumption that, in the famous words of Lord Acton, power tends to corrupt and absolute power corrupts absolutely. Hence the idea that, most of the time, power must be distrusted and resisted through a judicious mix of principles and institutions (separation of powers, rule of law, etc.). Liberal principles affirm faith in human progress and reason and acknowledge imperfection and human fallibility. The stated aim of liberal institutions – at least on paper – is to protect the rule of law, people's rights, and dignity and provide a framework for tolerating minorities and protecting dissenters.

Now, it's important to point out that what makes the liberals' agenda original and bold is that they insist on pursuing all these principles simultaneously.[8] Many of liberalism's critics tend to see in the attempt to uphold all these principles at the same time a form of doctrinal incoherence. They take liberals to task for being confused and/or dangerous when they fail to deliver on any of these themes. I believe, though, that they may have missed something important. For liberalism's attempt to pursue all these ideas simultaneously and with equal firmness can be seen as a form of courage, strength, and endurance. It shows that far from being incoherent, liberalism is a "fluid, capacious even if not indiscriminate story" that displays "a recognizable degree of unity and continuity."[9] It is also based on a series of moral sentiments – remember Adam Smith's book on this topic – and fosters a distinctive political temperament essential to maintaining freedom and dignity in modern society.

Lauren: This may be so, but doesn't this conceptual fluidity reflect liberalism's internal incoherence and its greatest weakness? For the radical Left, liberalism is a utopian project that promotes the reorganization of international capitalism with the aim of consolidating the power of economic elites. We believe that liberal institutions are rotten to the core and cannot be reformed; they can only be dismantled step by step until a "successor ideology"[10] fills the void. What we need today is precisely such a new ideology that can replace liberalism altogether and successfully challenge its tradition of self-congratulation.

In my view, the problem faced by anyone declaring the death of liberalism is that the latter has not one, but several pillars and dimensions – legal, political, economic, and moral (or religious) – that must be kept distinct. The weakening or disappearance of one pillar would not be enough to declare liberalism as a whole dead. For example, conservatives may express skepticism toward liberal principles such as the commitment to individual agency and individual choice, while maintaining a firm allegiance to freedom of expression and the security of property rights. In the same vein, people on the radical Left may be skeptical toward unregulated markets or trade but they may also embrace at the same time other essential features of liberalism such as non-discrimination under law, separation of powers, and freedom of choice and movement. All these are *liberal* principles.

Keep in mind that liberals may endorse free markets and free trade but they often disagree with one another over how free markets and trade should be. As far as I can see, very few of them think they should not be regulated at all – laissez-faire is a straw man mostly used by liberalism's critics for rhetorical purposes –

or that they should be centrally planned by experts. Remember also that liberals differ over how strongly to protect property rights against competing interests and, more generally, they disagree about the size and scope of the state's intervention in economy and society at large. I prefer to regard these disagreements as illustrating the internal diversity and complexity of liberalism rather than its alleged decline.

Lauren: Isn't liberalism, after all, one of many "isms" of our political and philosophical vocabulary, and like all of them, equally polysemic and ultimately ambiguous, given its many facets and meanings? We need to be as clear as possible on this point. Emphasizing the internal diversity of liberalism may be a good thing and a clever strategy, but it should not obscure the centuries of global violence and dispossession made possible by liberal principles in the name of liberal ideals.

Rob: From my point of view, the problem is deeper than that. Conservatives tend to see the incoherence of liberalism as a consequence (or abuse) of Enlightenment principles, among which the belief in personal autonomy and the infallibility of individual reason come first. Perhaps they are right after all, don't you think so?

In this regard, it seems that you are in full agreement with your opponents on the other side of the aisle. Seven and a half decades ago, two German philosophers, Max Horkheimer and Theodor Adorno, while living in comfortable exile in sun-kissed California, far from the war front, wrote a book about the "dialectic of Enlightenment." They claimed that for all the open-minded ideals of the Enlightenment, its instrumental rationality had produced triumphant calamity, "a state of affairs in which the enforced power of the system over man grows with every step that takes it out of the power of nature."[11]

Today, on both sides of the political spectrum, critics of liberalism follow in their footsteps, whether they have read Horkheimer and Adorno or not, and sometimes unbeknownst to them. They do so when claiming, for example, that the liberal project is ultimately self-contradictory and unsustainable, culminating in the depletion of moral and material resources upon which it has relied for a long time, without being able to renew them.

And let's not forget those who speak about our contemporary "carnage"[12] that requires a radical change of course. The world they describe in their columns and speeches is dominated by crime, gangs, and drugs, mothers and children trapped in poverty in inner cities, and rusted factories "scattered like tombstones" across the landscape of our nation. They speak in gloomy terms of our country as a hellhole, facing a serious existential threat. Would you be comfortable in their company?

Lauren: Let's face it: "it's even worse than it looks"!*[13] *Consider, for example, the growth of polarization, extremism, populism, and tribalism that accompany the new fights over education, the critical race theory, the "Great Replacement" theory, and the rewriting of the past. Or consider the "don't say gay" bills, and the controversies about abortion and gender equality that led to the overpoliticization of some of our most sacred institutions such as the Supreme Court. It would be difficult to avoid the impression that our system has reached an inflexion point and has begun its inevitable decline. Why try to save then liberal democracy when it's plain that it can no longer deliver the promised goods? We should not be afraid to admit that "failure is an option"*[14] *when all the other possibilities are exhausted.

You may be surprised to learn that your ideological opponents from the Right share similar views. In a widely acclaimed book, University of Notre Dame professor Patrick Deneen offered a sweeping critique of the liberal culture and institutions. In his view, they create a political and social order that renders our world bereft of meaning. "The underpinnings of our inherited civilized order," Deneen wrote, "would inevitably erode under the influence of the liberal social and political state. … A political philosophy that was launched to foster greater equity, defend a tapestry of different cultures and beliefs, protect human dignity, and, of course, expand human dignity, in practice generates titanic inequality, enforces uniformity and homogeneity, fosters material and spiritual degradation, and undermines freedom."[15]

Deneen's analysis contains many other striking and unsettling statements, among them the claim that the real and serious problems we are facing today across the world, from excessive globalization to high levels of inequality, mobility, or social disruption brought forth by it, exist not despite liberalism, but precisely *because* of it. And not because liberalism has failed, but because it has triumphed. According to this view, the liberal faith in progress, diversity, and toleration is seen as the main culprit for the disintegration of national states, the decline of family life and traditional religions. Societies are increasingly fractured, institutions are weakened, and democratic norms are slowly being eroded. Social conservatives regard all these disturbing phenomena as "the direct consequence of the embrace of liberal dogmas as a kind of universal salvation creed throughout much of the West."[16]

Rob: And isn't that really the case? For many on our side, liberalism's agenda seems unsustainable in every respect. They don't believe that our present ailments can be fixed by implementing more liberal principles and values. The (neo)liberal road leads to a dead end. The outcome of decades of liberal bromides is "the metastasis of woke ideology," endorsed by an arrogant ruling-class oligarchy that despises the "deplorables" unwilling to swallow the neoliberal pill.[17]

It might surprise you to note that radical critics in both camps differ in many respects but they seem to share one belief: liberal therapies are no longer desirable or possible given the current political reality of the world. The Left points to rising inequality, environmental havoc, and deep polarization. The Right deplores weak or disintegrating national states, ruined families, and eviscerated religious traditions. All these critiques have as their target much more than the exclusive form of humanism that has allowed the knowledge of human beings to free itself from nature and turn against the divine. They worry that liberal principles based on a bankrupt philosophy offer unstable foundations and lead us to committing slow suicide, both cultural and demographic. To put an end to this self-destructive trend, to paraphrase Lincoln's words, we can no longer rely on the dogmas of the past, because they are inadequate to the needs of the stormy present.

But what if the critics of liberalism miss a big part of the picture after all? What if what they describe as a tragedy and irreversible decline is, in fact, the outcome of economic growth? This is precisely what a prominent (and provocative) economist,

Deirdre McCloskey, calls "the Great Enrichment." In her opinion, "the fact of the Great Enrichment is a crucial element in showing that humane true liberalism of the modern sort ... is good and enriching, in every sense."[18] If we adopt this view, then it is not possible to explain the rising and unparalleled material prosperity we have been enjoying in the last two centuries other than as an outcome of economic and political liberalism.

Why do so many dislike liberalism then? One hint is given by McCloskey herself. The propensity to see gloom everywhere may be a reaction against Whiggish history which tends to see steady progress everywhere. For reasons that may not be immediately obvious, many like to hear that the world is going to hell, although when it comes to economic predictions, pessimism has traditionally underdelivered.[19]

Lauren: Really? When a house burns – and there is no doubt that ours is burning right now under our own eyes – the firemen cannot stay passive. Ignoring the current crisis would be as irresponsible and destructive as a fire department ignoring a fire, allowing it to spread until it consumes everything, leaving behind a pile of ashes and smoke, poisoning the atmosphere and the land. We are literally running out of time. The fire is consuming us, and we must fight it with every useful tool we have. But liberalism, I believe, is not one of them. "Liberalism doesn't account for power, and the differential in power."[20] That is something we must never forget.

We should be careful not to embrace a caricature of liberalism. What distinguishes the latter from other doctrines is that no one version of the liberal outlook has ever became canonical at any point in time. Unlike socialism or communism, liberalism has no accredited Church, no standard liberal manifesto similar to Marx's *The Communist Manifesto.* There is no standard liberal Bible, although there are, of course, classical texts in the liberal canon that everyone refers to, from Locke's *Second Treatise on Government* to John Stuart Mill's *On Liberty.* In the end, liberalism offers a big tent for many different conceptions of the good life, in accordance with its commitment to pluralism, liberty, and individual choice.

Some have seen this feature as a weakness of liberalism, others as a strength. As for me, following in the footsteps of

Ortega y Gasset, I prefer to view liberalism as the supreme form of generosity. What do I mean by that? Liberalism, he claimed, is unique among all other ideologies because it is grounded in the determination to share the political stage with an enemy that sometimes is weaker than you. Not surprisingly, such a noble, paradoxical, and civil attitude took a long time to appear and impose itself. It emerged in the eighteenth century and developed into a full-fledged doctrine a century later.

In many respects, Ortega y Gasset was prescient. "It is not to be wondered," he wrote in the late 1920s, "that this same humanity should soon appear anxious to get rid of it. It is a discipline too difficult and complex to take firm root on earth."[21] If you think about that for a moment, you will realize what a unique accomplishment liberalism is (or can be), when it is true to its original intent. According to the latter, the majority, which has power on its side, concedes to weaker minorities the right to live on their own terms, thus announcing the determination to share existence with – and respect– those who have a different view of government and the good society in general. That is truly exceptional and unique in history, no?

Rob: It may be exceptional and unique, but not entirely in the good sense of those terms, and certainly not forever.

I admit that settling on this broad definition does not preclude acknowledging the existence of a variety of liberal languages that emphasize different things in various degrees: human capacity, privacy, individual responsibility and creativity, toleration, limited power, separation of powers, the pursuit of greatness and excellence, equality, equal respect and dignity, social justice, and so on. That is why contrary to what many radical critics believe, liberalism should *not* be identified with a dogmatic campaign for liberty and small government (laissez-faire capitalism). When liberals speak for liberty, they are not all standing up for the same things; the same goes for defending the individual and the free market.

That is why you may want to be a little more skeptical toward the wholesale rejection of all the values and ideas subsumed under the word liberalism. You should not forget that liberalism has had a hard time affirming itself and faced many critics and enemies over time. And yet, liberals have been determined to follow democratic principles even when they clashed with some of their interests. So, let's be generous and recognize that despite all these challenges, liberalism – or liberal democracy, as we call it – has worked reasonably well and managed to defeat its main ideological rivals: fascism and communism. It allowed more and more people to pursue their own projects without coercion and replaced unjust hierarchies with more fluid and fair ones. It made possible "a massive explosion of economic betterments for ordinary people."[22]

Lauren: This apology for classical liberalism begs the real question. In my view, McCloskey argues more like an ideologue than an impartial scholar; she gives a simplistic explanation why neoliberal ideas emerged triumphant in the last decades of the twentieth century. She fails to note that liberal ideas, beginning with the free market, have been used as a system of justification and legitimation of actual practices that have reconfigured global capitalism.

Rob: It seems to me that perhaps unbeknownst to you, you are making an argument against your own critique of capitalism. For it is the ruling class of our oligarchic regimes that plays a big role in the spread of the woke ideology. The latter is abetted "by the rise of a new socio-corporate 'private'-sector tyranny adept at wielding and weaponizing the most sophisticated communications networks ever known to man."[23]

I am prepared to admit that liberalism's greatest illusion has been to regard itself as the inevitable and historically ordained culmination of a long historical process. Any serious student of liberalism (and capitalism) must carefully examine what defects and imperfections are to be imputed to the liberal economic system rather than to other historically more or less incidental variants and circumstances. It would be absurd to attribute to the capitalist economic system alone the entire blame for the current overpopulation, the armaments race, the world wars, inflation, revolution, and mass epidemics of all kinds. On the contrary, as Karl Popper and others have remarked, over time, in the part of the world where liberal principles existed, many of life's greatest challenges and evils, including slavery, poverty, unemployment, race, class, and religious discrimination, have been eliminated or greatly ameliorated.[24]

Lauren: If Karl Popper said it, it doesn't mean that we should accept his assessment as a dogma, no?

Of course not! But what he says should make you think about what liberal policies have achieved over time. There is another important point you may want to keep in mind when judging liberalism's successes and failures. Today, when the liberal system is attacked from all sides, it is distorted by a host of initiatives and interventions that interfere with the complex economic structure of modern society (tariffs, regulations, premiums, subventions, etc.) and alter the logic of competition and the functioning of the free market. In truth, many economic liberals have insisted that, left to itself, the market cannot generate its own moral prerequisites autonomously. Liberals understand that these conditions are *beyond* the realm of the economic exchanges and transcend the sphere of the market. They presuppose a set of fundamental "bourgeois virtues"[25] such as prudence, thrift, courage, respect for tradition, a sense of duty, civic-mindedness, propriety, and honesty, to name only a few. Without them, there can be no genuine and effective free market.

In reality, as the German economist Wilhelm Röpke so well put it, the vital things that give meaning, dignity, beauty, and richness to life will always be *beyond* the supply and demand of the market and the sphere of private property. "Man simply does not live by radio, automobiles, and refrigerators alone," Röpke wrote, "but by the whole unpurchasable world beyond the market and turnover figures, the world of dignity, beauty, poetry, grace, chivalry, love, and friendship. The world of community, variety of life, freedom, and fullness of personality."[26]

Lauren: I am still struggling to figure out how anyone can defend in good conscience a heartless system which simultaneously produces so much misery along with so much wealth. Moreover, since the liberal understanding of liberty is purely Western, it is alien to non-Western civilizations and cultures and, most of the time, unfriendly toward them. Do you have anything to say about that?

To be sure, there is a long debate on this issue. To all those who think of liberalism as extinct and incapable of renewal, I want to say the following. Before we try to relinquish the extra cargo, we should be clear in our minds as to what constitutes the cargo itself. For it includes many valuable things without which the existence of our free societies would be unimaginable: separation and balance of powers, the rule of law, equal justice under the laws, toleration, value pluralism, inalienable individual rights, economic liberty, the sanctity of the private sphere and property, the recognition of the equal dignity of all individuals, the belief in reason, freedom of thought, freedom of opinion and press, fair play, discussion and debate (in lieu of violence), trial by jury, publicity of proceedings, opposition to arbitrary power and fanaticism (religious, political, moral). Again, these are not merely Western values – they are values and principles embraced and praised throughout a good part of the world. That all these ideals would come to be seen one day as obsolete should greatly concern us.

Rob: One might reach precisely the opposite conclusion from your argument. These are old ideals that must now be replaced by new ones.

Never forget that maintaining our civilization is an endless and complex task, one that requires fine tuning and judicious reforms. From its early days, liberalism made a bold bid, namely that we can live according to the principles of reason that we can all embrace, solve our differences through rational debate, public argument, and compromise, limit power, avoid violence, and combine liberty and equal dignity. This is, I am sure you will agree with me, an ambitious wager, and one that it is likely to inspire and frustrate at the same time.

Granted, liberalism's critics have the right to be disappointed, but they must also provide a fair balance sheet. They may not rely on a caricature of liberal principles that distorts their nature and minimizes their contribution to the maintenance of our open societies. To claim that communism and liberal democracy "stem from the same root," that is, from the same inclination of modern individuals to assert their autonomy and proclaim it as the supreme good, is an obvious exaggeration that should not go unchallenged.[27] It is alarming that so many intellectuals no longer seem to see the merits of the liberal system that allows them to speak, think, and move freely.

Rob: You began by reminding us of the great transformation that occurred in 1989. The fall of communism had important unintended consequences, good ones as well as not so good ones. It has left liberalism without a global rival against which it could compete and define itself. Perhaps that is the main reason why liberalism has lost much of its steam in the last decades and is in deep crisis today. Don't you think so?

Maybe. But let's not be too quick to announce the final hours of liberalism; remember that it had managed to triumph over its rivals (communism and fascism) in darker times. Moreover, keep in mind that liberalism is a project that has not been – and can never be – *fully* completed. But let's not delude ourselves and believe that we might be able to solve our problems *only* with liberal ideas and principles. We shall not be able to properly address our dilemmas if we discard liberalism altogether. Liberal principles and ideas need to compete with their rivals and critics.

Lauren: This may be so. Yet, looking at the world right now, it is hard not to believe that liberalism has outlived its purpose in a world in which the free market is expected to function as an infallible guide for all spheres of life, as the sole director of the fate of human beings and their natural environment.

Rob: I endorse your conclusion – liberalism has outlived its purpose and must be replaced now – but for entirely different reasons than you. One could say that liberal democracy, at least in its present form, offers a more insidious ideological mystification of reality than communism did decades ago; hence, it is as dangerous as the latter, if not more so.[28]

Oddly, this is exactly what Vladimir Putin said in an interview with the *Financial Times* in June 2019.[29] Obviously, he is not an unbiased observer, and his words should not be taken at face value. Our current situation is quite concerning, but it has not – or at least not yet – sunk to the depth of the crises that engulfed Europe in the interwar period. It is interesting to remember what Röpke thought about intellectuals in Germany in 1933. "Rarely in history," he said, "has a group of people been so busy helping to saw off the branch on which they sit."[30] That statement was made on February 8, 1933, a little over a week after Hitler had been appointed Chancellor on January 30. The rest is history.

It is not difficult to resonate with Röpke's words today when liberal democracy is again under assault. Liberal principles have created the free and open society that most of us in the West take for granted. They have brought with them a level of freedom and prosperity unparalleled in human history. To reject liberal democracy as an insidious form of inverted totalitarianism, especially in this hour of crisis, would amount to sawing off the branch upon which we all sit, some more comfortably than others. It would amount to "attacking the imperishable through the perishable"[31] and throwing away the precious cargo that made possible the best of what civilization has to offer.

Lauren: I still don't get what all this has to do with our critique of liberalism from the Left.

In the end, it is important to remember that liberal democracy does not promise any ready-made solutions to our problems and cannot deliver any panacea. Liberal principles should not be viewed as a shorthand for guaranteed bliss, nor are they, with their insistence on universal rights, a purely utopian project. The truth is that liberal democracy will always be accompanied by the legitimate doubts we feel about its progress, but those doubts should not cause us to fall into despair. They ought to help us find the best means of maintaining and improving our open societies. As a wise commentator once put it, "after everything that liberalism endured and survived, after the unimaginably savage assaults of fascism and communism, we must steadfastly fight for it all over again, and we must begin again at the beginning."[32] There is simply no other choice.

Perpetually contested, liberal democracy is in constant need of being reinvented and saved. That is why I would like to end our conversation for now by quoting Mahatma Gandhi's apocryphal response to the question what he thought about Western civilization. After pausing for a moment, Gandhi is reported to have said: "It would be a good idea." This time, let's apply the same words, slightly amended, to liberal democracy itself. It, too, would be a truly great idea if only we were prepared to fight for it.

PART II

WHAT KIND OF VIRTUE IS MODERATION?

There is nothing therefore in the world more wholesome, or more necessary for us to learne, then this gracious lesson of moderation. . . . This is the centre, wherein all both divine, and morall philosophy meet; the rule of life, the governesse of manners, the silken string that runs through the pearl-chain of all vertues, the very Ecliptick line, under which reason and religion move without any deviation: and therefore most worthy of our best thoughts, of our most careful observance.[1]

Joseph Hall

Interlude

AS I WAS REREADING THE LAST EXCHANGES, I realized that an important idea had been left out of our conversation. It is possible to think of moderation as expressing a genuine and firm commitment to an inclusive vision of a *decent* society, with its own values, rules, procedures, and institutions. It is this sense of moderation that I seek to outline in the following pages. Yet, before I attempt to describe the political vision and ethos of moderation, it is important to explore what kind of virtue the latter is, so that we can better understand its underlying philosophy and institutional implications that often go unnoticed.

You might wonder why we need to begin with the tradition of moderation. The answer is simple: moderation is an old virtue with many faces and a rich history that must be properly understood before we pass judgment on it. We cannot grasp what moderation implies until we figure out what moderates stood for over a long period of time and how they defended their ideas. We must go back to subjects which although old, remain surprisingly relevant and fresh. After all, we always stand on the shoulders of giants who are ready to share with us their insights and wisdom.

Here is what one of them wrote 2,000 years ago:

> By the toil of others, we are led into the presence of things which have been brought from darkness into light. We are excluded from no age, but we have access to them all; and if we are prepared in loftiness of mind to pass beyond the narrow confines of human weakness, there is a long period of time through which we can roam. We can argue with Socrates, express doubt with Carneades, cultivate retirement with Epicurus, overcome human nature with the Stoics, and exceed its limits with the Cynics. Since nature allows us to

> enter a partnership with every age, why not turn from this brief and transient spell of time and give ourselves wholeheartedly to the past, which is limitless and eternal and can be shared with better men than we?[1]

I doubt anyone might be able to convey this better than Seneca, the author of these lines. Yet, I also believe that we should speak of the ancients without worship and of the moderns without insolence. It is in this spirit that I invite you to read the next letters.

1

Rediscovering Moderation in Our Immoderate Age

Without the great political virtue of humility, patience, and moderation, every man in power becomes a ravenous beast of prey.[1]

(John Adams)

YOU ENCOURAGED ME to say a few things about my upbringing and trajectory. It is always difficult to speak about oneself without succumbing to the temptation of vanity and self-righteousness. I will honor your request but promise to be brief and to the point.

Those like me who grew up on the "wrong" side of the Iron Curtain during the Cold War differ in some important respects from those raised in freedom in the West. For obvious historical reasons, we are more inclined to accept that political moderation is a real and indispensable virtue than those born on the "right" side of the former Iron Curtain. For us, embracing moderation is a legitimate reaction to the previous age of extremes that had torn apart our world and deprived so many of freedom and dignity. We do not need to be convinced of the truth of John Adams' words, for we know quite well that when moderation is absent, those who exercise power tend to turn into ravenous beasts of prey.

As I was reflecting on my own political ideas, hopes, and beliefs, I recalled the moment when the Berlin Wall fell a little over three decades ago, on November 9, 1989. I was twenty-three then and living on the other side – arguably the wrong side – of the Iron Curtain, resigned to remain there forever. We lived our lives in fear and were too often willing to make compromises to survive. Communism appeared like a dark eternity to which we were condemned. We were listening to Radio Free Europe to learn not only what was going on in the free world, but also what was happening in our own countries. For most of us, the open society and its principles such as the rule of law, freedom of the press, free speech, freedom of movement, and free political contestation, were mere abstractions. Yet, they also represented powerful ideals that appealed to us, even if the project of building liberal democracies on the other side of the Iron Curtain seemed utopian.

I wish you had been in East Berlin on that historic night to witness firsthand the euphoria and optimistic mood that dominated the scene. I wish you could share, at least for a few moments, the belief in the institutions and promises of liberal democracy that filled the souls and hearts of all East Berliners that day. Alas, a lot has changed since then. History is again on the move, and the liberal euphoria of 1989 is incomprehensible to younger minds today.

The reasons are obvious. Far from witnessing the end of history and the triumph of liberal democracy in 1989, our world has entered a new era of global disorder marked by "the terrible and pathetic encounter of the fanatic and the zombie."[2] Today, litanies of what has gone wrong are published almost every day, and the public sphere is awash with articles gleefully announcing the death of liberal democracy. Yet, we must not give up on the latter and should be prepared to defend it against its enemies. We must also regard cruelty as an absolute evil and should seek to limit the physical brutality and humiliation inflicted upon others.

All this is – I am sure you will agree with me – an endless task. The attacks on the principles of the open society along with the propensity to violence spring not only from a misplaced desire for more power. They also derive from the attempt to change the makeup of society, and the fact that people's minds are often far more susceptible to falsehood than truth. There is a thirst for catechisms and political gospels mixing religion, morality, and politics. Yet, while the absolute must always remain the preoccupation of each, it is not the concern of all, and should never become a controversial political issue.

As we all know, the last century saw powerful states using extensive propaganda techniques and brainwashing methods to create mass-scale terror, forced labor, and extermination camps.

All those tragedies represent the dark side of history that millennials or the members of Generation Z may be inclined to underestimate. It is therefore important that you never forget that our civilization has produced monsters such as Hitler, Stalin, and Mao whose abominable ideas and crimes would have been unimaginable in previous centuries. The ruthless Ayatollah Khomeini and the cruel Pol Pot lived for a long time in bourgeois France before they returned to Iran and Cambodia to perpetrate acts of cruelty from which their countries have yet to recover. If Voltaire's Candide were to read, for example, a few pages from *The Black Book of Communism*, even his sunny optimism might give way to dark pessimism.[3]

Are you surprised that after a bloody century which had seen millions of people sent to gulags and concentration camps, we have yet to recover from the profound trauma that resulted? Are you shocked to learn that moderates do not want any new revolutions and are skeptical of any radical social and political experiments? They are wary of virtue committees set up to identify and punish the traitors, the impure, the lukewarm, or the uncommitted ones who need to be reeducated. They are afraid to see new proscription lists of alleged enemies or agents of evil who must be eliminated to make way for a bright future. Moderates don't want any new training sessions to teach others the right way of thinking how to bring about "true" justice and "real" freedom. They dream of something much less heroic, less grandiose, and much more prosaic. They dream of little more than a "a patchwork of compromise and good sense."[4] Is that too much to ask? Or perhaps too little?

Of course, you might reply that the Cold War ended more than thirty years ago, and we now live in a different age. Our priorities are different, and so are our fears, dreams, and expectations. I agree. Who doesn't want, after all, a new and just society rid of the problems of the past? For that to happen, you believe that moderation is no longer necessary or desirable. Such a claim depends, of course, on what type of moderation one has in mind. Don't forget that this virtue has many faces, not just one, and they must all be taken into account. If you think of moderation as a timid or opportunistic attempt to carve out an uncertain middle ground between the extremes, you have a good point. Bear in mind, however, that it is also possible to think of moderation as a *fighting* creed sustained by a spirit of rebellion. This is what I want to emphasize now. History shows that appearances notwithstanding, this type of "animated moderation"[5] *can* be successful in practice.

Consider the following examples. This type of bold moderation was at the heart of Mahatma Gandhi's non-violent civil resistance, and Vacláv Havel's theory of resistance that inspired the opposition to the communist regimes in Czechoslovakia and Poland in the 1970s and 1980s. I encourage you to read Havel's essay on the power of the powerless originally published in 1977. The velvet revolutions in Central and Eastern Europe (except Romania) twelve years later were, to a great extent, revolts led by bold moderates that successfully challenged the power structures and brought down the communist regimes in the region. If anything, they remind us that moderation can still be a winning card. One may go a step further and add that moderation as a fighting (and rebellious) creed is more needed today than ever.

Now, you may wonder whether the civil and ethnic wars of our recent history bear any resemblance to past wars. I think that the follies of our time might be easier to understand if seen against the background of past events. I would like to remind you of a bloody episode that took place in the Greek city of Corcyra in 427 BC, described by Thucydides in the *History of the Peloponnesian War.*[6] His story is a warning lesson to all those who still take our civilization for granted. It's a story of internal strife and civic hatred between supporters of democracy and oligarchy between whom no compromise was possible. Almost overnight, extreme polarization tore the city apart, and atrocities that had been inconceivable until then became common and were committed in broad daylight. Words changed their ordinary meanings, and a new language was created to justify previously unimaginable crimes. Irrational boldness and sudden fury passed for prowess and courage, while prudence and caution came to be regarded as cowardice. Intrigues, quarrels, and plotting for one's own sect were encouraged, and identified with reasonableness. Violation of established laws was regarded as acceptable behavior. Praise was lavished on those who started quarrels and denounced others, while those who sought to avoid fights and build bridges were denounced as traitors. Taking revenge on others was deemed acceptable, and preferable to pity and reconciliation. People were cheered if they committed crimes with impunity before anyone else did the same, or if they encouraged others to steal, maim or betray their fellow citizens.

This is a story about events that took place more than 2,000 years ago, but you might be tempted to believe that they happened only yesterday. The civil war that erupted in Corcyra can happen again under our own eyes, here and now. The twentieth century turned out to be the bloodiest in history, despite its innumerable advances in science and technology. It was not a time known for its commitment to moderation. Anyone who examines the events of the last century becomes aware of the catastrophic effects of the unrestrained pursuit of power on people's lives.

What history teaches us time and again is that beneath the thin surface of civilization always lurks the specter of cruelty and savagery. It would be enough to remember the ethnic wars and the genocide of Srebrenica in former Yugoslavia from the 1990s or see the ruthless bombing of Ukrainian cities in 2022 to realize that the spirit of barbarism has remained alive even in the middle of civilized Europe. The 1994 genocide in Rwanda is another sad reminder that we can always relapse into barbarism if we ignore the lessons of reason, prudence, and moderation.

Observe carefully what guides the actions of the fanatics. Civilization cannot survive when moderation is replaced by extremism, desire for revenge, and greed. When moderation is missing, the language becomes debased and violence is regarded as legitimate. Fierce sectarian battles are waged among people who start seeing each other as irreconcilable enemies. In the end, a new state of nature replaces civilization, allowing the dark demons of human nature to prevail over its better angels.

There are times when irrational passions gain total control over human affairs and the voice of reason is muted or powerless.

Then, the attention of the public is focused mostly on what extremists say and do to inflame the imagination and expectations of their followers. A return to barbarism becomes possible. Have we already reached that point?

Nobody can tell for sure. Yet, there are many reasons to be very concerned about the current hyper-partisanship and extreme affective polarization. New forms of sectarianism have emerged, allowing political, religious, sexual, and racial identities to sort themselves into mega-identities that challenge the future of our democratic way of life. In some cases, people are fighting for a specific cause or group they believe in and are ready to die for. In other instances, partisans are banding together to fight a collective enemy, whether real or imagined. In most cases, they work with a Manichaean worldview and display a disquieting urge to purge and reeducate, sometimes in the name of promoting diversity and equity, at other times for the sake of strengthening the unity and homogeneity of their groups.

This style of politics is all the more dangerous because it encourages ruthless demagogues who promise quick answers to intractable questions. Their "my way or the highway" pattern of thinking fulfills the atavistic craving to belong to certain in-groups and helps manufacture solidarity by displaying irrational animosity toward out-groups. It also promotes cynicism and a self-defeating tendency to apathy and pessimism.

We have seen where this trend led in ancient Greece as well as in Rwanda or the Balkans. Politics became a zero-sum conflict in which every available tool was weaponized and there was no room left for middling or moderate positions. In turn, this gave everyone the feeling of being engaged in an existential all-out war between the forces of light and darkness, a battle that allowed for no nuances, no truce, and no compromise. Do we want this tragedy to return? Or are we prepared to do anything in our power to prevent it?

I will have a chance to address all these issues in more detail soon. Until then, farewell! Yours, . . .

2

The Skepticism toward Moderation and What Its Critics Miss about It

Extremism in the pursuit of liberty is no vice, moderation in the pursuit of justice is no virtue.[1]

(Barry Goldwater)

I SHOULD LIKE TO SHIFT GEARS today and start with something closer to us in time. I have in mind Barry Goldwater's memorable words from his acceptance speech for the nomination as the Republican Party's presidential candidate at the GOP's National Convention in San Francisco in the summer of 1964. Goldwater uttered that famous phrase – the epigraph for this letter – almost six decades ago, in an entirely different domestic and international context from the present one. His comment did not serve him well in the 1964 presidential election, which he lost by a landslide to Lyndon Johnson. Yet, Goldwater's famous sentence has secured him a front seat in the long history of skepticism toward moderation.

His rejection of moderation may have been witty and unforgettable, but I wonder how much it resonates with our present concerns and discontents. Today, the young seem more attracted to another critique of moderation that can be found, for example, in William Lloyd Garrison's stance against moderation in the fight against slavery. Here is what he said more than a century and a half ago on this subject:

> I do not wish to think, or speak, or write, with moderation. No! no! Tell a man whose house is on fire to give a moderate alarm; tell him to moderately rescue his wife from the hands of the ravisher; tell the mother to gradually extricate her baby from the fire into which he it has fallen; but urge me not to use moderation in a cause like the present. I am in earnest – I will not equivocate – I will not excuse – I will not retreat a single inch.[2]

This appears to be the spirit that speaks directly to the hearts and minds of your generation much more than Goldwater's libertarian rejection of moderation in the name of an extreme form of liberty.

Should we then be surprised that, given the hyper-polarization and politicization of every corner of our lives, there seems to be no market for moderation today? As media outlets become primary vehicles for demonizing opponents, moderate voices are no longer effective in fighting against hyperbolic narratives competing for attention, votes, and influence. Moreover, moderation has sometimes been hypocritically invoked to delay or block necessary reforms meant to address racial and economic forms of injustice. How can we still believe in moderation then?

When trying to answer this question, it is important to be clear about what the terms *moderation* and *moderate* imply. Let's briefly examine their etymology. It is worth noting that as a descriptor, *moderate* has various connotations and can be used simultaneously as a noun, adjective, or verb. Confusions often arise because the term can be applied either to means or to ends, to goals or to values, to individuals or movements. Distinguishing among them is never easy but it is important.

As a noun, *a moderate* can be defined in several ways. It can designate someone who is reasonable and self-restrained, opposes violence, and eschews extremes. Moderate can also be used to describe anyone willing to find common ground, or who prefers the middle ground. In turn, the verb *to moderate* can mean many things at once: to make something less intense or severe, to regulate, to soften, to temper, and to restrain. It can also signify to act as a moderator or compromiser, to pacify or keep within bounds. As an adjective, *moderate* can be used to mean frugal, temperate, mild, gentle, fair, and balanced, but also as a synonym of mediocre, average, and intermediate.

Finally, a small but important point to consider. Moderates should not be regarded merely as liberals or conservatives in disguise, though they may have liberal or conservative proclivities. There are undeniable affinities between moderation and certain tenets of classical liberalism or conservatism, but there are also some nuances and differences that are not unimportant.

Furthermore, some describe themselves as moderates simply because they tend to disagree with the more radical elements of their own political or religious spectrum.

Confronted with so many meanings and nuances, you might conclude that the word *moderate* becomes irrelevant when applied to such a wide array of views. You might also be tempted to believe that the phrase "I am a moderate" sounds like a neutral catch-all statement that doesn't convey anything substantial. After all, everyone is a moderate on some issue. Yet, this is *not* how I understand moderation and I will try to explain why.

It should be plain by now that even if both Goldwater and Lloyd Garrison referred to moderation, they had, in fact, different things in mind. For Garrison, moderation was entirely inadequate in the fight against slavery. In his eyes, there was no acceptable moderate position on slavery: one had to be either an abolitionist or a partisan of slavery. Moderation would have only perpetuated unacceptable forms of racial and political injustice. As a conservative, Goldwater should have been more inclined to see the brighter side of moderation connected to prudence. Yet in the end, he preferred to endorse a "creative" form of extremism in the pursuit of individual liberty and rights, the polestar of his libertarianism. Like Lloyd Garrison, he had no faith in moderation.

Do you think our situation is much different today? Those who identify themselves with the radical Left regard moderation (and most often dismiss it) as a reactionary or hopeless virtue, out of sync with the exigencies of our time. On the hard Right, moderation is identified with cowardice or resignation to the agenda of the woke progressives. On the radical Left, the consensus is that we cannot put a moderate roof on a house whose foundations are rotten; the roof alone, albeit in good condition, would not be able to hold the house together. The implication is that we need rip out the foundations and start to rebuild entirely from scratch, even if there is hardly any agreement on how to do it.

As you know, skepticism toward moderation doesn't end here. For those who believe that their mission is to build an entirely new society, moderation is an unappealing bourgeois virtue, incompatible with true greatness, passion, and enthusiasm. In turn, those who long for authenticity in politics may think that the problem with moderates has always been that they lack a "magnetic" idea. Moderation, they claim, is another name for mediocrity, an expression of the middling mind that levels everything, forcing everyone to conform to the deadening norms and prejudices of society. On this view, moderation stifles creativity and stands for a sparkless conventional world.

You might ask now: is not a certain degree of excess involved in all forms of greatness? Aren't moderates, by definition, incapable of enthusiasm without which nothing great and enduring can be achieved? Isn't the idea of the "moderate middle" most often only a rhetorical weapon to marginalize radical policy proposals?[3]

To answer these questions, it may be necessary for a moment to think of all the tragedies caused by misplaced enthusiasm and excessive zeal in history. Do I need to remind you that magnetic and grandiose ideas can be deceiving and sometimes plainly dangerous? If by magnetic idea one means class struggle, racial or ethnic purity, or something like that, it is true that moderation lacks such a strong ideal and is, in fact, fundamentally opposed to it. Only extremist ideologies offer such catchy slogans and ideas that can mobilize millions of people. Moderation does not do that. It lacks an emancipatory message and does not offer cheap promises of fraternity or solidarity (I will explain more later).

All this, I'm afraid, wouldn't be enough to convince the critics of moderation like you to revise their views. The most vocal opponents of moderation argue that people handicap themselves with all kinds of virtues, like decency and moderation which often work against their true interests. In their view, the ideal type encouraged by modern civilization is a superficial and shallow individual, easily satisfied with material comfort and ready-made solutions to life's complex questions. Young radicals believe that solving these questions requires a different cast of mind and a policy agenda that has little or no room for moderation. Others insist that moderation failed to deliver in times of extremes and did not work against tyrants such as Mussolini, Hitler, Stalin, Mao, and Pol Pot. Why would our situation be different today when the security of the free world is threatened by the irrational ambitions of Vladimir Putin and his enablers?

Moreover, it is alleged that moderation entails an ad hoc approach to political affairs that can never be universally applicable; it may be appropriate to some contexts and circumstances but not to others. Like the center, moderation, its critics claim, shifts constantly and has no clear location on the political map. It is unlike a true virtue that is universally good and praiseworthy regardless of circumstances and time. Since moderation is context-bound, so the argument goes, it cannot be regarded as a virtue in the proper sense of the word.

There are several objections here that need to be considered separately. I ask for your patience as I am going to address them one by one. First, it is important to emphasize that we should not conflate moderation with centrism, even if there is a certain affinity between the two (I will discuss this issue later). Moderates can be found on *all* sides of the political spectrum, including on the Left; the center has no monopoly on moderation, although there is an affinity between the two.

Second, many of us have a bias in favor of ideal theory and straightforward schemes. By comparison, the universe of moderation appears fuzzy and messy and excludes simple algorithms and abstract theories. Moderates prefer complex answers that leave room for nuances to simple explanations that focus on a single aspect of a problem or cause of an event. They deal with second best solutions and lesser evils, while ideal theory focuses only on the best.

Third, because moderation requires constant adjustments and compromises, one may legitimately speak of "the extenuating intransigence of moderation."[4] Although it accords with nature, it is *not* a virtue for everyone and all seasons. Like prudence, it is a circumstantial virtue that requires constant effort, attention, judgment, and proper discernment. Never believe those who argue otherwise!

You may now begin to understand then why it is so hard to talk about moderation and why it is difficult to practice it in a society in which the level of partisanship has become toxic and each side believes the other camp is dangerous or immoral, posing an existential threat to the survival of the regime. But if we take a broader historical perspective, we can easily see that there are different ways of acting like a moderate and that it is possible to recommend moderation as a valuable strategy in a conflict-ridden society. Of course, this type of moderation does not imply conformism or complacency, nor does it seek to appease the forces of tyranny or dictatorship. Embracing true moderation is, in fact, the *opposite* of being a conformist bystander, guilty of committing passive injustice by remaining indifferent to various forms of suffering and injustice in the world.

So, let me be crystal clear on this important topic often misunderstood by moderation's critics. The moderate response to those who pose threats to our democratic institutions and norms is *not* complacency, indifference, or apathy, as some believe. When moderates detect lies or fake news, they call them by their name rather than misrepresenting their nature. Sometimes, to be true to the spirit of moderation, one must act with a grain of boldness and even immoderation. While being open to negotiation and compromise, moderates can also be unbending without betraying their principles and nature. There are times when they recognize that they must stand firm and refuse any concessions.

Such moments, for example, occur when key liberal democratic principles, norms, and institutions such as civil equality, the rule of law, checks and balances, and political opposition are threatened. On all these issues, moderates agree that there can be no reasonable compromises with those who endanger the democratic way of life, its institutions and norms. Complicity with evil and a willingness to condone unpardonable acts of violence and injustice are incompatible with the exigencies of true moderation. Only a false type of moderation would put up with them or try to hide them. At the same time, moderates try to build bridges with opponents who disagree with them on important issues but agree on the fundamentals.

If we look for a classic statement on this topic, an exemplar can be found in Martin Luther King Jr.'s *Letter from the Birmingham Jail* (1963). You may be surprised to find his name invoked in this context, but you shouldn't really be. Here is how he denounced the cowardice of the white moderates, mainly the white clergy, who stood in the way of advancing racial justice:

> I must confess that over the past few years I have been gravely disappointed with the white moderate. I have almost reached the regrettable conclusion that the Negro's great stumbling block in his stride toward freedom is not the White Citizen's Councilor or the Ku Klux Klanner, but the white moderate, who is more devoted to "order" than to justice, who prefers a negative peace which is the absence of tension to a positive peace which is the presence of justice.[5]

Dr. King was right to be skeptical about self-proclaimed "white moderates" who would not challenge those who tried to curtail civil rights and deny justice and equality to all. Theirs was a "sandbagging moderation"[6] that sought to pass for responsible citizenship but neither understood nor resonated with the pain of those who suffered injustice and faced racial discrimination.

Critics of moderation are right to denounce *this* type of moderation as an impediment to overdue social and political change. They are correct to point out that it is most often a rhetorical posture used by those who hold power to consolidate their privileged positions and disguise their ambitions for more power. I agree that there would be no point in calling these people moderates and siding with them just because they pretend to be concerned about preserving social order and preventing anarchy. By the same token, it would be a costly mistake to assume that those who advocate democratic reforms should distrust everyone who preaches moderation. Those who organize to challenge the excessive power of elites and to give ordinary citizens a say in public affairs need to be aware of this virtue.

Let me briefly explain why I hold this view. Properly understood, moderation often entails a *rebellious* and *firm* attitude that welcomes tension and contradiction – for example, between justice and order, or between equality and liberty. It does not put up with injustice or discrimination and has no patience with abuses of power and violence. This type of moderation is a pillar of any decent society; it offers hope and a concrete path for improving people's lives through piecemeal reforms. That may not seem compelling enough for some, but for those who have suffered injustice and oppression at the hands of leaders and movements that claimed to possess "magnetic" ideas, such a vision does hold a lot of promise and appeal.

That is why it would be incorrect to assume that moderation is a merely reactive virtue, a middling temperament or agenda entirely dependent on the initiatives of the extremes. Moderation has a substantive core as well as a distinctive political, moral, and philosophical vision that follows its own logic. You may perhaps remember me saying that moderation does not fit well with any "*isms.*" I should add that moderates reject simplistic (either–or) choices in public debates and seek to go beyond conventional dichotomies that oversimplify reality. There is also a certain moderate *style* and *ethos,* characterized by skepticism, prudence, eclecticism, pragmatism, propensity to incremental change and piecemeal reforms, civility, toleration, dialogue, modesty, and humility. We will have a chance to talk more about all that later.

One more thing is worth noting here. In addition to studying moderation as character trait and moral virtue, it is also important to examine its *institutional* faces. When we refer to moderation as embodied in institutions, what we have in mind is something different from the moderation illustrated by the behavior of leaders and citizens. The institutional and constitutional implications of moderation are usually neglected both by its critics and friends, but they are quite important, and I'd like to encourage you to pay due attention to them. They include checks and balances, pluralism, veto power, bicameralism, bipartisanship, federalism, and polycentricity to name only a few.

Still, you might say, it is difficult to be enthusiastic about a virtue so lacking in charisma and that is often characterized as a bland doctrine with no appeal to the young. Yet, you should know by now that charisma is an ambiguous concept, especially when allied with ideology. Ambitious and power-hungry leaders use their charismatic skills to intoxicate minds and spread falsehoods, hatred, and prejudice. Skeptical of charismatic leaders, moderates attempt to disintoxicate minds and calm fanaticism, whenever possible. They are aware that it is often impossible to demonstrate the truth in political affairs, and we must therefore content ourselves with approximations and nuances. Yet, moderates believe that it is always possible to make sensible and reasonable decisions based on the limited information and resources at their disposal.

Does moderation have any room for martyrs, liberators, and saints? some critics wondered. Where are the brave moderates? someone once asked. History offers a few good lessons on this point. During the French Revolution of 1789–94 and the Russian Revolution of 1917, moderation was denounced as a device used by alleged intriguers and traitors to the nation to cover their ploys to destroy the work of the people and further the cause of tyranny. Moderates were signaled out for their presumed lack of patriotism and endorsement of dangerous ideas. Many of them ended on the guillotine or in labor camps in the name of the permanent revolution needed to bring about the radiant future. They were the real martyrs and saints.

I hope you will not look upon these issues as trifles. In reality, it takes a lot of bravery to remain moderate when everyone around you is immoderate and rude. As Edmund Burke once put it, moderation must be distinguished from "the counterfeits of pusillanimity and indecision" and requires "a deep courage" and resoluteness when one must stand up against the voice and wishes of the majority.[7] History demonstrates that moderates are not to be ranked among the cowards, the ambivalent, and undecided ones, those who are lukewarm in their beliefs. They do not belong with Dante's neutrals or ambivalent ones as described in Canto III of *The Inferno.* Dante's lukewarm spirits were neither faithful nor rebels; they stood apart and lived without praise. Unlike them, true moderates do have the courage to proclaim their ideas and do not seek to hide their convictions.

Try to emulate their example and stand up for your beliefs. Farewell! Yours, . . .

3

The Archipelago of Moderation (I)

The Old World

"*Mēden agan*" [*Nothing in excess*] (inscription from the Temple of Apollo, Delphi)

SOMETIMES IT IS USEFUL TO START with a bold generalization or platitude – wisdom implies moderation in all things.[1] This is precisely what the ancients believed. "Nothing in excess" was inscribed on the gate of the temple of Apollo at Delphi in ancient Greece. Looking back at what ancient authors wrote about this virtue, it becomes apparent that there is an entire tradition of moderation which forms a complex and diverse archipelago with many islands, some more exotic than others. You may see some of them and ignore what connects them. Such a view of moderation is at light years' distance from what its contemporary critics have to say about it. Should we be surprised by that?

When you read the writings of ancient Greek and Roman historians and philosophers, you notice that for them, nothing could have been courageous, generous, just, and wise in the absence of moderation. Horace thought that moderation is rooted in nature, while Tacitus regarded it as the most difficult lesson of wisdom. Stoics like Marcus Aurelius, Cicero, or Epictetus believed that excess can never lead to the good. They recommended moderation as a way of living in accordance with nature and reason by achieving "a due measure in all things."[2]

You should not be surprised that the ancients considered moderation as a cardinal virtue that directs all other moral virtues, a synonym of practical wisdom and reasonableness. They viewed it as being opposed to the spirit of the barbarians, whom they considered to be incapable of following a rational path in life. The ancients also believed that ethical moderation understood as a character trait has something important in common with political moderation and the institutional framework in which the latter is embodied.

Consider, for a moment, Plato's dialogues. He is often regarded as the philosopher entirely committed to the pursuit of wisdom, ready to leave behind the world of shadows and darkness for the realm of pure forms and light. He, too, believed that moderation is the very foundation of all other virtues, from prudence and justice to courage and practical wisdom. If you have read *The Republic*, you have noticed that moderation is granted there the status of an architectonic virtue. Why is this the case? Plato defined moderation as the virtue that allows us to regulate, control, and temper our passions, emotions, and desires. It enables us to put our souls in order and bring order and harmony in the city at large. Plato also equated moderation with self-restraint and self-knowledge; for him, being moderate amounts to being aware of what one knows and what one does not know.[3] It also implies acting with propriety in public, being able to temper one's impulses and desires, and adjusting one's words and actions to avoid excess and remain within the limits prescribed by reason.

You may also turn to Plato's most famous disciple, Aristotle, for whom moderation was neither science nor knowledge and represented more than a mere virtue of character. In his view, there is a strong connection between moderation and the mean that preserves social order. Every judicious or reasonable person seeks "to avoid excess and deficiency" and chooses "what is intermediate – but intermediate relative to us, not in the object."[4] The detail is essential because it points to the contextual nature of moderation and its dependence on judgment.

As practical wisdom, moderation implies having the right feelings "at the right time, about the right things, toward the right people, for the right end."[5] We must apply our judgment and instinct to find the mean between excess and deficiency in each case. Sometimes, we should incline toward excess, at other times, toward deficiency. For example, it is easy to spend money, make promises, or form casual relationships; anyone can do that, more or less. What is truly difficult is to know how to do it "well," that is, at the "right" moment and for the "right" end.[6]

Let's pause for a moment and reflect on what Aristotle means by that. He reminds us that all questions about finding the mean between extremes are complex and hard to solve. For unlike the middle, the mean can never be ascertained with geometrical precision; it requires attention and discernment. Moreover, the good and bad often run gradually into each other, making them difficult to identify and distinguish from each other. This skill, the ancients believed, is always the outcome of practice, not theory. Not surprisingly, Aristotle insisted that moderation is rarely to be found among the young who lack experience. Yet, they, too, can learn it in incremental steps, through exercise and patience. Finally, arguably the most important thing about Aristotle's moderation is that it was part of a larger political architecture, connected to limited power and the rule of law within the institutional framework of mixed government.

The knowledge of how to combine harmoniously all the elements, interests, and classes in society was one of the keys to the success of the Roman republic a few centuries later. There is no better name to invoke here than Cicero, whose writings form another major island in the archipelago of moderation. In his political works, he examined moderation (modesty or temperance) in relation to the other cardinal virtues (justice, fortitude, and wisdom) and believed that the key to living a good life lies in finding a proper balance between extremes.

If I may, I'd like to encourage you to read Cicero if you haven't already done so. You will notice that for him, too, moderation was connected to reason, seemliness, restraint, and modesty. It implied, among other things, "the knowledge of opportuneness, that is, of the fitting occasions for doing something."[7] In Cicero's view, moderation went hand in hand with temperance, restraint, a sense of shame, orderliness, and constancy. As for those who want to succeed in politics, Cicero believed that moderation was an indispensable virtue that allowed them to perform proper and honorable actions in the service of the republic. Moderation implies doing what is proper, which, Cicero insisted, can never be separated from what is honorable: "what is seemly is honorable, and what is honorable is seemly."[8]

You might wonder now how all this informed Cicero's conception of republicanism and statesmanship for which he is remembered today. First, he argued that maintaining *decorum* is a duty to nature, to our fellow citizens, and to the res publica at large. A cardinal virtue, moderation points out what is proper to do and what should be avoided in every context. Some things are so disgraceful and outrageous that no responsible citizen or leader may do them even to protect their country. Second, Cicero assigned a key role to the moderate statesman – the *rector rei publicae* – whose main duty is to keep the ship of the state on an even keel. Since this task requires constant changes, statesmen must act like trimmers who make the necessary adjustments to the institutions of the republic to achieve concord between various ideas, interests, and groups in society. They resemble the composers who arrange their notes to create beautiful melodies and are not unlike the directors of a choir who manage to bring about harmony out of a plurality of voices.

Third, Cicero emphasized that moderation was inseparable from and embedded in the institutional framework of the Roman republic, a mixed regime based on an "equitable balance in the state of rights and duties and responsibilities."[9] As such, for him moderation was much more than a simple trait of character, a certain state of mind, or a mere disposition; in addition to all this, it also had significant institutional ramifications.

I would like to end this letter with a bold claim about the centrality of moderation made by a modern with an ancient soul: the Anglican theologian Joseph Hall. Here is how he described moderation in a book published in 1640, just as the Civil War was about to start in England. "There is nothing therefore in the world more wholesome, or more necessary for us to learne, then this gracious lesson of moderation," he wrote. "This is the *centre*, wherein all both divine, and morall philosophy meet; the rule of life, the governesse of manners, *the silken string that runs through the pearl-chain of all vertues*, the very Ecliptick line, under which reason and religion move without any deviation: and therefore most worthy of our best thoughts, of our most careful observance."[10]

"*The silken string that runs through the pearl-chain of all vertues*" – if there is a "magnetic" idea of moderation, that should be it. In my view, it is the best and most beautiful definition of moderation ever penned. Think about it and let me know what you make of it. Until then, farewell! Yours, . . .

4

The Archipelago of Moderation (II)

The New World

My earnest wish and my fondest hope, therefore, is that instead of wounding suspicions and irritable charges, there may be liberal allowances, mutual forbearances, and temporizing yieldings on all sides.[1]

(George Washington)

THANKS TO A FORTUNATE turn of events, I have some free time today which gives me the opportunity to continue exploring the tradition of moderation with you. I promise not to abuse your patience. This time, I'd like to turn to the American political tradition, which has recently been the subject of renewed controversy. I know this is of interest to you.

One view is that the Americans have always been concerned primarily with what works rather than what should work, thus seeking a pragmatic middle between realism and idealism. There is, however, an alternative line of interpretation according to which moderation has rarely, if ever, played an important role in America's political tradition. Some historians have gone so far as to speak about the "paranoid style" of American politics,[2] while others have insisted that the founding act of the country should be 1619, the year when slaves first set foot on the soil of North America, rather than 1776, when the country declared and won its independence from Great Britain. Is there any room left for moderates in this debate? Did they exist at all? If so, where is the book of great moderates in American history? as a controversial conservative pundit once asked.[3]

Let's think about all these questions for a moment. It is not a mere accident that the epigraph of this letter is taken from Washington's writings. A moderate political persuasion began with our first President and has been a basic feature in American politics ever since.[4] Washington played a key role in the new experiment of creating good government from reflection and conscious choice as opposed to accident and force. If his polestar was political moderation, it was not a weak virtue by any means. Washington's moderation required a good dose of courage and willingness to swim against the current, and combined prudence and self-restraint with a conciliatory temper and firmness of character. When he judged it necessary, he did not hesitate to take risky decisions such as declaring the neutrality of the United States in the war between France and England, a decision that met with criticism from a good part of the press and even several of his allies.

You will remember that Washington repeatedly warned against the dangers of hyper-partisanship that could create gridlock and impair the Congress' ability to pass legislation. Remember his *Farewell Address* (1796)? As he was about to leave the presidency after two trying terms, Washington wrote this text to remind his fellow citizens that the fledgling republic needed to cultivate the spirit of compromise and moderation to avoid falling prey to the pernicious effects of the spirit of faction. The latter, he maintained, has "its roots in the strongest passions of the human mind." In popular governments, though, the spirit of faction is seen in its "greatest rankness" because it fosters the "alternate domination of one faction over another, sharpened by the spirit of revenge."[5] It risks tearing apart the social fabric and might bring the ruin of the commonwealth.

Washington was right to focus on this important point. Of all corruptors of moral sentiments, the spirit of party has been by far the greatest and most dangerous.[6] He knew that zeal and excessive enthusiasm for political or religious causes can overturn a settled power and are apt to beget a like spirit in antagonists. "I was no party man myself," Washington once said, "and the first wish of my heart was, if parties did exist, to reconcile them."[7] While he tried to be non-partisan, he avoided being neutral or indifferent. He was concerned about the emergence of major disagreements between prominent politicians within his own administration and he tried to reconcile them, as he strongly believed in the importance of "liberal allowances, mutual forbearances, and temporizing yieldings on all sides."[8]

There is another reason why you should reread Washington's *Farewell Address* today. It is no accident that during and after the Constitutional Convention in Philadelphia in 1787, Washington acted like a trimmer seeking to keep the ship of state on an even keel and prevent it from capsizing in rough seas. He was convinced that liberty and prosperity depend on the existence of a wise balance between various groups and interests in society. He agreed with Madison that factions are indispensable in free societies but also insisted that all parties must act in an institutional and constitutional framework imbued, as much as possible, with the spirit of compromise. It is this fragile equilibrium that ensures that power is exercised with judicious moderation in keeping with the rule of law.

I trust you get my point, but there are other examples of moderation in American history that might be worth mentioning here. John Adams believed that all those entrusted with power must exercise it with moderation, lest they risk turning into birds of prey. Moderation also loomed large in Benjamin Franklin's career, along with another twelve bourgeois virtues like order, industry, sincerity, and humility which he deemed essential to anyone's moral improvement. As Franklin wrote in his acclaimed *Autobiography*, he made a little book (with mottos from Addison, Cicero, and the Bible) in which he allotted a page for each of his thirteen virtues, marking daily the progress or lack thereof in practicing them. You should not be surprised to learn that moderation was central to his practice of improvement, as a cardinal virtue that allows us to avoid extremes and find a much-needed compass in daily life. Along with temperance, it procures "coolness and clearness of head" and makes us vigilant "against the unremitting attraction of ancient habits, and the force of perpetual temptations."[9]

Now, if you want an example of Franklin's political moderation, consider his statement in support of the proposed federal Constitution. On September 17, 1787, he asked James Wilson to read a speech he had prepared for the Constitutional Convention. Franklin justified his approval of the final draft submitted to the vote of the fifty-five members of the Convention while also confessing that there were several parts of the text which he did not approve of. Experience had taught him not to be a perfectionist and made him reluctant to reject the constitutional text in search of a better one, as many others were ready to do. "I doubt too whether any other Convention we can obtain may be able to make a better Constitution," Franklin admitted. "For when you assemble a number of men to have the advantage of their joint wisdom, you inevitably assemble with those men, all their prejudices, their passions, their errors of opinion, their local interests, and their selfish views."[10] From such an assembly of imperfect and passionate men, he concluded, no perfect outcome could ever be expected.

Can you find a more candid acknowledgment of one's fallibility and a stronger rejection of perfectionism than Franklin's statement? I doubt it. While openly admitting the new constitution's limitations, he consented to it because, as he put it, he expected "no better" and was uncertain "that it is not the best."[11] In this regard, Franklin was a political moderate, not sure that he was right, but hoping, based on the limited information he had, that the imperfect constitution would promote the common good and the long-term interests of the country. "The older I grow," he admitted, "the more apt I am to doubt my own judgment, and to pay more respect to the judgment of others."[12]

You might say that two or three examples, great as they may be, are not enough to prove the existence of a solid tradition of political moderation in America. That would be true. But then there is also the towering figure of Abraham Lincoln, who steered a middle course between radical abolitionism and the radical doctrine of states' rights. It is no accident that he regarded Henry Clay, known as the "Great Pacificator" or "Great Compromiser," as his beau ideal of a statesman.[13] As a disciple of Clay, Lincoln knew when to be bold and when to make necessary concessions while maintaining a strong commitment to a set of fundamental principles, including equal rights. He had initially placed the goal of maintaining the Union above abolishing slavery and was (for some time) open to finding a compromise with the South. Lincoln abhorred slavery, which he always considered as an absolute evil, and categorically opposed its extension into the Western territories. At the same time, he was not an abolitionist in the proper sense of the word and did not share the zeal of the radical abolitionists. Yet, a moment came in 1861 when his moderation drew a red line as the time for compromise had run out. Lincoln was quick to embrace extreme measures, including the suspension of habeas corpus, once the Civil War became inevitable. He signed the Emancipation Declaration two years later, putting an end to slavery.

You might, perhaps, point out that these illustrious examples were not always moderate in the regular sense of the word. Or you might think that if they were moderate, their moderation can only have limited relevance for us today. I confess that I have chosen these figures because they illustrate how a muscular form of moderation can help us deal with the challenges of deep disagreement and partisanship in our society today. They embraced a pragmatic form of politics that acknowledged human imperfection and was open to compromises that would benefit the country in the long run. Lincoln often sought to find common ground and limit the scope of dispute, but he also recognized that there are moments when we can no longer escape history, when caution and prudence become liabilities, and debate must be followed by resolute action. In those moments, inflexibility and firmness become necessary in the name of a higher form of prudence and moderation. To paraphrase Lincoln's own words, while it is understandable that a limb may be amputated to save a life, it is never wise to sacrifice a life to save a limb.[14]

There are a few valuable lessons you might draw from this brief historical foray. Moderates prefer to adopt a philosophy of gradual improvement and uplift that seeks to maintain a judicious balance between liberty and order capable of tempering social conflict and advancing the cause of justice. They are convinced that liberty has little or no real value without order and individual responsibility. They fear demagogues capable of inflaming passions and subverting order and liberty, pandering to the lower impulses in human nature. That is why moderates appeal to people's rational faculties to counter their base appetites and help them cultivate higher virtues like self-discipline, temperance, and compromise.[15]

The writings and careers of moderates like Washington, Adams, Franklin, Clay, and Lincoln also warn us that democracy can be fatally weakened if we allow rancor, "ill-founded jealousies and false alarms" to dominate the political scene, opening the door to "foreign influence and corruption."[16] The smooth functioning of democratic institutions depends on political actors exercising common sense, self-restraint, prudence, and moderation. These politicians are expected to pay heed to public opinion and learn to respect those who disagree with them, without believing that their opponents are dangerous people who must be eliminated. Let's constantly remind ourselves that we all should display "mutual complaisances, attentions, and sacrifices of little conveniences"[17] if we want to remain a civilized and free people. Even today, the surest way of producing moderation in every party is to increase the commitment to the common good, the res publica, the things we share and deeply care about.

The ancients knew it quite well, but do we still believe in this idea? Are you really prepared to take the ancients' lessons seriously? In the next letter, I will invite you to reflect on moderation as an alternative to ideology. Rest assured of my most cordial sentiments. Yours, . . .

5

An Alternative to Ideology

Aligning oneself with the Left, as with the Right, is only one of the numberless ways open to man of being an imbecile: both are forms of moral hemiplegia.[1]

(José Ortega y Gasset)

ARE YOU POLITICALLY HOMELESS? you asked me after reading my last letter. As a matter of fact, I might very well be, considering the events of the last two decades. To be frank, I have always been intrigued by Ortega y Gasset's quote (see above). Some may find his words unsettling, incomprehensible, or simply offensive. Others may dismiss him as a reactionary who has nothing to teach us today. To properly understand his words and before we rush to criticize him, we need to know a little about the context in which they were written.

Ortega's claim appeared in the Prologue to the 1937 French edition of *The Rebellion of the Masses* originally published in Spain in 1929. He wrote those words during dark times, when his country was torn apart by a bloody civil war and stormy clouds were gathering all over Europe. Ortega was concerned about the threats posed by extreme ideologies to the liberal values undergirding Western civilization. Alas, what happened a few years later proved him right.

Still, I would understand if you were unsettled by Ortega's caustic words. That would be your right. Note, however, he did *not* say that one should never hold views that belong to the Left or Right. That would have been incorrect and absurd. He warned against something else. Ortega's target was those captive minds who always think ideologically and who never change their views once they adopt a certain framework. The Spaniard took to task the fundamentalists who blindly defend the values and agendas of their political tribes and refuse to consider alternative points of view, being convinced that they possess secret access to the ultimate truth. They do not adjust their belief systems to the constantly changing reality and instead try to understand the present world through the lenses of old theories and concepts.

Since the word *ideology* always triggers strong emotional reactions, it is appropriate to begin by clarifying what it means. Whether thin or thick, ideologies embody a set of principles, aspirations, and values held by different groups or societies. As political belief systems, they give an account of the political evils and problems to be addressed and map out ways to tackle them. They are meant to foster unity and solidarity and give purpose and a sense of direction, while also identifying the enemies to be vanquished. Ideologies filter information and shape messages addressed to particular audiences, justifying them in taking charge of their destiny and shaping the future. They also lay out a plan for bringing about the desired changes. In the end, they tend to discourage critical thinking and foster motivated cognition and echo chambers. Those who embrace ideological thinking are inclined to use purity tests and promote intransigence toward alternative viewpoints.

You might ask: does this imply that *all* ideologies are nothing but means of deliberate manipulation of public opinion to advance particular class interests? I prefer to leave this question open for now. Because they are constantly changing, it is impossible to judge their legitimacy by referring to an objective and timeless standard of truth. The point I want to stress is that ideologies oversimplify and reduce reality to one single factor, principle, value, or axis – whether class, race, the invisible hand of the market, the survival of the fittest or the dictatorship of the proletariat. Because they are deterministic, they may easily become "the antibiotics of the intellect"[2] by discouraging nonconformism and creativity.

If ideologies are so problematic, you might ask, why can't we live without them? Let me remind you that it is the Marxists who believe that all ideologies as elements of "superstructure" are deceptive. I believe that trying to build a world free of ideology would be a futile and utopian endeavor. Here is where moderation comes in as an alternative to ideology. It does not give voice to the ideas of any dominating class or group in society, nor does it seek to justify the legitimacy of any claims to power. Moderates do not assume any monopoly of truth, nor do they seek to manufacture false consent. They offer something else: a way to keep our minds flexible and watchful, so that we can see the world around us with fresh eyes.

As an alternative to ideology, moderation combines humility with awareness of our limits and the fallibility of all things human. Moderates believe that a certain degree of inconsistency is natural and required to navigate political life. They refuse to accept that there is a single objective political standard or yardstick of truth against which ideas and policies can be judged and evaluated. That is why moderates refrain from offering comprehensive theories of the existing order or detailed blueprints for bringing about radical political change.

I can imagine your objection at this point: doesn't their position verge on relativism after all? How do moderates differ from those who claim that there are only subjective perspectives and points of view? The answer may be simpler than you think. Moderation does *not* imply moral relativism; it needs principles and a moral compass as much as principles need moderation. While moderates cherish their freedom to question settled issues and conventions, their views do *not* imply absence of principles.

Always look at the larger picture. Moderates are realists who follow the facts, refuse to misrepresent them, and avoid false premises to draw misleading conclusions. They never accept any arguments at face value without subjecting them to critical scrutiny. When facts change, they believe that their opinions must be revised accordingly. It doesn't matter whether someone began as a socialist, a conservative, or a libertarian; everyone must remain open to adjusting their ideas when the realities around them contradict their beliefs. As such, moderates are prepared to swim against the current when needed and avoid any complicity with official dogmas and propaganda. Furthermore, they refrain from deliberately using an ambiguous language that seeks to deceive by hiding their real intentions and goals. They speak in plain words that are never arrogant or sanctimonious.

I also want you to be aware of another way in which moderates differ from the proponents of ideological politics. They take the latter to task for their propensity to monomania and their self-righteous belief that they possess an infallible measuring-rod allowing them to judge all regimes and policies. Moderates believe that life can be seen through many windows that offer different perspectives and views. No single value or principle can, without loss, be made the center and circumference of all political and social life. To give a few concrete examples, in modern society, neither the First Amendment nor the Second Amendment, neither the pro-life nor the pro-choice agenda may be elevated to the single and supreme criterion for deciding how we ought to live in a free and open society. A balance is needed between all these principles and interests, and no ideology alone is able to offer it.

One other thing might be worth pointing out here. Acting like a moderate implies that one's views are often unpredictable and cannot be fixed in one single column or along one single ideological axis. It is neither contradictory nor impossible to be moderate in politics by defending limited government and individual freedoms and rights, conservative in religion, and radical in other spheres of life such as culture or private life. From the point of view of ideological thinking, such a heterogeneous combination may appear incoherent. Yet, from the perspective of moderation rooted in experience, it is possible to hold two or more different ideas at the same time, and still retain the ability to function properly (more about that later in my letter on eclecticism).[3]

I expect you would object to my account of ideological thinking and my interpretation of moderation as an alternative to ideology. Moderation, you might say, is primarily a conservative virtue that advances a conservative agenda. It overlaps with the major themes of conservatism such as affection for the variety and mystery of life; opposition to uniformity, leveling, and egalitarianism; the belief that civilized society requires the existence of orders and classes; private property as a prerequisite of political freedom; opposition to utopian social engineering and recognition of the need for slow change in keeping with the demands of tradition. As such, the argument goes, moderation is merely a face of conservatism.

I do not want to deny the affinity between moderation and conservatism, but the truth is that moderation overlaps only *partly* with the conservative tradition and disposition. To explain this point better, I'd like to start with the similarities between them. It is true that moderates are keenly aware of the fragility of the institutions of our open societies and are strongly determined to fight against those who seek to destroy them. They believe that the task of government must always be a limited one, "namely the provision and custody of general rules of conduct, which are understood, not as plans for imposing substantive activities, but as instruments enabling people to pursue the activities of their own choice with the minimum frustration."[4] On this view, as the conservative political philosopher Michael Oakeshott put it, it is not the business of government to inflame passions and give them new objects to feed upon,

> but to inject into the activities of already too passionate men an ingredient of moderation; to restrain, to deflate, to pacify and to reconcile; not to stoke the fires of desire, but to damp them down. And all this, not because passion is vice and moderation virtue, but because moderation is indispensable if passionate men are to escape being locked in an encounter of mutual frustration.[5]

I cannot recommend Oakeshott's words highly enough to you. Nonetheless, there are notable dissimilarities between moderation and conservatism that should not go unnoticed. For one thing, moderates do not idealize tradition, a complex and slippery term, and are reluctant to mix religion, morality, and politics. They combine epistemological modesty and skeptical temperament to a greater degree than conservatives who believe that "political problems, at bottom, are religious and moral problems."[6] Politics, economy, morality, and religion follow different laws and belong to distinct spheres that must often be kept separate. There is another related point that often gets neglected. Moderation does not commit anyone to holding any particular beliefs about the universe, the existence of a providential order or the human condition in general.

So, where are the moderates located on the conventional political map? Here the data might surprise you. What opinion polls tell us is that more than a third of American voters today call themselves neither liberals nor conservatives. There are reasons to believe that a surprisingly high percentage of the current electorate have a more positive view of moderation than generally assumed, even if some of them may not describe themselves as moderates. Quite a few of them see themselves as independents belonging to the group of swing voters skeptical about the relevance of the traditional categories of Left and Right. The independents are particularly annoyed and concerned by demagogues, warmongers, and rabble-rousers prone to spread violence and chaos. They also tend to see parties as overly ideological and engaged in a pernicious cultural warfare that delays or impedes necessary reforms on key issues such as healthcare, immigration, education, gun control, and abortion.

Where does all this lead us, you might want to know? For one thing, moderation should be seen as an invitation to focus the conversation on concrete social and political issues with a view to finding workable (if imperfect) solutions to them.[7] The tradition of political moderation attracts those who distrust ideological thinking, are sensitive to crisis and prioritize the problem of maintaining the complex and fragile legacy of rules, procedures, and civilized habits that provide the framework within which our democratic way of life is possible. Simultaneously too liberal for conservatives and too conservative for progressives, moderates are between sides in politics. Although they share important affinities with the conservative and liberal traditions, neither of them can fully claim moderates as its own reliable representatives. Conservatives find them lacking in zeal and too skeptical to be allowed into their family, while progressive liberals regard them as too hesitant and excessively wedded to the status quo to be welcome in their midst.

To return to the epigraph of this letter, moderates – and here I take the liberty of including myself among them – have strong reasons to be (and remain) politically homeless. Unlike the proponents of ideological politics who suffer from "moral hemiplegia," they are hesitant to take up arms in the name of a single political cause or faction and are reluctant to adopt a certain political creed forever. Their caution is both a strength and a liability. It is a strength in that moderates excel at trimming between extremes, seeking to facilitate compromises between various constituencies. But it is simultaneously a liability insofar as moderates lack a single doctrine to which they could attach their names, and prefer to remain eclectic even when their decision comes at a high price. To many voters, not to have a simple political doctrine that can be summarized in a few lines is often a disreputable thing.

You might be intrigued by the hybridity of moderates, and with good reason. It is manifested not only by their fluid political commitments, but also by their belief that life can be practical without being excessively materialistic; many-sided and colorful without being shallow; profound and spiritual without any trace of religious zealotry. They are aware of the inevitable plurality of social, moral, and political values and refuse to define the political good in one single way. Unlike the proponents of rationalistic policies seeking to apply a strict set of rules and techniques to achieve specific goals, moderates believe that the political good is always multidimensional and underdetermined and cannot be achieved merely through technical knowledge. Constitutionally, they are skeptics who stop short of assuming that constitutions are bedrocks of eternal wisdom demanding absolute reverence. At the same time, they refuse to admit that constitutions and political norms are like houses that we are free to inhabit for a while and then free to leave when they no longer suit our changing tastes. Hence their image as conservatives.

But it is already late, and I must stop here. Nothing might make moderation more appealing to you now than a good rest after a long and busy day. Whatever you are doing and believe in, make sure to first count your blessings, (still) living as you do in a free society where rival views of the good society are allowed to compete. Farewell! Yours, . . .

6

An Antidote to Fanaticism

I've got one aim in life. And I'm making straight for it.[1]

(Jean, a character in Eugène Ionesco's *Rhinoceros*)

BETWEEN OURSELVES, let's recognize there is no shortage of examples of fanatics these days. Our world seems to have plenty of them, wherever we turn, and they all are loud, grandiloquent, and menacing. We all know some of them and are worried about their ambitious plans and strategies. To illustrate the perils of fanaticism that threaten (again) our democratic way of life, I have decided to choose a less conventional type, Jean, a colorful character in Eugènen Ionesco's play, *Rhinoceros,* first staged in Paris in 1960. Rereading it today, in the context of our fractured and divided society, can be an eye-opening experience for anyone who wants to comprehend the nature of fanaticism and how to combat it effectively. The stakes are once again dangerously high; we – and your generation in particular – are no longer immune to fanaticism today.

The tragic events of the last century opened our eyes to the dangers of ideological fanaticism and immunized us for a while against it. Hitler, Stalin, and Mao's extremes of cruelty and inhumanity horrified the entire world and served as a warning signal to those who entertained radical dreams. Today, however, things are changing, alas, not for the good. "The partial immunity we absorbed is fading," the Israeli novelist Amos Oz warned us. "Hatred, zealotry, loathing of the other and those who are different, revolutionary murderousness, the zeal to crush all the villains in a bloodbath – all are rearing their heads again."[2] New fertile grounds for fanaticism have appeared all over the world, along with new means of propaganda and brainwashing. There are visible forms of fanaticism easy to recognize, but there are also invisible ones, more difficult to pinpoint but equally dangerous and unsettling. Is there a booster against the new forms of fanaticism that might become available anytime soon? I don't know, but probably not.

The remarkable thing in Ionesco's play is that all characters but one eventually become rhinoceros, an outcome of the collective paranoia that slowly dehumanizes and destroys our human nature and civilization. Like a pandemic virus, fanaticism is highly contagious and spreads very quickly. It can be prevented or mitigated but not without sustained effort and determination. Once started, it may be impossible to stop since it is so contagious, and its germs are everywhere. As Oz put it, fanaticism begins at home, among and within us: "The illness frequently begins with innocuous symptoms: not beheadings, not car bombs, not burning families alive in their homes, but rather in the bosom of the family."[3] No one is immune in the end to the virus of "rhinoceritis." The irony is that one might catch it even while fighting it. How so?

Although Jean is not the main character in the play – that role belongs to his friend Berenger – he plays an important role. In the second act, Jean slowly turns into a rhinoceros in his own house, under Berenger's bewildered and frightened eyes. His transformation is both insidious and shocking, and Ionesco paints it with his uncanny humor and exquisite eye for detail. It is worth pausing for a moment to explore this Kafkaesque transformation which can happen to any of us once we succumb to the siren song of ideologies.

In the first act, Jean appears as a rigid, arrogant, intolerant, and self-righteous character, excessively obsessed with order and duty. Fastidiously dressed – he wears a brown suit, red tie, stiff collar, and brown hat – he looks down at Berenger, who arrives late, is unshaven and hatless, and whom he calls "a bluffer" and "a liar." The contrast between Berenger's negligent appearance and Jean's stiffness is striking from the outset. The latter looks almost inhuman in his impeccable suit; his desire to be perfectly consistent also strikes the reader as awkward. Jean is never wrong, entertains no doubts, and thinks of himself as the superior man who fulfills his duty and believes that everything in life is simple if one follows the rules. Unlike Jean, Berenger sometimes wonders if he exists and is not afraid of contradicting himself. "Solitude seems to oppress me," he confesses, before adding: "And so does the company of other people."[4]

At the outset of the second act, Jean's first symptoms are pretty mild. When Berenger comes to visit him, he finds him in bed, with a mild cough. Although Jean seems unwell, there is no reason to suspect anything grave. Yet, his condition slowly deteriorates, and his attitude becomes contradictory. "I don't feel well at all," he tells Berenger, while refusing to admit any weakness. "My nervous system is in perfect order," Jean goes on, "I'm sound in mind and limb. . . . I'm master of my own thoughts, my mind doesn't wander. I think straight, I always think straight."[5] Soon, we learn that he has a slight migraine, his voice becomes hoarse, and his forehead starts hurting. Berenger notes a mysterious tiny bump on Jean's forehead, just above his nose; although it seems innocuous for the moment, it will eventually grow into a horn. His skin becomes green, and his breathing is very heavy. As the act progresses, Jean's voice turns into the unsettling groan of a strange animal. He stubbornly refuses to see a doctor, being convinced that he can look after himself and knows best what's good for him.

As Jean's language deteriorates, his skin becomes increasingly greener, and the horn on his forehead gets bigger and bigger. He becomes annoyed with Berenger whom he no longer recognizes as a friend. It is at that moment that the potential for violence appears, and all bets are off. The dialogue between the two friends becomes increasingly difficult, until Jean threatens furiously: "I'll trample you down!" At that very moment, Berenger discovers to his great surprise that his friend has turned into a real rhinoceros. "I never would have thought it of him – never!" Berenger admits, perplexed. His dismay grows when he looks out of the window and sees in the street many other individuals turned into rhinoceros. A whole herd of them, he admits, resigned. They invade the public space, leaving no safe place to hide. There is no way to escape the rhinoceros' menacing presence. They have taken over.

In the end, Berenger is the only sane person left standing. He refuses to capitulate, being determined to remain human and fight against the collective paranoia around him. All his friends and acquaintances have been infected by the virus. Berenger discovers that even good people (like Dudard) can at some point turn into rhinoceros. Lacking the courage to confront the evil, they give in to it. They are particularly good at finding justifications for their cowardice and hide their weaknesses under various pretexts.

Compare for a moment Berenger's straightforward determination to fight against evil with Dudard's self-defeating strategy. The latter claims that all he has to do is to be realistic, keep an open mind, and look the facts unemotionally in the face. He plays with words, pretending that it is difficult for him to distinguish between normal and abnormal. "Can you personally define these conceptions of normality and abnormality?" he asks with a smile. For Berenger, this is an unacceptable sophism for which he has no patience. "Lunacy is lunacy," he says, "and that's all there is to it! Everybody knows what lunacy is. And what about the rhinoceros – are they practice or are they theory?"[6]

What does this all have to do with us today and what lessons can we draw from the play? I believe that the message of *Rhinoceros* can be interpreted in different ways that speak to our present concerns. At the individual level, fanaticism may be contained when detected in time; if that happens, its effects can be limited and may not be harmful to others. But once it becomes a collective phenomenon, fanaticism is highly contagious and hard to control. The spread of group fanaticism is extremely dangerous to open societies that protect freedom of speech and association. It causes large numbers of people to behave in ways that are injurious to others.

Arguably the most unsettling message of the play is that the fanatic is present as a potentiality in *all* of us, without exception. The fanatic lurks in our souls, waiting for a moment to come out of the dark. No one – is entirely safe from or immune to the virus of fanaticism, everyone has the potential to become a rhinoceros. There is no herd immunity in this case. Some manage to escape the virus, through their conscious efforts or simply by accident. Others succumb to the bug and never recover from it.

Who is most likely to get "rhinoceritis" and how should we to fight against it? Is it possible to build at least some partial immunity to religious and political fanaticism? And how can we do that? It is difficult to answer these questions because many fanatics don't look insane or extreme at first sight; on the contrary, they look quite normal, like most of us. There are great fanatics and small ones, all of whom have maniacal obsessions and grand designs for a radiant future. Some may even look happy, though others may be profoundly dissatisfied with their lives in the most secret corner of their hearts.

You will note that all of them are extremely serious and lack humor. They are incapable of making fun of themselves and fail to perceive the relativity of all human endeavors. For them, life is *always* a serious matter, and any sense of levity is deemed sinful. Many have hidden inferiority complexes and resentments. A few may hate their superiors, others show disdain for their fellow citizens, or are simply uncaring or uninterested in others. As for Jean, he confesses cynically: "I'm indifferent to them – or rather they disgust me; and they'd better keep out of my way, or I'll run them down."[7]

Lacking the ability to understand and empathize with others, fanatics tend to be monomaniacs, focused exclusively on themselves or one single aim in life. Their priority, as Jean remarks, is to stay focused on their mission and make straight for it, no matter what. They prefer to interpret the world through a single lens and insist that their particular lens be applied everywhere. The fanatics believe that something is deeply wrong with the decadent world around them which they loathe profoundly. The objects of their hatred can change over time, from Western-style pluralism and freedoms to multiculturalism and identity politics. As self-appointed saviors, they feel called to bring the cure to a sick (and despicable) world and are convinced that their noble ends justify any means and medicine. "When we've demolished all that," Jean believes, "we'll be better off."[8]

If you read the play, you will also note that fanatics are accustomed to living in permanent tension or conflict with the outside world. Like Jean, they are easily excitable and obsessed with orderliness and duty. They are unable to debate rationally and tend to speak in clichés like Jean; they shout rather than talk calmly to others. They see themselves as impartial and free of bias, while they regard everyone else as victims of prejudice and partiality. Since they feel persecuted and constantly under siege, they look for tensions and threats and thrive on them. Fanatics like Jean need a permanent enemy at the gate whose presence increases their vigilance and mobilization and reinforces their sense of identity and cohesiveness.

Not surprisingly, fanatics spend their energy and time trying to figure out how to rebuild the world from scratch by purifying it of villains and rogues. "I'm sick of moral standards," Jean exclaims. "We need to go beyond moral standards. ... We've got to build our life on new foundations. We must get back to primeval integrity."[9] For fanatics like Jean, there is no time to rest: the seeds of corruption and the traitors are everywhere and must be eliminated without delay. Even moral standards, when they stand in the way of their plans, must be abandoned for the sake of the final victory. They are prepared to use any means that may be needed, including intimidation and violence, to advance their agendas.

Above all, fanatics feel an irrepressible urge to burn and destroy. In their view, every issue is simple, has only one side, and admits of simple and decisive solutions. They are convinced that the world must be interpreted according to one single and simple dimension. According to this view, one can only be pro-life or pro-choice, for low taxes or high taxes, for protectionism or globalism. Choices are definitive and allow no nuances. Furthermore, one must be on guard all the time since every moment of inattention or relaxation might be fatal. That is why, as Amos Oz remarked, "the fanatic is always in a hurry to fall on your neck to save you, because he loves you. ... But conversely, he might grab you and strangle you if he discovers that you are beyond redemption. Lost. And if that is the case, he is obliged to hate you and rid the world of you."[10] For fanatics of all kinds, everything is now-or-never, all-or-nothing.

It should be obvious to you by now that fanatics long for simple salvation formulas and oversimplify the world at the cost of making it uniform and destroying its colorful variety.

Their agendas seek to bring universal happiness on earth but often lead to massacres and executions ending with universal misery and suffering.[11] Fanatics like Jean replace love of real people with abstract love of humanity and view everything – both social and private life – through a single prism that destroys the beautiful and authentic things in the world.

There is another thing that strikes me as important in this regard: fanatics are skilled at trading faiths and camps. They can also easily move from extreme optimism to total pessimism and back. Emotionally unstable, fanatics are ready to serve a particular cause or party without reserve. At the same time, they are ready to quickly change camps when they feel abandoned or betrayed. Fanatics can easily replace the love of God and charity toward all with the love of their own religion and the adoration of their own tribe. While pretending to love truth, freedom, or justice, they are ready to trade them for an ideology, doctrine, or sect that promises to translate these values and principles into practice.

Now, let's turn our attention to Berenger, apparently the only sane character in Ionesco's play. How do we explain that he manages to remain human to the very end in spite of everything going on around him? Why is Berenger alone capable of resisting the collective madness and maintaining his humanity and integrity intact? Why isn't he infected by the virus like all others? And what are the values and principles that can make us immune to fanaticism in the end?[12] I believe that what saves Berenger from being contaminated by the virus of rhinoceritis is not a miraculous vaccine against fanaticism – alas, such a thing does not exist and will not be found anytime soon – but his imperfection and plainness, along with his moderation. He is not dressed as impeccably as Jean, lacks his punctuality, and longs for real relationships and love. He is often not sure what to do and even doubts himself – "I sometimes wonder if I exist myself"[13] – being unsure who is normal and who is abnormal. Yet, despite all that, Berenger never loses his humanity and common sense, and this quality saves him in the end.

Perhaps unbeknownst to him, Berenger instinctively seeks to preserve something vital to human life. But what exactly is that, you might ask? I believe he wants to protect the moral standards derided by Jean, that is, those principles and values that make possible a civilized and free way of life. As a sort of moderate, Berenger also has respect for limits, tradition, and unwritten norms, and wants to maintain them as much as possible. He does not wish to wipe the slate clean of them, nor is he willing to risk everything to build a novel and allegedly better life on entirely new foundations. Only those who are entirely committed to a particular cause will set no limits to their large-scale revolutionary plans. As such, Berenger is the true conservative while Jean is the fanatic who believes that "when we've demolished all that, we'll be better off."[14] For zealots like him, big words such as humanism and morality are mere slogans meant to further their political cause. But not so for Berenger, who takes those principles seriously and believes in them to the end.

Berenger's example shows how to fight fanaticism and why moderation, too, may be a realistic, if arguably solitary, strategy for combatting extremism. For him, the sight of fanatics is upsetting and does not – indeed, it cannot – leave him indifferent. "The shock is too violent for you to stay cool and detached," he confesses. "We must attack the evil at its roots."[15] One may not simply turn one's back or pretend it doesn't exist or it will go away by itself. That is what Dudard chooses to do. He is not an evil person, but he is good at finding justifications for his excessive tolerance of evil and lack of courage. I find his example unsettling – and I hope you will as well – because it shows that even decent folks like him, animated by good intentions, may sometimes become rhinoceros. As Berenger puts it, "Good men make good rhinoceros, unfortunately."[16]

I have chosen to write to you about *Rhinoceros* because literature and humor can often serve as effective antidotes to fanaticism. They enlarge our imagination, make us curious, and invite us to question our beliefs, even to make fun of ourselves at times, something that fanatics seem incapable of. Humor combined with a sense of irony and a touch of skepticism allows us to contemplate ourselves, at least for a few moments, as others see us. They invite us to let the hot air out of any excessive sense of self-righteousness and self-importance that we might well have.[17] They help us put things in perspective and teach us about the relativity of all things. They also warn us against turning all disputes and controversies into either–or choices that leave no room for ambiguity.

Humor may be a powerful solution to fanaticism and fundamentalism, but it is not the only one. Since fanaticism begins "at home" and its germs are present everywhere, the best antidotes to it are still the natural and simple ones: modesty, humility, and a sense of the relativity of all things human – in other words, *moderation.* "Being immune to fanaticism," Amos Oz remarked, "entails, among other things, a willingness to exist inside open-ended situations that do not come full circle and cannot be unequivocally settled. A readiness to live with questions and choices whose resolutions hide far beyond the hazy horizon."[18] He was right, and I have little to add to his words.

You should then have the courage of nuances and be on guard against self-righteousness. Avoid ideological conformity and stand firm for the freedom to speak your mind, without any form of self-censorship. Stay away from publicly shaming others for their beliefs, no matter how different they might be from yours. Above all, do not try to force them to change the way you want. Just let them be and go on with their lives as they think fit as long as they seem harmless. But be prepared to say no and fight against them with all your power and conviction if and when they threaten our free way of life and our democratic institutions.

Adieu! Yours, . . .

PART III

DO MODERATES HAVE A POLITICAL VISION?

The virtue of moderation (which times and situations will clearly distinguish from the counterfeits of pusillanimity and indecision) is the virtue only of superior minds. It requires a deep courage, and full of reflection, to be temperate when the voice of multitudes (and specious mimic of fame and reputation) passes judgment against you.[1]

Edmund Burke

Interlude

AFTER READING THE PREVIOUS letters, Lauren and Rob remained unconvinced about the benefits of moderation. Here is a short note I received from them that I take the liberty of reproducing here in full.

You wrote about moderation as an alternative to ideology and antidote to fanaticism. We know now what moderates are against, but the question remains: what do they stand for? Do they have a real and coherent vision of what a good society might look like, or are they simply against any radical ideas and plans broadly defined? Do their agendas have any fixed points or lodestars? Or it is rather the case that they change constantly and have no such fixed points? If so, can then moderation be viewed as a real virtue rather than a merely circumstantial strategy?

It is troubling and disconcerting to see moderates dismissing radicals who fight for justice for all as inexperienced idealists. But isn't it true that radicals fight against various forms of injustice precisely because moderates lack the moral imagination and courage to do it? While it is true that most moderates acknowledge the existence of some forms of injustice, they tend to underplay their severity or misrepresent them. They prefer to remain in their comfortable bubbles rather than speak up for all. When they decide to leave their echo chambers, they only pay lip service to justice and equality for all.

That's why instead of using the term moderate to describe those who reject radical plans and ideas, perhaps we should call them by their real name: enablers and partisans of the status quo, "corporatist mouthpieces"[1] *who want to maintain current hierarchies and perpetuate existing forms of injustice.*

My first instinct was to point out that there is a wide range of viewpoints among people who call themselves moderates and this diversity matters a great deal. Then I realized that my younger interlocutors might want to learn more about the political vision of moderation. The next letters will explain why moderation is much more than a private virtue, as commonly perceived. It also has significant *institutional* and *constitutional* implications that often go unacknowledged or underappreciated.

1

The Limits of Moral Clarity

No great nation can abandon the obligations of moral clarity for the convenience of situational ethics.[1]

(Senator John McCain)

YOU MAY REMEMBER that I have previously voiced skepticism about achieving moral clarity on controversial and complex social and political issues. It is time to examine closer this catchy concept. Calls for moral clarity have been made from various quarters, predominantly from the radical Left lately. The Left has made the fight against all forms of domination and racism a priority in the name of moral clarity. Yet, demands for moral clarity are not exclusive to the Left. To demonstrate that, I have chosen as the epigraph of this letter the words of the late Senator John McCain (R-AZ) from a speech he gave in 2002, in the early phases of the war on terror. Nobody can question the moral probity of the late Senator, who was a true patriot and served his country with honor and dignity. Although animated by noble intentions, might it be possible that he expected too much from moral clarity in political life?

To be sure, there are situations when choices are clear and leave no room for doubt or hesitation. For example, in wartime, we can clearly recognize who are our enemies and we can effectively mobilize to defeat them. When Winston Churchill gave his memorable speech in the summer of 1940 asking his fellow citizens to rise and fight with all their might and determination against Hitler, that was a memorable moment of moral clarity. But let's recognize it: such moments when moral clarity is possible and necessary are (fortunately) rare in history. Not every conflict can or should be depicted as a cosmic gigantic battle between the forces of good and evil. Luckily for us today, the stakes are not as high as in 1940, when the world was fighting against Nazism.

I don't want to deny that moral clarity might be an attractive concept that can sometimes help us make the right choices. Yet, I want to warn you that it is prone to being abused and might easily turn into a cliché. It is also a polemical term rhetorically used to support various political agendas, some more controversial than others. Let's remember that moral clarity was initially introduced on the Right in the 1980s, in the fight against communism. Two decades later, it was invoked to justify the use of evil and inhuman means – torture – in the name of national security.[2] Today, many activists on the Right tend to use this term to condemn the "dictatorship" of moral relativism as a serious threat to the survival of Western civilization.

Consider, for example, a widely publicized speech at the University of Notre Dame on religious liberty given by former Attorney General William Barr in October 2019. Describing the present state of our politics and culture, Barr opined: "This is not decay. It is organized destruction, ... an unremitting assault on religion and traditional values."[3] Note the key words here – "organized destruction" and "unremitting assault." You might be led to think we are engaged in a total war of survival in which no second may be lost, and the doom can be averted only if we get involved in the fight right away. Barr ended by calling for moral clarity and a firm response to the new barbarian invasions that are threatening the values of our Western civilization.

If all this might sound strange to you, don't forget that moral clarity has also become an obsession on the Left lately. In the name of achieving it, some have argued for abandoning objectivity and reliance on real facts in the fight against injustice. They delineate a wide spectrum of privileged to oppressed and place people along it according to various groups and categories. In the end, each receives a score and a certificate of good or bad behavior. The partisans of moral clarity on the Left believe that to be "woke" is to wake up to the truth, to free oneself from all forms of false consciousness, in particular from the belief in the legitimacy (and goodness) of liberal principles. For them, liberal society is profoundly hypocritical and never lives up to its professed ideals.

Everything in it, from our daily interaction to our institutions and schools, can be interpreted as a form of power and oppression that must be unmasked, condemned, and resisted.

According to this radical view held, among others, by Wesley Lowery, the American view-from-nowhere, objectivity-obsessed, both-sides journalism is a failed experiment. Social justice warriors must therefore abandon neutral objectivity which should be replaced by moral clarity.[4] What we took to be an objective perspective was an exclusively white and male one, an oppressive (and often racist) lens that distorted reality and led us astray. It has failed and must be abandoned in the name of moral clarity.

It may not be immediately obvious to you, but in some regards, the logic embraced by radicals on the Left resembles the one adopted by right-wing radicals. I don't intend to draw any strong equivalences between them, so please keep that in mind before you begin criticizing me. What concerns me here is that those who are ready to abandon objectivity for the sake of achieving moral clarity (broadly defined) tend to dispense with distinctions, nuances, and complexity, and work only with stark contrasts and alternatives. Such a tendency may be motivated by good intentions but it encourages hyperbole, self-righteousness, and intellectual complacency.

This happens, for example, when in the name of moral clarity, certain laws are adopted that restrict the right to privacy and infringe upon individual rights. It also occurs when strident affirmation of group identity and solidarity prevents open exchanges and contestation and replaces the common pursuit of truth and justice with a one-dimensional narrative about the course of history. Moderates are wary of ever assuming that God or history is infallibly on their side. They know that those who believe themselves to be invested with a divine or holy mission are often inclined to stop at nothing, including sacrificing other people's lives, when they feel that the time is ripe for fulfilling their task. Anything may then be deemed permissible in the pursuit of what is regarded as the right or just cause.

You might now think that moderates only believe that they must be skeptical of others' beliefs, but that's not really the case. They are also acutely aware that they should always hold their *own* views and ideas with a reserve clause. They are not oblivious of their own blind spots, especially when it comes to making bold claims about certainty and moral clarity on deeply divisive issues. Moderates know that brash assertions encourage crude hyperbole and simplifications and leave little room for debate and contestation. Once you believe you have achieved moral clarity on a certain subject, then it seems no longer necessary to explore it any further. You acquire an unshakeable certainty about the truth of your theories. No more questions are necessary, debate becomes superfluous, sometimes even dangerous, and the case is declared closed. What is there to debate anyway when it is obvious that there is only one (right) side to the story, and everyone who is reasonable must embrace it?

To be sure, there are other problems with high-minded calls for moral clarity. Consider, for example, the repeated warnings (from the radical Right) that our society is totally decadent and corrupt, and moral clarity is entirely lacking in our homes, businesses, schools, and government. Or take the claim (advanced by the radical Left) that we must judge the past not on its own terms, but solely through the expectations, norms, and mores of the present that (alone) afford us an opportunity to achieve total moral clarity. Removing the statues of George Washington and Abraham Lincoln from our public squares in the name of moral clarity and restorative justice is an example of such a crude form of ideological thinking leading to perverse outcomes. Banning textbooks or destroying the civil service as part of the "deep state" in the name of moral clarity is another.

Such claims and actions, different as they may be, have something important in common. They lack nuance and are often the expression of reductionist thinking that tends to overreach. Everything turns into an auction for popularity in which those who shout louder carry the day. Then, under the cover of moral clarity, it becomes possible for individuals and entire groups to be publicly defenestrated and declared immoral and guilty by association with the alleged sins of their parents or relatives.

But this is not all; there are additional problems and ambiguities surrounding the concept of moral clarity.[5] The obsession with achieving it now may lead people to believe that most political and social things are simple, plain, and easy to understand, and that a select few may be able to come up with straightforward solutions to difficult and complex problems. As such, calls for moral clarity, even when they start from good intentions, tend to ignore the fact that the world is a mixed bag and a messy house, in which what is pure and spotless is always accompanied by what is coarse and unwholesome.

In such an imperfect world, ideas, beliefs, and interests constantly clash with each other. Even good ideas and proposals, arising from good intentions, can have – and often have – unintended and perverse consequences. Sometimes, using the term moral clarity may help figure out which ends and means are desirable and acceptable, while at other times it does not. Some initiatives that seem questionable or bad might, in fact, lead to good outcomes, and vice versa.

Let me explain this paradox with the aid of a few other concrete examples. It is appropriate to endorse a modicum of welfare provisions that ensure that individuals cannot fall below a certain threshold, but it is not acceptable to create (in the name of moral clarity) a system that levels everything and punishes individual creativity and spontaneity for the sake of creating a fictitious solidarity. It is always necessary to defend free speech, but it is unacceptable to claim (again by invoking moral clarity) that free speech is "violence" when used by the "wrong" people to advance allegedly pernicious agendas. It is perfectly legitimate to try to figure out the original intentions of the Founding Fathers to understand better what they set out to achieve and how we may continue their unfinished work. But it is not realistic to endorse a strictly originalist interpretation of the US Constitution seeking to discern its single "true" meaning that may be applied *tale quale* to solve our present problems. And the list could go on.

My message to you is *not* that the term moral clarity ought to be abandoned altogether; it certainly has its own undeniable merits, as the civil rights struggle showed decades ago. That was a moment of moral clarity, after all, that was effectively used to promote far-reaching reforms and fight against the hypocrisy, philistinism, and pseudo-realism of those who were comfortable with the establishment. What I want to stress, however, is that this concept ought to be viewed with a necessary grain of skepticism. If you still want to invoke it, do it, but be aware of its limits and potential overreach.

Avoid, above all, its self-righteous rhetoric and politics of self-indulgence that may give your conscience the false assurance that you are on the right side of history, allied with the forces of the good against those of evil.[6] That rhetoric is often a trap because it feeds hubris and self-righteousness, making you feel entitled to bring intelligibility, purity, and order to a world you believe to be immoral, decadent, or in disarray. Such claims inspire the false confidence that you alone are able to see things as they really are, while everyone else lives in a dark cave, under a thick veil of false consciousness.

As for me, I have another reason to be skeptical of loud calls for moral clarity, couched in simplistic soundbites and slogans that promote peer pressure and conformism. Such demands often have a bellicose tone and display excessive ardor, seeking to make us all share in the culture of repudiation (on both the Left and Right) and participate in the fierce battles that rage around us. A surprising number of those who call for moral clarity are highly confident that they are invested with a special vision, mission, and power, denied to other mortals, and that they are better, purer, and wiser than their opponents. Their activism knows no limits. They invent new social codes and pretend to see farther than everyone else. Overconfident in their power, good intentions, and expertise, the new Puritans believe they need no restraints or limits. Everything fits perfectly with their preconceived ideas, which eventually become indistinguishable from slogans and crude headlines. Their judgment is swift, decisive, and merciless. They no longer feel the need to listen to or tolerate dissenters and critics, whose views are declared *a priori* wrong, evil, deplorable, stupid, and toxic.

But slogans and headlines are no more complex than bumper stickers that convey a superficial message in few words for hurried eyes. When we settle for a single headline or story, when we choose to see reality only through one prism and window (freedom/equality, justice/oppression, racism/anti-racism), we risk losing any sense of balance and proportion. Then, our minds may become "wide shut"[7] and we undergo a personality change, turning into "captive minds." We enter an alternative reality from which, in the end, there may be no exit. Certain topics are declared beyond debate, critics are pilloried, and dogmas replace the search for truth.

It is always easy (and tempting) to denounce the others – always the others, never ourselves – for lacking a clear sense of what is right and wrong, for being confused, indifferent, misguided, or lacking moral clarity. Nonetheless, this tendency comes with a high price tag. When we are overconfident about our beliefs and, in the name of moral clarity, no longer acknowledge the need to see all sides of a story, or declare certain topics taboo, we give up any pretension to objectivity along with willingness to weigh the pros and cons on every issue. Open-ended questions and nuances are replaced by categorical, apodictic answers that prevent free exchange and contestation.

It might not be such a bad idea, from time to time, to cultivate doubt and learn to appreciate the beauty of nuances.[8] I fear those who never doubt, because they tend to be fanatical. But I am also skeptical at the same time of those who go to the other extreme and doubt everything. For doubt, too, can be narcissistic to a fault and might lead to cynicism and arrogance, if abused.

So, I urge you to beware of intoxication with your ideas and stay clear of the temptation of invoking moral clarity to advance your political agenda. You should always let your skepticism fight against your proclivity for self-righteousness. It is better to be strict and rigorous with yourselves and generous toward others than vice versa. Above all, it is important to never settle into a single ideological costume that promises moral certainty or clarity. Remember that all we can do is to try to edge ever closer to the truth with the humility and moderation that come from the heart.

But more about all that in another letter. Farewell! Yours, . . .

2

Against the Politics of Warfare

Charge the cockpit or you die.[1]

(Michael J. Anton)

YOU HAVE CHASTISED me in the past for being somewhat elusive and coy about contemporary politics. Rest assured though that even if I wanted to do that, it would have been impossible, given the current level of hyper-polarization and anger which greatly concerns me as well. I propose we start today from a controversial essay by Michael J. Anton, a prominent right-wing figure and former official in the Trump administration. He is the author of the (in)famous "Flight 93" article published in the September 2016 issue of the *Claremont Review of Books*, under the pseudonym Publius Decius Mus.

I have chosen Anton's essay because it is a good example of the politics of warfare that moderates like me categorically reject. If you haven't already read it, I recommend it to you. Not because I agree with its theses – far from that – but because the author has a provocative style that teaches us something important about the radical politics of the Right. As a libertarian critic put it, "Unwittingly (no doubt) and perhaps quite tragically, Michael Anton is the super carrier who brought the virus of the reactionary Right into the bloodstream of the conservative intellectual movement."[2]

Of course, Anton didn't discover a new political planet. A similar point had previously been made by many others, including Carl Schmitt, Fascism's most prominent legal scholar. In a famous book published in the 1920s, he argued that "the specific political distinction to which political actions and motives can be reduced is that between friend and enemy."[3] Schmitt wrote these lines during the last years of the Weimar Republic. Then Europe was enjoying a brief peaceful interlude, although dark clouds were gathering on the horizon, foretelling devastating thunderstorms. A decade later, Schmitt's theoretical distinction between friend and enemy became the leitmotif of world politics, as the entire civilized world quickly descended into the abyss of barbarism and fanaticism.

It didn't have to be that way. The foundations of modern politics were laid in the sixteenth and seventeenth centuries, when a clear demarcation between the spheres of politics and religion was drawn. The aim was to turn people's minds away from the fear of invisible spirits and supernatural powers in order to limit or eliminate the inconveniences and the uncertainty of the violent state of nature. In the eighteenth century, attention turned to refounding politics on universal reasons and principles, accessible to all, that could be verified and certified properly. The consensus was that it was necessary and possible to lower the stakes of politics so that the latter would no longer be directly connected to religion and personal salvation.

According to the modern view, politics should never be about searching for certainty or the meaning of life, nor should soulcraft be its main goal. In times of crisis, when societies are threatened by chaos and anarchy, politics takes center stage and is expected to help reduce or eliminate the risk of a war of all against all. Even then, it is important to remember that its main task is *not* to endow life with splendor and greatness like literature, philosophy, and art, but more modestly, to provide a stable framework for the gradual readjustment of human relationships. In normal times, it is literature, art, music, and philosophy rather than politics that should be the outlets for individual creative energies and skills.

In this regard, I'd like to recommend to you the following definition of politics given by Michael Oakeshott. "In political activity," he wrote, "men sail a boundless and bottomless sea; there is neither harbor for shelter nor floor for anchorage, neither starting-place nor appointed destination. The enterprise is to keep [the ship] afloat on an even keel; the sea is both friend and enemy; and the seamanship consists in using the resources of a traditional manner of behavior to make a friend of every hostile occasion."[4] His message is crystal clear. Politics ought to always remain an ancillary, second-rate activity focused on making prudent and constant adjustments to an imperfect reality in permanent flux. Because its realm is a limited one and involves a certain degree of mental vulgarity and a narrowing of horizon, politics should never be allowed to become the central focus of our lives. Oftentimes, a general and constant interest in and feverish preoccupation with politics may very well be the surest sign of a general decay in society. Moreover, for Oakeshott, any person who has "a passionate interest other than politics will be disposed to be a conservative in politics."[5]

You may disagree with this last point, but I am sure you would endorse his point that politics must always remain a limited activity. In an over-politicized era in which the stakes have been raised to dangerously high levels, we are treating again politics as a form of religion and all-out warfare. Our ideological warfare represents the contemporary equivalent of seventeenth-century religious zealotry. The paranoid style of warfare politics has increasingly dominated and shaped our public life over the past few decades, posing significant threats to America's constitutional principles. While both sides have contributed to this climate change that has raised the general political temperature, the radical Right bears a great(er) responsibility in this regard.

Whether or not we agree on this issue, a few things seem beyond dispute. In 2017, the authors of a study comparing levels of political polarization in several developed nations discovered that partisan hatred was strongest in the United States. They noticed that Americans have become accustomed and addicted to receiving and consuming information slanted through political lenses that blur the lines between real and "alternative" facts. Political elites, too, bear a large share of responsibility as they have embraced radical rhetoric that inflames passions and deepens sectarianism. The study concluded that "a poisonous cocktail of othering, aversion, and moralization" poses significant threats to the survival of democracy and warned that something must be done to mitigate the growth of political distrust and hatred.[6]

It won't be easy, to use a polite understatement. Politics as warfare has become a staple in our national political discourse and mass media in the last few decades. Today, it is a common style of argument and political strategy with obvious electoral benefits. Note that the language of the practitioners of this type of scorched-earth politics is often apocalyptic; it employs a bellicose, paranoid, and uncivil tone that plays on people's fears and worries. It calls for enforcing purity and litmus tests to weed out alleged traitors and lukewarm members from all groups. This sectarian and vindictive form of politics, a type of Fox News on steroids, enhanced by the dramatic use of hyperbole and anathemas, goes hand in hand with the constant demonization of opponents and heightened ideological intransigence.

Now let's take a closer look at Anton's "Flight 93 Election" essay, a masterful illustration of this type of politics. Written to endorse Donald Trump's presidential run in 2016, it provides a clear and powerful example of the galvanizing rhetoric of warfare politics. The text was praised as a home run in the conservative media for its acerbic tone and incisive content. There are many things one could say about this striking essay that gave voice to the fears and hopes of many on the radical Right. Anton's pugnacious style confidently drew stark Manichaean contrasts, stoking a sense of danger and raising the stakes of electoral politics to a very high level. Those who embrace this style of politics believe they are engaged in an all-out holy war, martyrs for a just cause and ready to die for it if need be. They regard themselves as part of a larger fight for redemption in which there is no place for moderation, nuances, or compromise. On their view, to be cautious and prudent is itself a form of treason and lack of heroism.

There is also a repeated warning that time is running out, and the choice we are facing is presented in the simplest possible terms: "You charge the cockpit, or you die. You may die . . . there are no guarantees. Except one: if you don't try, death is certain."[7] The conclusion is that we must fully commit ourselves to saving the soul of the country which is jeopardized right now. If we stay passive, we acquiesce in our collective demise. Nonetheless, the goal is to achieve much more than that. What Anton and his friends want is total victory over the "evildoers," an inclusive and broadly defined category; almost anyone may be included in it at some point. Equally important, anything seems justified in the pursuit of these maximalist goals, from disseminating fake news and sowing civic distrust and paranoia to inciting to insurrection, civil unrest, and even violence.

You may think now that Anton's apocalyptic rhetoric, meant to arouse passion and militancy, is an isolated case, but the reality is different. This type of rhetoric has since become common among the hard Right, defining both the Trump administration and the post-Trump era.[8] Shortly following Joe Biden's victory in November 2020, the editors of the same *Claremont Review of Books* penned a chilling open letter in the *American Mind* that read like another apocalyptic battle cry, urging followers to challenge and reject the election results.[9] Its message was unambiguous, evoking Anton's passionate exhortation from 2016. There is no time to wait since America is headed off a cliff; everything is at stake in this war, it is now or never. The letter deliberately distorted the facts and flouted the rule of law, declaring one side – the Democrats who allegedly tried to "steal" the election – entirely corrupt and … anti-American. The editors also went to great lengths to demonize the "weak sisters on the right," calling for the character assassination of moderate Republicans who stood up to the wild and fantastical claims about election fraud.

You might also want to read another essay, titled "Conservatism Is Not Enough," in which Glenn Ellmers, a senior fellow at the Claremont Institute, went a step further. "Let's be blunt," he wrote. "The United States has become two nations occupying the same country. When pressed, or in private, many would now agree. Fewer are willing to take the next step and accept that most people living in the United States today – certainly more than half – are not Americans in any meaningful sense of the term." As you might expect, the list of suspects is diverse and quite inclusive. Many native-born people, Ellmers warned, may technically be citizens of the United States, but "they are no longer (if they ever were) Americans." The reason is simple: "They do not believe in, live by, or even like the principles, traditions, and ideals that until recently defined America as a nation and as a people." And Ellmers concluded peremptorily that "these citizen-aliens, these non-American Americans" are not real American citizens, "they are something else."[10] But what are they, one is tempted to ask, if not citizens of the United States, the diverse and imperfect country that has always aspired to be a beacon of hope and liberty for the entire world?

Such overheated and apocalyptic language should not leave us indifferent. It peddles dangerous fantasies of salvation and conspiratorial theories that illustrate what historian Richard Hofstadter once called "the paranoid style" in American political life.[11] Its radical embrace of an extreme form of the "politics of faith" and the open call for a crusade to cleanse the body politic of those who are not "real" American citizens fly in the face of reality. Even the specter of civil war is invoked to mobilize the base.

If you think I exaggerate, listen also to another ultra-conservative critic of the controversial "1619 Project." "You and I," he wrote, "are in the middle of what has been a two generation-long civil war, in which the Left is determined to replace America with a different system."[12] In the eyes of those who conceive of politics as total war, the objective is not reaching compromises and building coalitions in order to govern for the common good. In the end, they become "so preoccupied with who or what they are against that the foundation of their politics is reflexive opposition rather than first principles of reason."[13] The new crusaders believe that they must fight the culture and political wars with the aim of winning big and crushing their enemies. They see the other side as an existential threat that must be annihilated without delay.

We find similarly fantastical claims in the apocalyptic politics promoted by influential conservative radio hosts who claim that the Left is engaged in a systematic shredding of norms and the undermining of the rule of law. This crude language is also applied to chastise those conservatives who refuse to embrace a scorched-earth brand of politics and are therefore denounced as traitors or RINOs ("Republicans-in-name-only"). The listeners are encouraged to stick to their own imaginary facts, no matter what, and ignore the evidence and real facts when they contradict their ideological priorities. On this view, even the rule of law and the Constitution are seen as (little more than) mere conventions that people may defy when they seem to go against their interests and convictions.

I must add though, without wanting to draw any false equivalences, that the demonization of opponents and conspiratorial thinking are key tropes of the politics of warfare that transcend ideological boundaries. The fight is described as being against an enemy that is "different from us" and, as a result, a very dangerous one that must be neutralized. The adversary does not always fight in the open but often lies in hiding and resorts to cunning and dishonesty. Equally important, the enemy is international, ubiquitous, and "does not have its own homeland but feels it owns the whole world."[14] It is easy to see that there is no limit to this conspiratorial way of thinking. The plot is universal and the pressure of the enemy relentless. Fighting against it requires being on constant alert and in a state of permanent mobilization.

What is noteworthy about the practitioners of this bellicose type of politics ready to storm the cockpit is that they see themselves as manning the barricades of civilization against the new barbarian invasions led by the partisans of moral relativism on the Right and the most radical among the social justice warriors on the Left. They share an understanding of politics as a gigantic Manichaean battle, waged on multiple fronts (political arena, deep state, education, culture) and leaving no room for bargaining or political compromise. They may be motivated by nostalgia, which can be delusional but ultimately harmless, or by prudential skepticism toward large-scale social and economic changes, which can be a healthy attitude. The real danger appears when their leaders are willing to relinquish key liberal principles like the rule of law, toleration, pluralism, and constitutionalism to achieve their reactionary goals. The actual threat arises when they come to believe that reactionary politics is the only salutary path, and their motto becomes: "To hell with liberal order!"[15]

Now, you will ask, what exactly does all that have to do with political moderation? I hope the answer is not difficult to surmise. For one thing, if left unchecked, "partisan teamsmanship"[16] is a major danger to – and vulnerability of – democracy because it raises the temperature of the political game and fosters the rise of extremism. Moderates refuse to believe that America is only right-wing and left-wing people, fighting against each other. They are skeptical toward claims that the mere existence of the other side poses an existential threat that justifies an all-out battle, making concessions impossible and foreclosing the possibility of reaching any compromise or common ground. Even when moderates get to exercise power, they refrain from rewriting the rules of the game to suit their momentary advantages. They reject as utopian and absurd the claim that the members of a certain party can get everything they want when they are in power. Moderates also dismiss as a dangerous fantasy the idea that half of the country may be conquered or controlled largely by means of gerrymandering, redistricting, court appointments, and voting restrictions.

You may disagree with me on this point, but I still want to remind you that the stakes in politics are rarely either–or, a matter of life or death. Most often, they tend to be smaller, of the more-or-less type, leaving room for bargaining and compromise. That's why moderates believe that what really matters is to try to build bridges and maintain open venues for dialogue and collaboration among opponents committed to the rules and norms of the democratic game. What is important is to critically engage with one's opponents and learn (as much as possible) from their ideas and proposals rather than attempting to score a decisive victory with a view to establishing a permanent majority and enjoying the spoils. I believe that anyone seeking to achieve total victory in politics pursues an impractical and self-destructive goal. It can only foster civic distrust or hatred, shutting all avenues that might yield compromises and help find common ground.

Between opponents competing for power in free elections, trust is possible, but between enemies seeking to destroy each other, it is not. In the first case, democracy works, the rules of the democratic game are obeyed, and key norms are respected. The language used by political actors tends to be civil. In the second case, democracy ceases to work and politics degenerates into an uncivil game of hostage-taking, invectives, and blackmail. Many will have the tendency to constantly magnify their differences and turn them into fundamental differences of beliefs, identity, and values among which there can be no compromise.

When this happens, the politics of personal destruction replaces dialogue, and ideological intransigence – "my way or the highway" – takes the place of compromise.

If you think I exaggerate, listen to an academic-turned-politician, Michael Ignatieff, who has experienced firsthand the rough edges of politics in his native Canada, as well as in Hungary where he served as the President of the Central European University, which was forced by the Hungarian government to move from Budapest to Vienna for political reasons. "Once adversaries think of democracy as a zero-sum game," Ignatieff wrote, "the next step is to conceive of politics as war: no quarter given, no prisoners taken, no mercy shown."[17]

This style of politics as perpetual and total warfare is incompatible with any civilized political creed. It fosters a siege mentality and apocalyptic tone that reinforce extremism and fuel sectarianism. Everyone feels emboldened to show their total and unconditional loyalty to their party when their identity is under attack. Politics thus becomes tribal warfare that demands constant vigilance and permanent mobilization. It generates an addictive and toxic form of partisanship that brings to light atavistic instincts and dubious forms of solidarity under threat. For those who embrace this form of politics, there can be no room for compromise with the forces of evil broadly defined. Every second is – or can turn into – a dangerous Flight 93 moment.

That, you will certainly agree with me, would not be a pretty picture. For this type of warfare politics represents a big threat to our free way of life and is incompatible with any civilized creed. It renders public debate extremely difficult, opening the door to political paralysis, violence, and chaos. It also encourages disappointed citizens to disengage from normal politics or, worse, to mentally secede from our democratic institutions and way of life. In the end, it degrades the political sphere by eroding informal and formal rules of behavior.

Nothing is more revealing of the pernicious long-term effects of this mode of politics than the unwillingness to accept the democratic outcome of elections if one's side were to lose. This phenomenon should not be taken lightly because it threatens America's civic foundations. Promoted by irresponsible leaders seeking to satisfy their own ambitions, it can trigger a sharp decline in civic trust when citizens lose faith in the democratic process and come to question their government's legitimacy simply because they reject the outcome of the elections. It also promotes ideological intransigence that undermines longstanding democratic customs and procedures. In opposing everything that stands in the way of their ambitions, the leaders who promote this type of warfare politics declare war on democracy, sometimes paradoxically in the name of more democracy or the will of the people.

What can or should we do then? Are we condemned to powerlessness when this type of politics is normalized? Can moderation save us from our current predicament? I know you don't believe in the power of moderation, but I am more sanguine than you in this regard. At the same time, I, too, admit that there are no guarantees that moderation can prevail in the current context, and am aware that moderation alone might not be able to do much. What moderates can do, however, is help lower the temperature and the stakes of politics, whenever possible, and encourage others to start working together on concrete issues, often at the local level, to bridge ideological divides. By seeking to build civic bridges, moderates can also show how to effectively oppose any form of politics that sanctions norm-breaking for short-term partisan advantage. They can effectively warn against false alternatives and dichotomies that promise (without ever being able to deliver) straightforward solutions to complex moral, social, cultural, and political problems.[18]

Make no mistake. Political decisions may sometimes appear as simple matters of right and wrong, but that is often a costly illusion. In real life, there are no easy choices, only difficult trade-offs between rival values and principles and different shades of gray. There are very few reliable litmus tests (if any), and achieving total clarity is an impossibly high bar on most political issues. Beware then of the prophets of doom who divide the world into irreconcilable camps and want to convince you that you must storm the cockpit or be resigned to die.

But more about all these topics tomorrow. Till soon! Yours, . . .

3

No Manichaeism and No Litmus Tests

There are two peoples in France, the one is the mass of citizens, pure and simple, moved by justice and lovers of liberty. These are the virtuous people who spill their blood to establish liberty, who prevail over enemies within and topple the throne of tyrants. The other is the collection of factions and intriguers.[1]

(Robespierre)

HISTORY IS OFTEN – though not always – a good teacher that can offer wise counsel if we know how to listen to and interpret it. I have previously invoked historical examples to justify the need for moderation. I propose now to take another step away from contemporary politics and invite you to reflect together on the example of one of the most famous leaders of the French Revolution, Maximilien Robespierre (1758–1794), whose words serve as the epigraph of this letter. He was the leader of the twelve-member Committee of Public Safety elected by the National Convention which governed France at the height of the most radical phase of the French Revolution (1793–94).

Robespierre's unique political trajectory and exquisite oratory are great examples of the curse of political purity and the dangers of Manichaeism in politics. The peaceful enjoyment of liberty and equality and the reign of eternal justice and virtue were his avowed aims. Robespierre became famous for his oracular style that cleverly combined abstract statements with personal notes and bold policy proposals. Few of his contemporaries could match his exceptional rhetorical skills, and even fewer could rival his political radicalism in the name of moral clarity, equality, and justice. Robespierre despised venality and was frugal and inflexible in the pursuit of virtue, which he regarded as the soul of democracy. He believed that virtue "is always in the minority on this earth."[2] Robespierre's speech on the principles of political morality from February 5, 1794 expressed his radical conception of virtue that owed a lot to Rousseau's ideas. It's one of his best discourses that allows us to better understand his political Manichaeism and political radicalism. If you haven't already read it, don't hesitate to do it. You won't regret it.

Robespierre reveled in his oratorical skills which often gave him the exhilarating feeling of playing king. Here is how he described his revolutionary goals in a famous passage that illustrates well his lack of moderation:

> We want to substitute in our land morality for egotism, probity for a mere sense of honor, principle for custom, duty for propriety, the empire of reason for the tyranny of fashion, contempt for vice for contempt for misfortune, pride for insolence, large-mindedness for vanity, the love of glory for the love of money, . . . merit for intrigue, . . . truth for show, . . . the grandeur of man for the pettiness of grand society, . . . a people magnanimous, powerful, and happy for a people likable, frivolous, and wretched. . . . And in sealing our work with our blood may we be able to see at least the dawn of universal felicity gleam before us. That is our ambition. That is our aim.[3]

Worth noting here is the contrast between virtue and vice drawn in stark terms meant to leave little or no room for nuance or indecision. For Robespierre, the function of the government was simply "to guide the moral and physical energies of the nation toward the purposes for which it was established."[4] He used to state his maximalist goals in paired contrasts whose role was to simplify choice and eliminate doubt and hesitation. Robespierre deftly used paired opposites – morality/egoism, reason/fashion, truth/show, glory/money, or magnanimous/frivolous – to stress the profound abyss between virtue and vice. On his view, everything was – and had to remain – simple and clear. One was either on the side of virtue, defined as a total commitment to the cause of the revolution, or that of evil, defined as any form of opposition to the latter.

You might wonder how Robespierre and his Jacobin colleagues justified their Manichaeism and extreme pursuit of virtue, purity, and justice. This could be explained in good part by their strong belief that they were instruments of Providence invested with a holy mission: to build the temple of liberty and hasten the dawn of universal felicity on Earth. Robespierre's view of power rested on a radical conception of virtue and equality that paid no heed to tradition, history, and human nature. The Jacobins were entirely determined to set the house ablaze to save it from the plague of tyranny, corruption, and injustice. This radical task demanded total commitment and determination. "To stop before the end is to perish," he used to say.[5] Moderation was powerless and useless in this regard and represented a threat to the cause of the revolution.

If you think that conspiracy theories are a new thing, you are in for a big surprise. In the name of revolutionary justice, the Jacobins proceeded to eliminate all the factions formed by "charlatans" and defenders of tyranny accused of conspiring against the people. Suspecting the existence of corruption and spies in every quarter of the country, they saw everywhere potential murderers seeking to assassinate patriots, enemies that had to be annihilated before they could strike back. Led by their constant virtue and obsession with political purity, Robespierre and his Jacobin colleagues drew a sharp line between "good" patriots, committed to the goals of the revolution, and "evil" citizens, who allegedly sought to thwart the will of the people.

This sharp distinction between the two peoples was at the heart of Robespierre's political radicalism and immoderation. He admitted that he knew "only two parties, the party of good citizens and the party of bad" ones.[6] The first was pure, virtuous, reasonable, and simple, and entirely committed to justice and the republic; the revolutionary government owed these good citizens full protection and security. The second party was perfidious and corrupt, a collection of factions that endorsed tyranny, monarchy, and injustice; to these citizens, Robespierre insisted, the government owed no legal protection whatsoever. They had to be identified and destroyed so that the reign of justice, freedom, and virtue could be secured forever.

What Robespierre shared with the other members of the Committee of Public Safety was more than a mere fondness for purity, regeneration, and purges. They all espoused a Manichaean worldview in the name of the fight against tyranny and aristocratic privilege. Despotism, warned Saint-Just, "is like a reed that bends with the wind and which rises again."[7] The enemies of the republic are never fully vanquished and are capable of being reborn from their ashes: "The forces of tyranny gather the fragments as a reptile renews a lost limb."[8] That is why the Jacobins believed everything that opposed the republican institutions and principles had to be destroyed without mercy. For radicals like Saint-Just, the war on all the tyrants of the world began here and now, and compromise and moderation were two words absent from their vocabulary: "No consideration can stop the course of justice" which must reign supreme.[9]

Words always matter and, in this case, they did have momentous political implications. The revolution created extraordinary circumstances that, in turn, required that exceptional powers be entrusted to a select few, the vanguard of the people, the virtuous and pure ones. The Terror came to be justified in the name of the fight for liberty and virtue, and a novel language (in addition to a new calendar) had to be invented. As Saint-Just put it, "terror is nothing other than justice, prompt, severe, inflexible; it is therefore an emanation of virtue ... a consequence of the general principle of democracy applied to the pressing needs of our country."[10]

Moreover, the Jacobins were convinced that the cause and progress of the revolution demanded constant mobilization and vigilance to discover and neutralize the plots against the people and their leaders. As long as the last enemy of liberty still breathes, so the argument went, there is no hope for justice and freedom. Predictably, the list of enemies was long and expandable as circumstances demanded it: "You must punish not only the traitors but even those who are indifferent."[11] Since the sword of justice had to be quick and inflexible, the guillotine took care of separating the good and trustworthy citizens from the evil and dangerous ones.

How many times has this scenario played itself out in history and how often has the obsession with purity and virtue led to suffering and violence! Let's fast forward now and try to explain the psychological causes of the ever-present obsession with political purity, litmus tests, and Manichaeism. For many, resorting to litmus tests is often the outcome of fear and uncertainty, a strategy used when their sense of identity is endangered and skepticism toward out-groups is on the rise. Then people begin looking for imaginary culprits and conspiracies and maintain close ranks within their own factions and parties to avoid contamination by impure elements. As a result, they are determined to make no compromises with those who are outside of their sphere. They believe that tight control of power is indispensable to the success of their cause, until all the enemies will have been silenced and vanquished.

The case of Jacobinism is instructive because its radical style of politics still has many enthusiastic fans around the world, who regard their political adversaries as the embodiment of evil engaged in dark conspiracies and acting under the impulse of demonic influences. The uncompromising soldiers of virtue who embrace Manichaeism see themselves engaged in holy crusades meant to rid the sinful world of occult evil forces and demonic powers. Their inflexible style of politics demands total and unconditional allegiance – either stand with us and adopt our values or be against us and suffer the consequences. Like their presumed enemies, the virtuous warriors never rest, they all are always watchful and on constant alert against real or imaginary threats. Their insistent Puritanical admonitions about the need for self-discipline, sacrifice, and order are meant to convince the skeptics within their ranks that there is no room for any middle ground, no opportunity for bargaining and give-and-take with their critics and opponents. The real battle is ultimately a spiritual one: one may not bargain with evil, nor can one learn anything from wicked sinners under the spell of Satan. The latter must be demonized and crushed without mercy.[12]

You should not be surprised to learn that this is precisely the style of politics that the moderates who feel the complexity and uncertainty of all things human vigorously oppose. I include myself in this category. We are skeptical of Manichaean visions of politics based on litmus tests and calls for moral, political, or religious purity. Our instinct is to explore and understand what each side says and figure out what, if anything, might be derived from it that has some value. We are aware that in politics good and evil often coexist in such a way that nothing is so evil and degraded that it does not contain some grain of good, just as nothing is so good and pure that it does not contain some impurity.[13] That is why we reject purity tests and are willing to engage with political opponents who accept the basic rules of the democratic game.

The contemporary American political scene is a telling illustration of the curse of political purity and the price we all have to pay for the propensity to Manichaeism displayed by extremists and their supporters. It is no secret that litmus tests and appeals to political purity have become extremely popular among the extreme Right lately. Many of its members suffer, often unbeknownst to them, from the Flight 93 syndrome and see themselves engaged in a fierce combat to save civilization from ruin. They tend to paint with a broad brush and treat politics as a form of religion. The political sphere becomes toxic when adversaries resort to constant demonization and purity tests that leave no room for concession and moderation. This belligerent style gives oxygen to the winner-take-all politics of warfare that threatens our civic foundations and makes our civic life increasingly unbearable.

Do you need perhaps a few concrete examples? Here they are. When one argues that America is in the middle of a once-in-a-lifetime struggle, a "cold civil war"[14] between the traditional American way of life and identity politics, that person is undoubtedly already engaged in an all-or-nothing crusade that makes compromise impossible. Anyone who thinks that there are no other reasonable alternatives to the present crisis than endorsing authoritarian populist leaders ready to "drain the swamp" is already on board of Flight 93. When one believes that the conservatism demanded by the present moment must fight the culture war "with the aim not of neutrality, but of outright victory,"[15] then ruthless sectarianism replaces civility and moderation. Then, it no longer suffices to stand up to defend one's beliefs in a free competition of ideas; waging total war against one's adversaries becomes the priority. And war, as we know it, is not a time for bargaining and playing nice; instead, one must fight with utmost determination as if there were no tomorrow, or risk becoming irrelevant.

If you think I am exaggerating, listen to another prominent voice from the hard Right. "There simply can be no peace between woke communism and America," Thomas Klingenstein, the Chairman of the Board of the Claremont Institute claimed. "The essential thing I've tried to stress is for Republicans to understand we are in a war and then act accordingly. War is not a time for too much civility, compromise, or for imputing good motives to the enemy. Our generals must fight as if the choice were between liberty and death."[16] Note the dramatic language reminiscent of Robespierre – *as if the choice were between liberty and death* – that leaves no room for bargaining and the middle ground. Can anyone be more explicit about the high stakes of the present battle?

I suspect that when the former Attorney General William Barr gave his speech about religious liberty in October 2019 at the University of Notre Dame, his frame of mind was not very different. Referring to the liberals and secularists' corrupting agenda, he argued: "This is not decay; it is *organized destruction.* Secularists, and their allies among the 'progressives,' have marshaled all the force of mass communications, popular culture, the entertainment industry, and academia in an *unremitting assault* on religion and traditional values."[17] He, too, was embracing Manichaean politics and litmus tests. Organized destruction, unremitting assault: these words were carefully chosen to demonstrate the existence of a worldwide conspiracy led by wicked secularists and liberals against tradition and religion.

This militant style of politics is tailored to meet radical and hyper-partisan goals making moderation, negotiation, and compromise virtually impossible. It is born out of the conviction that politics must be a form of total warfare that politicizes every aspect of our lives, from education to economy, leaving no corner untouched. It requires that pledges be strictly monitored and enforced; everyone's commitment must be continually tested and validated by the self-anointed priests of the tribe.

"Republicans-in-name-only" (RINOs) or "Democrats-in-name-only" (DINOs) – for this is, after all, a tale of two parties, although much more prevalent on the Right – must be unmasked and denounced without delay. Everyone must demonstrate that they are reliable party members who follow the official line and whose credentials are to be measured by their unconditional obedience, zeal, and enthusiasm for the party's agenda. If you fail to do so, you are a traitor.

I don't want to be accused of one-sidedness and wish to avoid false equivalences. We must recognize that Manichaeism and litmus tests can also be found among the members of the far Left who display a different form of political Puritanism. They tend to be frustrated with the slow and patient exercise of politics that liberal democratic institutions and norms require. This exasperates the social justice warriors engaged in endless crusades for curing the country of all the sins of the past. The most radical ones are prepared to even purge the term "moderate," which, in their view, is a synonym for treason.

Consider, for example, the letter penned by the leadership of the Democratic Socialists of America (DSA) in May 2020, which justified its decision *not* to endorse Joe Biden in the November presidential election of that year. The letter unambiguously stated that Bernie Sanders was the *only* acceptable presidential candidate, reminding the DSA members that endorsing anyone else would be an unacceptable rotten compromise, corrupting the purity of their organization's cause and ideals. "We believe that *the only way to beat the radical Right once and for all,*" the signatories wrote, "is through a socialist movement that draws millions of disillusioned working-class people, here and abroad, into the political arena."[18] Worth noting here as well is the maximalist goal of scoring a total victory once and for all, and enlisting the support of "millions of disillusioned working-class people" in the pursuit of a radiant future.

Let me put it to you frankly. The agenda of those who embrace Manichaeism, political Puritanism, and litmus tests on either side may score a few triumphs in the short run – remember the short-lived victory of Robespierre and his Jacobin colleagues – but it is imprudent and ineffective in the long term, because it lacks practical wisdom. It mischaracterizes the nature of the present challenges and offers unsavory solutions to social discontents. Those obsessed with purity and litmus tests in politics tend to act upon dangerous fantasies of salvation and conspiracy theories to identify and punish the non-believers. On their view, politics is nothing but a zero-sum game in which compromises are a sign of betrayal and enemies must be ruthlessly exterminated like vermin. These radicals use fear and invent conspiracies to motivate their supporters to act. Their politics of suspicion aims at creating a dedicated mass of zealots fully committed to – and ready to die for – the "right" cause as defined by their omniscient visionary leaders. Again, the Jacobins' hubris is a lesson and warning that must never be forgotten.

I hope that you will develop over time some immunity to the temptation of Manichaeism, which is a curse that must be resisted (as much as possible) in normal times. At the very least, your generation must be aware of its obvious dangers and costs. You should keep in mind that the role of politics is not to solve our inner dilemmas or spiritual longings for the absolute. It is the more modest one of setting and maintaining our house in (relative) order, a task that requires passion along with constant fine tuning, moderation, humility, and compromise. Through its apocalyptic and alarmist tone, the politics of Manichaeism inhibits negotiation and prevents necessary concessions to one's political opponents. It warns people that the impure ones – who often happen to be moderates like me – will eventually sell them out, when given the opportunity to do so.

So look beneath the surface and don't be fooled by those who practice the politics of Manichaeism based on purity tests. It is a form of aggressive evangelism or a crusade whose result is the hollowing out of the meaning of politics. Manichaeism and litmus tests are never able to foster a new sense of civic solidarity. On the contrary, they deepen the divisions in the body politic and fail to build civic bridges.

But more about all this another time. Bye for now! Yours, . . .

4

Compromise

Logic admits of no compromise. The essence of politics is compromise.[1]

(T. B. Macaulay)

I FEAR THAT ANY PRAISE OF COMPROMISE as the essence of politics might seem utopian today. So, let's examine a few more historical examples for the time being. The words chosen as the epigraph of my present letter come from the pen of Thomas Babington Macaulay, a prominent nineteenth-century British historian and politician. His speech on the Reform Bill in the House of Commons on March 2, 1831 was instrumental in the passage of the landmark legislation (by one single vote!) that modernized the antiquated and ineffective electoral map of Great Britain. Compromise worked well back then. What about today? Is there anyone who still believes that the essence of politics is compromise rather than the pursuit of social justice, freedom, or equality?

This seems a rhetorical question. Praising compromise may still look good on paper, but in practice such a view appears unrealistic and self-defeating. For many – and I believe you belong in this category – compromising with your opponents is nothing but a sign of weakness and betrayal. "We are in a 'no compromise' era and that's not changing any time soon," claimed the founder of Public Opinion Strategies, a Republican polling firm.[2] Some politicians who may privately be open to compromise are reluctant to publicly admit it. It is no accident that they find the word *compromise* dangerous to pronounce, preferring instead the more neutral phrase "finding common ground" or "working together."[3] Why is compromise such a dirty or dangerous word and how can we explain the reluctance to use it? And why is it so hard to rally people behind a message of compromise after all?

You may already know the answers to these questions, but I still would like to try to answer them. To begin with, there is the common view that compromise (like moderation) is a virtue only (or mostly) for weak and undecided minds. When we compromise, the argument goes, we are on a slippery slope and ready to abandon our principles for the sake of short-term benefits. The strong ones do not compromise, they stand their ground and affirm their views with confidence and firmness, without giving an inch. On this view, to compromise with one's opponents means to sell out, betray one's beliefs, acknowledge the superiority of one's opponents, and capitulate to them in an unmanly manner. As such, compromises are seen as a form of cowardice, duplicity or moral corruption and must be rejected without hesitation. Moreover, some believe that when they compromise, they negotiate with those who are immoral and impure and thus risk being corrupted by their contagious vices.

As you know, this negative view of compromise has become quite popular in contemporary American politics. On many topics, compromise seems increasingly hard or impossible to reach, given our profound differences along ideological, racial, religious, gender, and cultural lines. Sectarianism turns minor problems and differences into life-and-death issues on which no concessions seem possible or desirable. As a result, many view compromise and bargaining as betrayal or treason rather than reasonable ways of resolving their differences and disagreements.

This negative perception of compromise is particularly alarming as a particular type of polarization – *affective* polarization – is on the rise. A main driver of negative partisanship, affective polarization measures the level of distrust that people have toward members of other parties. In the 2020 election season, for example, nine in ten voters in both camps believed that a victory by the other party would inflict lasting harm on the future of the country.[4] Not surprisingly, the level of civic distrust is at an alarmingly high level as well, with one of the two main parties dominated by a majority of voters who are reluctant to admit the legitimacy of the results of our free elections.

Hence, you should not be surprised to hear zealots in all camps calling for constant vigilance and mobilization, nor should you be astonished to discover that a good number of our political controversies are not primarily about real policy issues or alternatives, but rather about reaffirming sectarian identity and reinforcing group unity or solidarity. Many actions, proposals, and initiatives are little more than forms of virtue-signaling, expressing simultaneously solidarity with those of the same kin and deep partisan animosity toward members of opposing political tribes.

One of the victims of ideological intransigence is compromise, the other, moderation. As a perceptive journalist has remarked, "even if members of the two parties are not especially far apart on substantive issues, their social, cultural, racial and ethnic conflicts and differences will preclude agreement on the selection of a centrist candidate as the presidential nominee of either party."[5] This trend has intensified in the last decade or so – it certainly began prior to 2016 – and risks making our polity ungovernable if it continues unabated.

Now, you might say, defending compromise sometimes makes sense, but a few essential questions about its desirability and relationship with moderation remain unanswered. If Franklin D. Roosevelt had been more moderate, would we have Social Security today? Would it have been wise to advise the Italians to try to find "common ground" and compromise with Mussolini and the Fascists? Should we have counseled the Germans living during the Weimar Republic to set aside their differences with the National Socialists and compromise with them to make Germany great again?

Obviously, the answer to all these questions is a resounding no. No one may partake of the table of the Lord and the table of the Devil at the same time. Accommodation was Neville Chamberlain's policy at Munich in 1938, when he struck a rotten compromise with Hitler. If he had been a bit more immoderate and refused to compromise with the evil then, where would we be today? The Yalta agreement of February 1945 between the United States, Great Britain, and the Soviet Union was another rotten compromise that paved the way for the later advance of the Soviets into the heart of Europe. Compromise did not work against Mussolini and Hitler and it won't work today either against the staunchest enemies of democracy.

You and I agree that normalizing the enemies of democracy by offering calm talk of moderation and accommodation in times of crisis is irresponsible. Toleration toward the intolerant ones seems absurd and unwise. But it is here that our agreement ends. You believe that we may not normalize our current political climate by embracing compromise and moderation. In your view, we need less compromise and moderation and more protests, marches, boycotts, and sit-ins. Moreover, you think that it is acceptable, even desirable, to shatter some norms to strengthen democracy, and are prepared to do it without a second thought.

You are also inclined to see in the monomaniacal pursuit of a single idea or principle a sign of strength and are convinced that being willing to think the unthinkable (when the house is not in order) is itself a source of power. For you, our present situation calls for bold actions and emergency measures; a half-hearted approach based on mutual concessions, comity, and courtesy would be self-defeating when trying to put the house back in order. That is your position, if I understand it well. Am I mistaken?

Let me try to explain the moderates' position on these issues, as I see it. They, too, may acknowledge that there is no value in conserving a burning or rotten house, but they would want to make sure the foundations are rotten before the work of demolition begins. The moderates are willing to sit down with all their political opponents committed to democratic norms to identify shared interests and try to find common ground. They are bridge builders, not fence sitters, and believe in the importance of building bonds and putting the country above party.

Nonetheless, don't assume that the moderates' willingness to compromise is a sign of weakness. It is not. It is rather a symbol of real power, if you think about their deeper reasons to embrace compromise.[6] While they are open to making reasonable concessions to pass much-needed legislation, they are uncompromising in their commitment to longstanding liberal democratic norms and institutions. As I have already mentioned, they draw the line when it comes to those who deliberately undermine the legitimacy of the rule of law and the key principles of the open society – above all, pluralism, open contestation, publicity, and toleration.

Does this imply that one must always embrace compromise to be reasonable? And who defines what "reasonable" means in each case? Let's be clear on this point: sensible political compromise should *not* be confounded with ignominious compromise over thorny moral and political issues. A rotten compromise such as the Molotov–Ribbentrop secret pact of August 1939 was anything but reasonable. It is also possible for a politician to espouse a compromising mindset at one point and an uncompromising mindset at another. In other words, it is possible to combine compromise and moderation with flexibility and firmness. Think of Lincoln's political career and you will see how this combination can be achieved in practice.

May I give you another example? It might come as a surprise to you and those who know only the title of one of his famous books, *Rules for Radicals*. Saul Alinsky was a legendary Chicago-based community activist known for his unique and unorthodox style. In reality, he was a much more complex character than people tend to think these days. Alinsky was firmly committed to pursuing a progressive agenda at the local level, but he also believed in the power of dialogue, bargaining, and negotiation in community organizing at the grassroots level. Yet he understood that compromise is never risk-free or easy. It requires a good dose of courage, non-conformism, eclecticism, and flexibility to engage in compromises that are both reasonable and necessary.

Alinsky was not a moderate, but his long and successful career as a community activist in Chicago shows that the strongest ones are in reality those who hold firm views and are still able to negotiate with their opponents to advance much-needed reforms. His case is challenging for several reasons, beyond his wit, quickness of mind, and unconventional language. Alinsky's ability and openness to work with individuals from all walks of life, secular and religious, were truly remarkable. He was petulant and occasionally impulsive, but also unpretentious. He was simultaneously forceful and amiable, militant, and open to finding pragmatic ways to solve urgent problems in the life of the communities on whose behalf he worked. His actions and words show that compromise, when practiced well, is not weakness, as many assume, but can be a muscular and principled form of pragmatism.

But what kind of compromise are we talking here, you might ask? Some claim 1+1=2, while others object that 1+1=3. Is then the "reasonable" compromise moderates are prepared to endorse something like 1+1=2.5? If that were the case, moderation would amount to relying on imagined or alternative facts. But the reality cannot be contradicted: 1+1 always equals 2, never 2.5. There can be no compromise on that (let's not forget that sometimes even admitting an obvious truth such as 2+2=4 may be risky or dangerous). But there is plenty of room for compromise when the question under consideration is, say, raising the minimum wage, providing fringe benefits to workers, lowering student debt, addressing climate change, or reforming our expensive health-care system by lowering the costs of prescription drugs.

The question remains: can we ever compromise our principles and seek at the same time a modus vivendi with others whose ideas we perceive as wrong or nefarious – I am not saying evil – without losing our integrity? Of course, it is possible and not uncommon to view compromise in general as a threat to personal honor and dignity but here, too, nuances and context play a significant role. I believe that it is counterproductive to judge politicians, who are supposed to legislate and represent a wide variety of interests and groups, *only* by what they are unwilling to compromise. It is also important to look at the concessions they are prepared to make to pass much-needed reforms. For we live in a diverse and pluralist society, in which multiple groups pursue different values and principles and are unlikely to agree on the existence of a highest good, narrowly defined.

The main point I want you to remember is a simple one. In any free society, all legislation and government are based not on the (revealed) Truth, as is the case for religion, but on bargaining, mutual concessions, and compromise. Politics and religion belong to different spheres. The holy is never negotiable; in its realm, faith is the vehicle of understanding, and it is impossible to compromise where the sacred is concerned. Such a compromise would be regarded as sacrilege. But politics is *not* the domain of the holy. Its role is to provide room for accommodation between individuals and groups who have different conceptions of the good life and personal salvation.

So, let us not be so naïve as to suppose that our principles should trump everything every time. If you hold such a strong view, your principles will inevitably become roadblocks to compromise. You must accept that moral, political, cultural, and economic differences are real and sometimes intractable, and you must learn to manage them as best as you can. If carried too far, any idea or value – be it justice, reason, equality, or liberty – can be distorted, and may turn into its opposite. That is why you must treat your ideas, values, and principles as being open to change and revision and should never forget that they are realized in practice only partially and imperfectly.

The uncompromising mindset that identifies politics with total warfare allows political conflict to spill from the political sphere into other areas of life and influence everything from abortion and taxes to healthcare, food options, and education. This, in turn, contributes to the emergence of a zero-sum atmosphere in which compromise and civil dialogue become virtually impossible, being replaced by intransigence and intolerance. This should concern all of us, since any society devoid of compromise is ultimately authoritarian.

While campaigning often requires an uncompromising style meant to discredit and outmaneuver one's adversaries, governance in democratic societies is based on mutual concessions and civility and demands compromise and conciliation, no matter what people believe. Finding common ground means setting aside the ideas that divide us and focusing instead on the issues on which we may agree or compromise.

How can we do that? I will try to address this issue in my next letter. Until then, be well. Yours, . . .

5

Trimming and Balance

This innocent word Trimmer signifieth no more than this, that if Men are together in a boat, and one part of the company would weigh it down on one side, another would make it lean as much to the contrary; it happeneth there is a third Opinion of those, who conceive it would do as well, if the Boat went even, without endangering the passengers.[1]

(George Savile, Marquess of Halifax)

After writing my last letter, I realized that there was another topic I wished to touch upon and didn't have enough time to do so. I am doing it now, hoping it might be of interest. You will, no doubt, wonder why I chose to speak about *trimming*, an unusual word rarely used in common parlance. The reason for that is simple: trimming is linked to balance which, in turn, is related to moderation and compromise.

I agree that trimming is one of those concepts that challenge our imagination, and this is not necessarily because we rarely use it. In fact, *to trim* can mean many things such as to put something in proper order, to clip, to cut something down to the proper size, to balance a ship by shifting its cargo or an aircraft by adjusting stabilizers. It can also mean to modify something according to expediency, to adjust one's opinions, actions, expenditures (to trim one's sails), to adapt (opportunistically or not), or to meet changing conditions. So, as you can see, it is a rich word that challenges our imagination.

The meanings I have in mind here, however, are somewhat different from the ones previously mentioned. As the epigraph of this letter shows, I am interested in political trimming understood as keeping the ship of state on an even keel. This implies, among other things, changing one's opinions, viewpoints, and actions to moderate the zeal of opposing factions, avoid violence, and maintain a middle-of-the-road policy through necessary and timely concessions. You might note that trimmers are, in general, difficult to place on the spectrum of political ideologies. Some may be seen as conservative, others as liberals. Yet trimmers go beyond these two ideological families and it is not easy to find a proper label for them. When trying to describe what they do, it is important to keep in mind what their final goal is: avoiding chaos and violence, preserving the equipoise of the state, maintaining the balance between social and political forces and economic interests on which political pluralism and freedom depend in modern society.

Let's consider now the classical definition of trimming given by George Savile, Marquess of Halifax (1633–1695), in a famous essay, "The Character of a Trimmer," written in 1684–85 and published in England in 1688. Halifax, who lived and wrote in a conflict-ridden period, made creative use of the classical image of the captain seeking to keep the ship on an even keel. This was *not* the meaning that most of his contemporaries gave to this term, which had a pejorative connotation derived from the intense religious controversies of that period. A trimmer was seen as a "neutral" and uncertain person, a "traitor" not to be trusted. To his credit, Halifax embraced his reputation as a trimmer and assumed it as a badge of honor while remaining politically unaffiliated. He attempted to reduce the differences between rival parties instead of adopting and inflaming their political passions. Halifax distrusted parties because he believed that most people adhere to a party out of ignorance, while "shame keepeth them from getting out of it."[2] He was also persuaded that the intensity of political contest gives men "a habit of being unuseful to the public by turning in a circle of wrangling and railing, which they cannot get out of."[3]

I am bringing Halifax's example to your attention because his conception of trimming remains relevant to us today. Trimmers like him tend to be demanding with their friends and seek to maintain civil relations with their opponents as much as possible. Their independence of mind and unpredictability are incompatible with party spirit which requires conformism and strict obedience. When the equipoise of the state seems endangered by overloading it upon one side, they trim the sails quickly, and add the weight of their reason to the other side so that the ship of the state remains on an even keel.

Equally important, when they support the ideas of a party, trimmers refuse to go all in for them; when they move away from a group, they do not fully turn against it either. If trimmers break ranks, they rarely go full apostate and tend to leave open the possibility of dialogue with their opponents. Their changes and transitions are never so absolute and drastic that they fly from one extreme to another. Nor do they regard the parties they have left with great animosity or acrimony. Instead of adopting and inflaming the passions of those whom they have just joined, they try to diffuse among them something of the spirit of the group which they have just left.[4]

You might say at this point: this sounds interesting but aren't trimmers, above all, mere opportunists who follow their self-interest in the pursuit of questionable short-term goals? What distinguishes them from ruthless and cynical speculators who trade colors, ideas, and camps as they think fit? How can trimmers be really trusted as long as they are flexible and open to revising their opinions? What about the accusation of being lukewarm, hesitant, opportunistic, timid, or inconsistent? Aren't trimmers often too ingenious in devising objections and pretexts for their changes of mind and don't they deal in contradictory and equivocating ideas?

All these are good and difficult questions. I propose we take a look at the image below featuring a real funambulist in action. It is, I believe, the best metaphor for moderation and it might have an answer to your questions. Why do I say that?

Tightrope walkers need many things to maintain their balance.[5] They must be opportunistic in the full sense of the word and stay focused on their short-term goals to avoid falling. They should always be able to change positions and tactics to remain up on the wire. Funambulists need not only skills, training, courage, and patience to do all that, but also determination, foresight, and intuition. They can neither go backward nor can they stand still – the only possible direction is forward. That is why tightrope walkers must have a vision of the final destination and never lose sight of it, while paying due attention to every single step, knowing that each miscalculation or moment of inattention may be fatal.

Illustration # 1
Credit: Chris Anaspitos Bullzini. Photograph by Joe Clarke.

I realize that my interest in trimming and funambulism might strike you as quixotic and you might think that trimmers are condemned to remaining marginal figures. Granted, trimming may be an exotic word, but it constitutes a distinctive political tradition and sensibility that may not be ignored any longer. Its singularity comes from the fact that it includes and accommodates individuals with different moral, philosophical, and political outlooks. It attracts those who are sensitive to crisis and concerned about maintaining the rules, procedures, and civilized habits that provide the framework within which the free competition for power is possible.[6]

Let's think now about how trimming might help us bring some sanity back into our politics. Isn't it the case that able politicians resemble good funambulists who know how to seize the opportunities to achieve their goals? They must be prudent and quick to seize the moment. They need intuition, self-discipline, a keen perception of the environment, and a good sense of direction. Like trimmers, they must also have the courage to swim against the current when necessary. They should also make sure that the other side is always heard and consulted on all controversial topics of general interest.

What should make trimmers agreeable to us is that they are neither saints whose virtue would be too demanding for us nor rabid ideologues who seek to change our lives according to their plans. As skeptics, they differ from those who embrace the "politics of faith" in the pursuit of perfection or salvation. As moderates, they refuse the litmus test of ideological purity and oppose all attempts to oversimplify political issues for short-term gains. As students of history, they have a good understanding of past experience and the multifaceted nature of politics.

Trimmers believe that their task is "to find some means of being at home in the complexity we have inherited"[7] without trying to artificially remove the inherent ambiguity of politics. They are also keenly aware of the tragic nature of politics and the plurality of social, moral, and political values and goods. They accept as inevitable the uncertainty of political and moral life and seek to avoid a single-minded fixation on one principle or dimension of politics.

Do you now see better the advantages of trimming as a face of moderation? Trimmers balance inconveniences and alternatives and start from the assumption that like most questions of civil prudence, political issues are "neither black nor white, but grey."[8] They distrust grand schemes and abstract theories and embrace a pragmatic approach that combines the disposition to preserve with the ability to improve. They understand that political matters demand modifications that must often be made according to the rules of prudence rather than categorical imperatives, abstract theories or apodictic axioms.

But don't assume that's all they do. Trimmers pay close attention to the survival of their communities; when the danger of civil war looms large, they do everything in their power to prevent or reduce chaos, anarchy, and violence. They are interested above all in maintaining common decency and saving human lives. Like Dr. Rieux, the beloved hero of Albert Camus' novel *The Plague*, they are concerned first and foremost with people's health and wellbeing.[9] As such, their attitude is characterized by a fundamental modesty that teaches them the sound order of priorities (I will say more about modesty later). Trimmers refuse the posture of seers or prophets and believe that the most important aim of politics is to reduce as much as possible the intensity of conflict and the potential for violence and chaos in the world.

You might imagine that trimmers are always condemned to remain powerless and isolated in an uncertain middle space between parties. History offers useful counsel in this regard. It shows that while trimmers are most of the time between political parties, trimming does *not* amount to maintaining a lukewarm equidistance between them. Trimmers choose one side or another, though not always the same side. Their proverbial flexibility does not prevent them from taking resolute stances against their former associates, nor does it condemn them to powerlessness and irrelevance when supporting unpopular causes. On the contrary, under some circumstances, it allows them to be real kingmakers rather than powerless voices in the wilderness. Are you surprised by that?

Now to the key point. Although trimmers' actions have a provisional and tentative cast and are unpredictable, they never lack a compass when making their choices. Their commitment is to the common good of the society in which they live, not to the narrow self-interest or short-term calculations of the parties or groups to which they happen to belong or support at some point in time. Justice always rests upon the existence of a balance of power which is always fragile and under threat. It can be restored only with the aid of a judicious mixture of institutions, ideas, and principles, which are imperfect and partial. Moreover, trimmers believe in the supremacy of laws and constitutions which they consider to be powerful antidotes to arbitrary power. While being devoted to their country, they stop short of idolizing the sacred gods of their tribes.

And here is another valuable lesson we all can learn from trimmers' examples. They assume that politics is often a messy and mundane business which has little in common with the romantic quest for ultimate truth and certainty. Many political issues admit of no ultimate solutions and involve difficult trade-offs. When making their decisions, trimmers seek to put all circumstances in the scale and refuse to oversimplify matters for the sake of expedience, or in the name of an ideology. In most political arguments, they admit that there are partially valid points of view and try to maintain "a rough proportion between them,"[10] while also recognizing that their own assumptions may sometimes be flawed or incomplete.

That is why trimmers tend to support that party which they dislike least, even when they do not entirely approve of its principles. Knowing the ways in which society lacks balance and needs reform, they seek to add weight to the lighter scale to restore its fragile equipoise. In so doing, trimmers sometimes prefer "a wise mean between barbarous extremes,"[11] while at other times they incline toward one party or another. They combine "a tough mind with a tender heart,"[12] and blend opposites, rejecting simplistic binary choices or superficial alternatives. By adopting the soundest attitudes and principles of all parties, trimmers seek to facilitate agreements between them that could prevent the country from slipping into anarchy. They are careful to avoid picking out sore places and overstating accusations against any group and are eager to find anything that may be healing and facilitate agreements among rival factions.[13]

I have digressed a little, but I hope you will forgive me for that. The question remains: does trimming have a cure for the hyper-partisanship, bullying, myopia, and growing incivility that afflict contemporary politics? One must not imagine that trimming can be the magical cure for our present ills. It is definitely not. My main reason for writing to you about trimming (as a face of moderation) is to encourage you to learn something from the trimmers' experience and understanding of politics. They are prepared to follow the facts wherever they lead and however uncomfortable they might be. They are also attentive to the unintended (and sometimes perverse) consequences of human actions, which may jeopardize the implementation even of the best plans and most generous intentions.

The bottom line is this. Trimmers acknowledge that in the political world almost nothing is good absolutely and forever, but only in a relative way. No question can ever be decided only by taking into consideration one single principle, viewpoint, or theory. There is little room for Puritanism in politics; you must sometimes put up with strange bedfellows to overcome grave crises and promote much-needed reforms. Are you prepared to do that?

You are right to be concerned about the state of our democracy as much as I am, but do not let your anger define everything you say or do. Remember that representative government always requires compromise and bargaining, adding and subtracting, multiplying and dividing. Take your distance from those who push their principles and ideas to extremes, rejecting compromise. Learn from those who seek to balance and weigh various principles and ideas rather than rely on a single set of values or a single ideology. Their presence in political life should be regarded as a true blessing rather than a nuisance. They form a party without banners, indispensable to any form of civil politics.

I encourage you to study the trimmers' art of balance without bias, even if your temperament is different, or precisely because of that. You will never waste your time and you stand to learn a lot from them. Bye for now! Yours, . . .

6

Centrism

Things fall apart; the centre cannot hold."

(W. B. Yeats)

The Center Can Hold.

(Niskanen Center)[1]

I AM MUCH OBLIGED TO YOU FOR HAVING carefully read my previous letters. Since I have promised at the outset that our exchanges would not be a monologue, I hope you will feel encouraged to openly voice your opinions, especially when you disagree with me. Today's topic – centrism – will certainly be such an occasion. This time, as you may have noticed, I have selected two epigraphs instead of one, and they come from two different domains. The first one is selected from W. B. Yeats' famous poem "The Second Coming," in which he lamented the defeat of reason and innocence, announced the coming of a new dark age, and claimed that the center could no longer hold.[2] The second epigraph is the title of a white paper outlining the moderate vision promoted by the Niskanen Center, a think tank from Washington DC with which I have been affiliated for some time.

With the benefit of hindsight, nobody can deny that Yeats' worst fears turned out to be entirely justified. Things fell apart several times, the worst characters were full of zeal and passion, and the center failed to hold precisely when it was most needed. But does this necessarily imply that the center will always fail? And what would it take for it to hold after all?

Now, let's remember that skepticism toward the center is nothing new. According to the *Oxford English Dictionary*, the word "centrist" was first used in 1872 as a term of derision by the correspondent of London's *Daily News* in France, who mocked the politicians who sat in the middle of the House and called themselves Centrists. Not much has changed since. For many, centrism remains an empty word, whose apologists have no concrete beliefs and no clear agenda. Centrists continue to be blamed for their inaction and small-minded commitment to moderation and are described as shallow, opportunistic, or ill-willed. As recently as 2018, one radical critic expressed this deep-seated skepticism in stark terms in *The Jacobin*: "Centrists look at a burning planet, a racist in the White House – and plead for moderation."[3] On this view, centrists don't really know where they stand and what they fight for until they figure out where the Left and Right are, so that they can comfortably position themselves between them. Thus, for most critics, centrism appears as "a political ideology built on a tautology – the center is wherever the center is."[4]

I suppose you will not be surprised by this claim and might in fact agree with it. Yet, you should not forget that there is another positive way of considering the center. According to it, the centrists are pragmatic individuals endowed with common sense and reason, who eschew radical positions and search for the golden mean between extremes. This is never an easy task. "To reach and not to pass the salutary medium is the province of sound judgment," Alexander Hamilton once wrote. "To miss the point will ever be the lot of those who, enveloped all their lives in the mists of theory, are constantly seeking for an ideal perfection which never was and never will be attainable in reality."[5] David Hume had made a similar point in his essays. He argued that there is no abstract reasoning or algorithm that can help us figure out where the mean is to be found in each situation. Finding it is always a difficult task "both because it is not easy to find words proper to fix this medium, and because the good and ill, in such cases, run so gradually into each other, as even to render our sentiments doubtful and uncertain."[6]

Furthermore, finding the mean may not always be possible or desirable. When fundamental matters of justice are at stake and we face stark choices, the mean might not be the best solution. For example, there is no acceptable mean between attempting to curtail voting rights and defending them; such rights are a pillar of democracy and, therefore, non-negotiable. The same goes for violence; there is no mean between condoning violence or murder and rejecting it. Aiming for the mean would be absurd in these situations.

To come back to the question of centrism, it is always hard to motivate and rally others behind a centrist message of moderation, pragmatism, and compromise. This is even more obvious in a hyper-polarized society like ours today. Can centrism help us deal with complex issues and existential threats such as climate change, intergenerational justice, joblessness, police violence, and deep inequalities when we disagree about basic, plain facts?

You may be tempted to regard this as a rhetorical question, but in trying to answer it, you should carefully consider not only the complexity of topics, but also the proper level at which they should be addressed. Some problems may be solved best at the local or state level, others at the federal or national level. The scope of governance unit always depends on the scope of the problem to address. On the one hand, a pragmatic centrist agenda based on common sense might work at the local and state levels, when it involves concrete issues such as taxes, education, or infrastructure, topics on which we deal with more-or-less choices rather than either–or ones.[7] On the other hand, cultural and religious disagreements can be exacerbated at the local level, where culture wars often start and thrive.

Now, I must remind you that like moderation, centrism comes in many shapes and colors. There is a faint-hearted soft centrism that imagines the possibility of a politics without conflict; on this view, reasonable people of good sense are always willing and able to agree on basic principles and calmly deliberate about everything else. On this rather optimistic view, controversies can always be settled through rational discussion and civil exchanges. I am sure you will agree with me that this type of centrism does not seem to be a realistic option in our age of ideological intransigence and partisan vitriol.

At the same time, there is a strong-minded and muscular form of centrism that does not shy away from controversies and may be instrumental in advancing essential political reforms under favorable circumstances. This is what might be called the "vital center"[8] which *can* be politically effective. It is a strong center that may be mobilized to elect candidates able to build common ground among a wide range of groups, interests, and perspectives, with a view to advancing a bold agenda for tackling structural, fundamental issues.

You might say now: this all sounds good but isn't such a "vital center" a thing of the past? It may have worked in 1949, during the first years of the Cold War, when Arthur Schlesinger Jr. published his book with the same title and the free world had a common enemy (communism), but today our mood, priorities, and opponents are radically different. How would the center work now?

You are certainly right that we are much less sanguine today about the desirability and effectiveness of the political center. Suffice it to take a look at some titles or headlines such as "Centrism is Dead," "The Third Way is a Death Trap," and "Centrists Are Pining for a Golden Age That Never Was." They all reflect where public opinion stands on this issue. The predominant view is that centrists won't be able to save democracy because they do not (and cannot) go far enough. On major issues such as Medicare for All, universal jobs guarantee, climate change, education, or culture wars, the opinion is that centrists have lost the debate and have nothing to contribute to it anymore. To do anything substantial in politics would require changing the old norms and moving past the center, which is, as the said article put it, a "death trap."[9]

Such a deep distrust of centrism should hardly surprise us, given how polarized our political elites are today and what a rare commodity bipartisanship is. Legislators, party officials, and lobbyists compete with media commentators and donors in being hyper-partisan and sectarian. The structure of our two-party system, the prominence of the primaries, or the exclusive focus on group identity on both sides prevents the center, where many moderates tend to be, from becoming a dominant force in American politics. And yet, what if the general public may not be as polarized and divided as our political elites appear to be? Would you be surprised to hear that there is still out there a large contingent of voters supporting the center and whose voices are rarely heard or counted?

Let's take a closer look and judge for ourselves. These are the politically homeless ones whose views on issues as diverse as racial equality, gender, immigration, or abortion are not matched or reflected by any party.[10] Many voters seem to prefer – at least in theory – compromise and accommodation to intransigent, all-or-nothing approaches. When it comes to top priorities such as affordable healthcare and jobs, infrastructure, education, and clean air and water, the possibility of finding a centrist middle ground seems more realistic. On these concrete issues, different from cultural or religious topics, pragmatism can prevail under fortunate circumstances. Centrists may also play a key role in putting forward concrete initiatives and building essential coalitions for preserving the constitution of the country, the rule of law, and defending individual freedoms and rights, including freedom of speech and voting rights.

I suspect you would want a few concrete examples. Let's start with education, a subject of common interest to all of us, regardless of our political differences. We all are crying out for good history that should liberate us from bias, cynicism, cheap sentimentality, and narrowness of vision. Some simplistic narratives – the novels of Ayn Rand come to mind – uncritically celebrate competition and self-interest and encourage naïve interpretations. Others like the "1619 Project" offer bold and controversial accounts seeking to entirely rewrite the history of the country along one single axis (racism, oppression, slavery, or colonialism). The goals of the "1776 Project," conceived of as a rejoinder to the "1619 Project," may be different, but its spirit is similar.

Centrists have legitimate reasons to be skeptical of both stories. They are uneasy about any historical narratives that flatten or misrepresent our historical landscape and heritage. There is a more sober way of approaching the past, without zeal or anger, that allows us to understand what we have achieved, where we have failed and why, and learn how to move forward together by strengthening the bonds of our union.

Now, consider competing views of the decent society and the good life. Centrists believe that there is more to living a meaningful life than being constantly engaged in a fierce competition with one's fellow citizens. In addition to justice, self-interest, and recognition, other virtues and values such as honor, prudence, roots, and loyalty are needed to create a good and decent society. They criticize those views that interpret everything that has happened in America as driven only by profit, crude individualism, and ruthless self-interest. While they admit that American history contains many controversial narratives, centrists refuse to see America as an unredeemable netherworld. As a moderate voice from the center-left once put it, "far better to acknowledge and wrestle with the strange and perverse dualities of America: the liberty and arrogance twinned, the bullying and tolerance, myopia and energy, standardization and variety, ignorance and inventiveness, the awful heart of darkness and the self-reforming zeal."[11] In other words, it is necessary and important to recognize what we have achieved thus far *and* seek to preserve the heritage we have received *and* continue to fight to improve our laws and institutions for the sake of future generations.

Would such a centrist agenda help us effectively address the challenges facing higher education today? I don't know. A centrist pragmatic policy might be able to effectively push against equating higher education with an industry and would oppose the idea that the chief task of our universities is to create skilled labor for the new economy. It would challenge the predominant obsession with efficiency and utility and insist that universities and colleges do not need to train foot soldiers, helots, or robots for the new economy. Rather, their main mission is to cultivate valuable citizenship skills and encourage students to let themselves by "ravished" by good books, art, and music and thus acquire a sense of larger vistas in life.[12] This is one of the ways in which we might prevent or delay the slow decline of Western civilization, whose values are always worth studying and engaging with, imperfect as they may be.

At the same time, a centrist agenda would also welcome attempts to spread learning widely, democratize privilege, and revisit the canon, but not with the exclusive intention of cancelling uncomfortable authors or texts that challenge our current perspectives. Instead, the animating idea behind it would be: dare to understand, open your wings widely, and learn to think independently. The spread of knowledge and the freedom of inquiry allow us to detect and eliminate errors, innovate, and free ourselves from dogmas.[13] Such an agenda would therefore seek to open the best of what humanities have to offer to anyone who wishes to have access to them.

Even if the current political climate disfavors centrists, and although you might believe that radicalism is a more effective strategy than centrism, I believe that at least some centrist ideas "beyond market and democratic fundamentalism"[14] remain relevant for addressing our present challenges. For example, sensible middle-of-the-road proposals on taxes and education can be effective in reforming our antiquated tax code or our poorly performing education system. Centrist proposals may also help tackle the increasing bureaucratization of our institutions of higher education and the high levels of student debt. A centrist agenda for reforming environmental and financial regulations may also be devised with a view to promoting social entrepreneurship and a fair allocation of scarce resources, while stopping short of excessive regulation and control.

You can also learn from centrists that free markets and various forms of social assistance are not always at odds with each other. In fact, they often go together and reinforce each other to form the framework of a "free market welfare state,"[15] relying on a middle-of-the-road agenda that combines a modicum of welfare provisions and socialized healthcare with the incentives provided by the free market. You do not need to use the term neoliberalism to criticize the limitations of the free market, which are real and cannot be ignored. A pragmatic and realistic platform starts from the assumption that competition, a key principle of free market economy, is essential to the smooth functioning of the market, along with real prices that convey essential information to all economic agents. Yet, when competition is perverted by the collusion of major economic powers and interests, monopolies and oligopolies arise, and resolute state action may be needed to restore the competition and rules of the free market.

The main lesson you can draw from here can be summarized as follows. One does not need to be a socialist to complain about the inequalities generated by the market, nor must one be a capitalist to criticize the waste of resources due to flawed welfare and social programs. Similarly, one does not have to be a committed left-wing activist to point out the moral costs of capitalism and its externalities, nor be a right-wing conservative or a committed libertarian to talk about the undeniable material benefits of capitalism and its underlying virtues that sustain economic progress. The center allows everyone to do just that, without becoming wedded to a single ideological perspective forever.

Let's return to where we began. I don't expect you to agree with me on the virtues of centrism as a face of moderation. You may have already made up your minds on this point. So be it. What I want to suggest to you is that even today, in our new age of extremes, the center can hold and is far from being dead, although its location is disputed and has shifted.[16] A few things, however, have remained unchanged. We already know that it is difficult to mobilize the people to endorse a centrist movement and political message. That much is clear. What is less clear is what the nature and content of the center can still be.

In my view, the "vital center" does not have to be entirely dependent on what happens at the extremes but can follow a logic of its own.[17] It starts from acknowledging the complex and intricate nature of our moral, social, and political universe and embraces hybridity. It rejects any form of single-mindedness that tends to degenerate into the fanaticism and zealotry of single causes (abortion, free speech, identity politics etc.). It does not oblige anyone to choose between the free-speech and pro-life positions (usually endorsed by the Right) and the right to protect difference and identity (usually advocated by the Left). Instead, it tries to see beyond such dichotomies which are oversimplifications that may further deepen our rifts. As moderates, centrists are aware that it is possible and necessary to celebrate differences and individuality and reject any form of discrimination and censorship at the same time.

We should have no illusions about another important point. We all live in our own world influenced by our dreams, fears, and hopes. In the imaginary corner of the universe inhabited by the spirits I admire for their lucidity and courage, there are few abstractions and lots of windows through which they can contemplate the universe. Politics occupies only a limited sphere in it. One finds there real people, fragile and fallible human beings searching for grace and beauty as well as freedom, equality, and justice. Their world is infused with the spirit of humility, generosity, and faith. It has a place for the sacred as well as the highest human capacities, such as generosity, love, and aesthetic sense.[18]

That warm and luminous space is my "vital center" I'd like to invite you to discover on your own. Farewell! Yours, . . .

7

Eclecticism and Pluralism

Few men are of one plain, decided colour; most are mixed, shaded, and blended; and vary as much, from different situations, as changeable silks do from different lights.[1]

(Lord Chesterfield)

If you have carefully read my last letter, you might have noticed that it is not easy to comprehend and assess centrist agendas by using the conventional categories of our existing political vocabulary. The main reason has to do with their eclecticism, a concept that I want to write about today. But what does eclecticism really mean in practice and how does it differ from centrism? Is it a mere noun devoid of content, or is there a coherent political and philosophical vision undergirding it?

In a passage written nearly four and a half centuries ago, Michel de Montaigne penned one of the most compelling accounts of eclecticism that complements Lord Chesterfield's words from the epigraph of this letter. Each one of us is a multiplicity of selves that cannot be reduced to one single dimension. "We are entirely made up of bits and pieces," Montaigne wrote, "woven together so diversely and so shapelessly that each one of them pulls its own way at every moment. And there is as much difference between us and ourselves as there is between us and other people."[2] No wonder we can hardly get to know ourselves, let alone know exactly what others think and who they really are.

How should it not be difficult for us and why should we be surprised by that? We are only just beginning to rediscover what Montaigne and Chesterfield knew so well: that we are eclectic individuals, drawn to different sides and constantly torn between competing ideas and beliefs. I would encourage you to take their insights one step further. Not only are we variegated and mixed creatures made of many disparate bits and pieces, but the world itself is eclectic in its own fascinating way. It cannot be reduced to one single formula, nor can it be seen through a single window, lens, or viewpoint. It is full of many lights, shapes, and colors and accommodates many conceptions and opinions.[3]

This would come as no surprise to those who study philosophy and religion. There are countless philosophical and religious texts that confirm this truth. You can judge for yourselves and draw your own conclusions, of course, but one thing is beyond doubt. Nature itself is an integrated process of such intricate complexity that eclecticism is an essential part of life. We must learn how to live with it and benefit from its advantages. It challenges us to try to reconcile our multiple identities, passions, and attachments and balance the advantages of some by the presence of others.

As you may guess, eclecticism has important implications for the ways in which we conceive of our political attachments and advocate for our values. First, there is a close connection with liberalism's commitment to pluralism and the claim that we live in a multiplicity of realms which follow their own logic and can never be reduced to one single principle. The diversity of these realms casts doubt on any "fantasy of wholeness"[4] under whose spell many still live. We must resist the temptation to embrace one single ideology, value or principle and should instead exercise our freedom to change our minds when facts change, and new truths are revealed.

The second important implication may be stated as follows. Whether we like it or not, in contemporary society it is impossible to identify a single overriding interest or value that ought to govern social life. There are many standards and rules that steer our lives and may be acknowledged as legitimate. Legislators are therefore faced with the difficult task of finding a balance between rival values and principles such as freedom, equality, justice, and efficiency. They must use prudence and practical reason when adjudicating the competing claims and interests of different groups, especially when the issues at stake are not so much about right versus wrong, but rather what is *partially right* against what is *partially wrong*.

That is why you will be well advised to distrust anyone who might tell you that any single overriding value or ideological principle, however noble and admirable it may be, can govern the intricate reality of modern society. Given the complexity of our social and economic relationships and institutions, no single story – and this applies, of course, even to moderation itself – can describe, and render justice to, the manifold nature of our world. If we try to reduce it to a single dimension and interpret it through the lens of a single system (capitalism or socialism), ideology (liberalism or conservatism), or value (liberty, equality, etc.), we risk distorting its nature. This was one of the main flaws of Marxism, with its ambition to understand history through a single prism (the inevitable triumph of communism) and in light of one single principle (the class struggle). That is why if our political homes are to be put back in order, they will have to be eclectic, hybrid, and heterogeneous and should resist all forms of ideological standardization.

You might reply, of course, that many people err in their beliefs or change them so often that calling them eclectics would make little or no sense. If you hold this view, then you would find it questionable to describe someone simultaneously as "a socialist in economics, a liberal in politics, and a conservative in culture."[5] Such a combination would appear to you as incoherent, if not utterly absurd. Yet, this is exactly what a perceptive sociologist did several decades ago. In *The Cultural Contradictions of Capitalism* (1976), Daniel Bell showed why and how such an ideological crossover is possible (and desirable) in the modern world. Let us take a closer look at his argument which runs as follows.

Our contemporary society is composed of three distinct realms – the techno-economic structure, the polity, and the culture – that follow different "axial principles" and regulative modes. For the techno-economic order, the axial principle is functional rationality, and the regulative mode is economizing. In politics, the axial principle is legitimacy, and the regulative mode is the free competition for power and government by consent. Other related principles are equality before the law, equality of civil rights, and equality of opportunity. As for culture, the axial principle is expressive symbolism, and the regulative mode includes the remaking of the self, personal authenticity, and self-realization.

The key point made by Bell is that in modern society, these different realms – techno-economic, political, and cultural – do not (and cannot) form an integrated holistic web. Between them, there is often discordance and disjunction rather than harmony and conjunction. The three major spheres are not congruent with one another and follow different rhythms of development and change.[6] Once we take eclecticism and pluralism seriously, we can no longer think of modern society in holistic terms or through the lens of a single value or principle, be that equality, liberty, or justice. There is no longer a single cockpit or central command station that everyone can recognize as legitimate. The free market is often described as such a commanding height, but in reality, many areas of life are and remain *beyond* the spheres of supply and demand.

You may wonder what all this amounts to in the end. I'd summarize it as follows. It is possible to simultaneously espouse progressive economic policies – say, a moderate welfare state and a redistributive network to uphold equality of opportunity – and accept key features of the market economy such as free prices and economic competition. It is conceivable to be a classical liberal committed to constitutionalism, pluralism, toleration, and the rule of law in the realm of politics and embrace at the same time a more conservative stance that opposes leveling trends in the realm of culture and education. After all, conservatism has never been devoted to freedom or tradition alone, but it has to do with the whole way of being made possible by our institutions, culture, history, and religion.[7]

Such a combination may appear as frustrating and oxymoronic, especially if you believe in the existence of a common value system and an integrated web between these different spheres. As for me, I doubt such a system exists, but this doesn't prevent many others from dreaming about it and seeking to realize it in practice. It is not a mere coincidence that fusionism – in the end, another name for eclecticism – is disliked on the Right today, nor is it a mere coincidence that the old type of social democracy – another hybrid – is viewed by progressives with great skepticism as insufficiently radical. A product of the Cold War, fusionism as formulated by Frank Meyer more than half a century ago, attempted to combine laissez-faire economic principles with social and cultural conservatism. It created a temporary but powerful alliance between social, cultural, and economic conservatives who joined forces with defense hawks to fight government overreach at home and the specter of Soviet tyranny abroad.

That eclectic fusion worked quite well for several decades but is rejected today by purists who seek a more muscular and unadulterated form of (national) conservatism.[8] Whether they turn for inspiration to the Bible, Edmund Burke, or the American Founding Fathers, these critics see fusionism as a weak philosophy suitable only for people with porcelain-fragile sensibilities and grounded in a problematic philosophy, which, in their view, removes from the political arena the fundamental issues concerning our humanity and civilization. For them, the eclectic synthesis provided by fusionism amounts to little more than another vacuous form of liberal bromide that cannot successfully resist and fight against the Left's alleged takeover of state institutions.

The question remains: assuming there is some wisdom in it, is there any chance of the emergence of a new type of eclectic fusionism adapted to our present context and needs? For that to happen, a few conditions must be met. First, we should recognize that our values and principles are plural and there is no single universal and definitive criterion allowing us to choose between them. We are sometimes called upon to make tough choices and trade-offs – for example, between liberty and equality, efficiency and spontaneity, justice and order – by taking into account different contexts and competing criteria.

Second, left-wing radicals must acknowledge that it is no longer possible to uncritically advocate the Marxist paradigm that emphasizes the supremacy of the forces and relations of production. Ideas always matter a great deal and should never be discounted as mere elements of superstructure. In turn, right-wing radicals may no longer embrace a strictly traditionalist view of society anchored in the past that ignores the plurality and fluidity of interests, values, and groups in modern society. Nor would it be prudent for them to stick to a strictly originalist interpretation of the US Constitution to pursue their present agenda and justify their priorities. As we have recently seen, tradition itself is a construct that can be manipulated for various political agendas and purposes.

So back to the old question: what are we to do then? We may try to embrace eclecticism and avoid all forms of "blueprint thinking,"[9] no matter who promotes them and with what goals in mind. Remember that there is no longer a single overriding principle of social organization that trumps everything else in modern society. What we have instead is a wide variety of institutional arrangements that go beyond the concepts of state and market. Sometimes, it may be the case that the market or local associations provide effective solutions to complex problems; at other times, it may be the state agencies that can tackle these problems most effectively. Some issues such as transportation or education are often best addressed locally or at the state level, while others like protecting voting and individual rights are best dealt with at the national level. In time, the situation may change and require a different approach.[10] Various problems may be solved at different levels and multiple scales that will usually transcend political ideologies and favor bargaining and compromise. And remember that while small can be (and is) beautiful, it is not always so.

This is a lesson that should not be ignored by our politicians and regulators. Many of the institutional solutions proposed by them are often naïve or inadequate because they are based on simplistic blueprints. A little familiarity with complexity theory might be of help here. Instead of sticking to old concepts such as *the* market or *the* state, or using traditional dichotomies such as Left versus Right, capitalism versus socialism, you should think about alternative ones such as polycentricity, federalism, and "power-with versus power-over."[11] Don't be afraid of this heterogeneity and don't imagine for a moment that it is a weakness of liberal democracy. In fact, what constitutes the strength of liberal democratic regimes is that they can include and accommodate many groups and agendas simultaneously pursuing diverse interests and priorities.

Second, on the policy level, it is possible to be left-leaning in economics (by defending moderate social provisions and programs), liberal in politics (by defending limited government), and conservative in culture and religion. A traditional conservative may defend limited government, patriotism, and the sacredness of the private sphere without feeling obliged to turn the issues of abortion, immigration, or same-sex marriage into definitive litmus tests. Similarly, a progressive liberal may defend individual rights and toleration in the political realm and support at the same time a sensible pro-life agenda and an enlightened type of patriotism that doesn't turn into jingoism.

It is also possible to combine economic and political liberalism with cultural and religious conservatism to uphold a vision of the decent society that promotes a reasonable and appealing vision of the common good.[12] The free market often – though not always – works as a reasonably efficient allocator of scarce resources and conveyor of information. Nonetheless, neither the market nor the indicators measuring economic growth and the GDP may be allowed to decide alone on how all the resources of society are to be distributed. Human beings do not (and should not) measure their happiness by the size of their refrigerators or car garages.

Third, you must have the courage to admit that the world is far too complex, puzzling, contradictory, and fast-changing to fit within any single belief system or ideology. The fact of pluralism teaches you how to live with doubt and uncertainty in a world in constant flux and obliges you to constantly revisit your beliefs. You must accept that most social and political questions can never be decided with the compass of a single set of principles, magical blueprint, or a one-size-fits-all theory, no matter how brilliant it may be. Remember what Montaigne and Chesterfield teach us. We all have many overlapping identities, attachments, and affiliations and are made up of diverse fragments that constantly pull us in different directions. None of our desires or motivations is pure and straightforward, and none is simple and unambiguous either. We must learn to live with them and turn their eclecticism into an advantage.

The reason I recommend eclecticism to you is that those who embrace it are usually in a good position to take a clear stance against crude blueprints and policy agendas that simplify our choices and offer a false sense of certainty and security. Eclectic minds have the courage to swim against the current and seek to restore complexity to our world. They refuse to follow the dogmas promoted by the self-anointed priests of their political tribes and believe that in politics, nobody has the final say; truth is to a great extent a matter of reconciling and combining opposites. Everyone is invited to contribute to the ongoing social conversation on what kind of society we want to live in and how to achieve that goal. There are no definitive solutions or victories, only small steps and, often, setbacks.

Finally, since eclecticism acknowledges the relativity of all human perspectives, it is a welcome invitation to modesty and humility, two unassuming virtues in scarce supply today. Let us, therefore, avail ourselves of this opportunity so that we may be able to avoid the extremes. Adieu! Yours, . . .

8

Dialogue

He who knows only his side of the case, knows little of that. His reasons may be good, and no one may have been able to refute them. But if he is equally unable to refute the reasons on the opposite side; if he does not so much as know what they are, he has no ground for preferring either opinion. ... He must be able to hear them from persons who actually believe them; who defend them in earnest and do their very utmost for them.[1]

(John Stuart Mill)

FROM OUR PREVIOUS EXCHANGES, I have noticed that you don't seem to have much faith in the power of dialogue as one possible cure for our present discontents. For your generation, anger and rebellion seem much more important, relevant, and urgent than discussion, bargaining, and piecemeal reform. Having taught many cohorts of students who worry that they would not enjoy a better future than their parents, I can understand why. Yet, I feel obliged to remind you that along with moderation and compromise, dialogue and exchanges of ideas are the lifeblood of liberal democracy. It is about them that I would like to write to you today.

John Stuart Mill is a good author to start from because his writings remind us that liberal democracy requires free exchanges and constant testing of ideas. It cannot survive without a reality-based network, in which real facts matter and not "alternative" ones. Relying on evidence, checking the accuracy of our views, amending them when the data contradict our beliefs – all of that demands sustained effort and does not come naturally. You should not be surprised to discover that most people would rather have minor surgery than confront new ideas and change their minds if their beliefs are proven wrong.[2] Too many among us are prepared to censor and punish dissenting or controversial views and too few think it necessary to take precautions against their own fallibility.

The truth is that we don't want to be forced to constantly examine and reconsider our beliefs, nor do we like being reminded or corrected when we are wrong. It is much easier to think that we are always right, and sometimes even that we have privileged access to the truth. As a result, we are inclined to talk mostly to like-minded people willing to confirm our biases and beliefs and dismiss those who think differently as unreasonable or deplorable.

Just look around and judge for yourselves. Should we be surprised to discover that so few among us are ready and willing to follow Mill's agenda, even when they profess to be open-minded and tolerant? Dialogue is difficult, and so is tolerating other people's views and ideas, especially when they are opposed to ours. It would be nice if we all could become unprejudiced and respectful of others' opinions. But, given the "crooked timber of humanity," to use Kant's famous phrase (from *Idea for a Universal History with a Cosmopolitan Purpose*), that rarely happens in practice. A world in which dialogue between people holding different viewpoints and principles would be effortless is not to be expected anytime soon.

Therefore, you should not be surprised to see many people arguing sophistically, suppressing facts or arguments, and misrepresenting others' opinions for short-term political gain. Be prepared to discover that many are prone to stigmatize their opponents and critics as bad and immoral individuals and infer their vices from the side they take. In reality, the exception rather than the norm is to give "merited honour to everyone, whatever opinion he may hold, who has calmness to see and honesty to state what his opponents and their opinions really are," and be willing to exaggerate nothing, "keeping nothing back which tells, or can be supposed to tell, in their favor."[3]

But, you might ask, why should we try to talk after all to those who start from erroneous premises, reach false conclusions, and contradict our opinions? How can we engage in dialogue with them without having any prejudices or biases on our part? Can dialogue really help cure or alleviate the human propensity to ignorance, deception, and malice?

These questions remind me how rare is the example of someone like Montaigne, who always embarked upon discussion and argument "with great ease and liberty" and admitted that no premises shocked him, no beliefs hurt him, no matter how different they may have been. How refreshing is his belief that we can only improve ourselves "by discord not by harmony, by being different not by being like," and that "in conversation the most painful quality is perfect harmony."[4] That is a high bar, indeed, but one that is not too high for moderates. They believe that there is always hope as long as people are willing to listen to both sides and their errors do not harden into prejudices or degenerate into falsehood leading to uncivil exchanges.

The openness to dialogue is only the first necessary step in the right direction; you must also be ready to treat your opponents with respect and civility, listen to them carefully, and take their views seriously. Let us be generous and assume for a moment that this might be done without much effort. Yet, genuine dialogue demands much more than mere politeness: it requires that you refrain from trying to cancel those views that you disagree with or find abhorrent.

Moderates know that the quiet suppression of half of the truth is a more formidable evil than the open struggle between all parts of the truth. They start from the premise that "truth has no chance but in proportion as every side of it, every opinion which embodies any fraction of the truth, not only finds advocates, but is so advocated as to be listened to."[5] Consequently, they are ready to engage and negotiate with their political opponents and are prepared to entertain the strongest possible arguments *against* their own views, so that the truth might eventually come out from their exchanges with their critics.

You may be wondering where the moderates' propensity to dialogue comes from. What makes them capable of talking and listening to others beyond the differences that separate them? Do they possess a magical power that others lack? The answer is simpler than you might imagine. Moderates refuse to become members of political sects and are determined not to live in epistemic bubbles and echo chambers. The latter encourage people to be self-righteous and overly confident in their beliefs and make them intolerant of or deaf to challenges to their views. Bubbles and echo chambers exclude alternative sources of information and promote dogmatism, intellectual passivity, and unconditional obedience. Slowly, those who live in them become prisoners, like the members of a cult, brainwashed and comfortably trapped inside, but unable to escape. They are not exposed to dissenting views and trust only those who share similar ideas. The ones outside of their bubbles are not to be believed because they are seen as evil and dangerous and threaten the tribe's solidarity and unity.[6]

Here is the real challenge to you and, frankly, to all of us. Can you throw yourselves into the mental position of those who think differently and try to see the world through their eyes? Are you prepared to give credit to your opponents and learn from your critics when they prove you wrong? If you can do all that, then you already belong to the moderates' camp, even if you might not be aware of it yet. But moderates go a step further and I wonder whether you are prepared to do it as well. They are convinced that "if opponents of all important truths do not exist, it is indispensable to imagine them, and supply them with the strongest arguments which the most skillful devil's advocate can conjure up."[7]

And here we come to the real sources of the moderates' openness to dialogue: their eclecticism, modesty, and epistemic humility. They believe that nobody can have a panoramic or telescopic view of life; we only get to know partial truths and often need the lights of others to interpret the facts. Given the imperfect state of human nature, "only through diversity of opinion is there … a chance of fair play to all sides of the truth."[8] And this viewpoint diversity can only come to light through dialogue and constant contestation of ideas.

There is a significant difference between true dialogue and mere discussion. Here is how a prominent physicist, David Bohm, describes it:

> "Dialogue" comes from the Greek word *dialogos.* Logos means "the word," or in our case we would think of the "meaning of

> the word." And *dia* means "through" – it doesn't mean "two." A dialogue can be among any number of people, not just two. Even one person can have a sense of dialogue within himself if the spirit of the dialogue is present. The picture or image that this derivation suggests is of a *stream of meaning* flowing among and through us and between us. This will make possible a flow of meaning in the whole group, out of which may emerge some new understanding. It's something new, which may not have been in the starting point at all. It's something creative. And this shared meaning is the "glue" or "cement" that holds people and societies together.[9]

Let's not be over-optimistic though: this glue doesn't last forever and should never be taken for granted. Great self-restraint, constant effort, and limitless patience are needed to become aware of one's biases and slowly overcome them. Most people are only capable of monologue and, as a result, rarely learn anything valuable from their opponents.

Let's recognize how difficult and rare it is to leave our echo chambers and epistemic bubbles and start a conversation with our opponents and critics. How often do you do it? It takes a lot of courage and resolution to face your adversaries and respond to their objections without anger, in a firm, calm, and civil manner. We may sometimes have cursory exchanges with those who hold different opinions, but forthright dialogue with our opponents is rather rare. Instead, we prefer to be coddled and look for safe spaces to avoid emotional injury and stress.

I believe that the propensity to "emotional safetyism" is a particular danger for your generation because it stifles your intellectual development and maturity by substituting ideological thinking for free thought. Not only does it distract you from tackling and solving real problems, but it risks transforming you into members of a sect, faithful and cheerleading soldiers of the army of the right-minded and self-righteous ones.[10] Be always on guard against the temptation to join their ranks; the price you will pay for entering any cult will be high.

Now consider what a great political blessing your opponents and adversaries can be. It is a mark of a person of intelligence and sound judgment to know how to profit from one's political opponents and critics. I would even be prepared to say that to be saved from making big mistakes, you need not only honest friends but forceful enemies who can act as gadflies that wake you up from dogmatic slumber.[11] We all stand to learn a great deal from those whose ideas differ from ours, who can identify weak points in our arguments so that we may be able to improve them.[12] After all, what would be the point of reading, and talking to, only people who hold roughly the same views as we do?

Dialogue with our critics and contestation by our opponents perform a salutary role: they prevent us from becoming too comfortable with our beliefs. They also help us plug the holes in our arguments and strengthen the latter whenever possible. Only by developing a steady habit of checking, doubting, correcting, and rounding out our ideas and opinions and collating them with those of others do we learn to cogently defend our beliefs and confidently stand our ground.[13] When we do that, we manage to think on our own. Only then do we behave as mature and responsible human beings rather than snowflakes.

But there are other significant benefits of dialogue that you may not be aware of. In a frank conversation, nobody is silenced and a wide array of opinions is voiced. As a result, everybody stands to win, and the biggest winners are often the minorities. They are always better off in an environment which encourages and protects dissent and open exchanges than in a society which seeks to coddle people by punishing dissent and protecting them from unorthodox views.

It is possible that my advocacy of dialogue might strike you as a sophism, truism, or, worse, as a pedantic and useless exhortation. Whether you agree with me or not, make sure that the world remains for you a vast school of inquiry and a constant source of information. Never forget for a moment that those who know only their own side of the case might not even know it that well. Your reasons for holding certain beliefs may be good and legitimate, but you must still be acquainted with others' ideas and reasons and should be able to understand why people hold those beliefs before trying to refute them. Denying a fair hearing to opinions and ideas that you have already condemned without proper examination does you lasting mental harm. It gives you a dangerous feeling of infallibility that only genuine dialogue and robust criticism might dissipate.

Therefore, you would be wise to imitate the example of moderates who, when facing opposition, refuse to censor or shun their critics, even when they find them disagreeable. Fight to end cancel culture and intimidation on all sides. Cancellation is not a word that ever appears in the moderates' vocabulary and it ought also to be absent from yours. Your adversaries and critics should provoke your curiosity rather than your anger. Instead of drawing up blacklists with real or imaginary enemies to be eliminated, avoid any form of ostracism and strive to create and maintain open spaces in which diverse ideas can freely compete and the spirit of curiosity and toleration may prevail. Take inspiration from those who like and cultivate "a strong, intimate, manly fellowship, the kind of friendship which rejoices in sharp vigorous exchanges."[14] Their companionship will foster fellow-feeling and develop your ability to make contact and empathize with others.

One more thing, if I may. You must make sure that exchanges are vigorous, competitive, and argumentative, but remember that they should always remain polite and civil. Imitate the moderates' genteel spirit that knows how to speak, what to say and what not to say, when to begin and when to finish, when to remain silent and when to avoid saying something unpleasant or hurtful. Theirs is a joyful and elegant disposition that knows when and how to push one's beliefs without offending or hurting others. It creates a friendly atmosphere in which difficult negotiations and necessary compromises become possible.[15]

At the same time, learn from the arrogance of those who believe they know all the answers before any questions are asked, the self-righteous ones who live in bubbles and fear unorthodox ideas. Make sure not to accuse your critics of committing microaggressions when they come out against you with solid arguments. Instead, keep your minds open to criticism and listen to all that could be said *against* you. Avoid building straw men and try to hear directly from people who actually hold the beliefs you are attempting to refute. To have a solid ground for preferring your own opinions, you ought to be able to throw yourselves into the mental position of those who think differently from you and learn how to make the strongest possible and the most persuasive case *for* them before trying to refute them. Dialogue is an essential prerequisite in this regard.

That is, undoubtedly, a high bar for all of us. We tend to shrink from controversies for fear of being cancelled, and cling to our views as dogmas, relying on ready-made formulae to validate them. The longing for paradise on our own side can sometimes turn into a bad habit, the suppression of truth in the name of loyalty to our political tribes.[16] You must always be on guard against that, no matter what. As a mental practice and discipline, dialogue is essential to fight against groupspeak and groupthink in a world in which sectarianism, ideological intransigence, and hyper-polarization thrive.

Cultivate the art of dialogue and civil disagreement and try to live in truth even when that might go against the short-term interests of your party or group. Time is short, but there are many opportunities to learn this valuable art. Do not hesitate to seize them before it is too late. Farewell! Yours, . . .

PART IV

THE ETHOS OF MODERATION

Moderation does not consist of saying that you have a half-belief when you fully believe in something. It consists in respecting opposing opinions and combatting them without excessive anger; refraining from engaging in personal attacks and not issuing condemnations or cancellations.[1]

Frédéric Bastiat

Intermezzo

The Lure of Radicalism

We have it in our power to begin the world over again.[1]

(Thomas Paine)

AFTER READING THE PREVIOUS LETTERS, my younger interlocutors were eager to reopen the live conversation and ask new questions.

Lauren: I continue to be intrigued by your ambiguous use of the word moderation. It is time to call a spade a spade; we should not add to the confusion that exists in our society today. We must denounce without hesitation any form of moderation willing to tolerate extreme forms of inequality and injustice.[2] In the end, our world does not need lukewarm souls; it needs instead "burning hearts," always concerned with fairness and unwilling to put up with reactionary interests. Our world needs tenacious hearts and minds, "ever vigilant, without illusions, immune to discouragement, disdainful of artful maneuvers."[3] What makes us sick to our stomachs is our political society in its entirety. The truth is that there will be no salvation until we are prepared to unambiguously repudiate our present system to begin looking for a path to genuine renewal. That is why we must continue to fight without moderation for our values and principles.[4]

Your youthful passion makes me think of two things. To begin with, I am reminded of the first part of a famous saying (attributed, I believe, to Georges Clemenceau) according to which any person who is not radical in her twenties lacks a heart. It would be hard to disagree with that. The second part of the aphorism, though, is more controversial and rather harsh; it claims that if you are not a conservative after thirty-five you have no brain.

I am not sure how to interpret these words other than as another provocative claim meant to stir controversy. Your passion is genuine and reminds me of the boundless enthusiasm of eighteenth-century revolutionaries like Thomas Paine whose confidence in the human power to "begin the world anew" was a classical expression of the Enlightenment's faith in the capacity of reason to create a new secular order. He believed that the state of civilization was as odious as it was unjust, "absolutely the opposite of what it should be," and called for revolution.[5]

Do you see the resemblance here? You, too, welcome the storm and the earthquake and see yourselves as inventing a new world with the aid of your passion and imagination.[6] Now, you may no longer think that you are able to "begin the world anew," but you, too, seem to believe that only a total revolution can solve our social, economic, and political woes. Is that true?

Lauren: Well said! First, we'll make the revolution – then we'll find out what for.[7] This is the spirit of our fight. What we need today is a bold New Deal. We need noise and disruption rather than cautious reform and halfway measures that don't go far enough. So, if you are a moderate, then . . . think again.[8]

Rob: I don't share all of Lauren's ideas, but I also believe that we must have the courage to recognize that our current system has ceased to function properly. It is highly dysfunctional and it's time to radically change it. We need to drain the swamp since the entire system is corrupt to the core. How can this be done with moderation?

I suspect that your rebellious attitude is motivated by little else than anger and youthful hope. You and your radical friends believe you are called to change the whole system and have your own reasons for thinking so. It is true that the temptation to embrace radicalism is sometimes irresistible. For one thing, radicalism seems to be in the DNA of the young for whom living authentically amounts to affirming one's will, often in competition with that of others. On this view, seeking a compromise with the principles and ideas of others would be a shameful admission of weakness, an act of violence against oneself, a blow to one's integrity.

Now, I'd like to remind you that there are many ambiguities surrounding the word *radical*. It comes from the Latin *radix* or *radicalis,* which means "root" or "having roots." Over time, it has been used both as an adjective and a noun. As an adjective, it means going to the root or the essence of a thing; this meaning that goes back to the mid-1600s does *not* imply entirely uprooting the system. The political sense of the word that equates radical with revolutionary can be traced back to the eighteenth century, the century of revolutions.[9]

Lauren: It is impossible to deny that some forms of radicalism and radical agendas have contributed to political progress across the world over time.

I get it. Your view is that civilization would not have advanced in many parts of the world (Athens, Paris, etc.) without the ideas promoted by radical spirits. Do you regard Socrates as the first "radical"? If so, you may have a point. After all, this view was confirmed by the majority of the 500 Athenian jurors in his trial, who condemned Plato's teacher to death for his dissent. They saw Socrates as a dangerous gadfly challenging the traditions, norms, values, and stability of their beloved city. But was he a radical in the same sense of the term we use today? I am not so sure.

Rob: It's interesting you brought up Socrates. If he were alive today, the woke Left would most likely try to cancel him immediately. Perhaps he wouldn't even be put on trial today. He would be found guilty by the vanguard of public opinion – the woke ones – as soon as he opened his mouth. He would immediately be declared persona non grata without having a chance to defend himself.

Lauren: These are mere speculations, so let's leave Socrates out of the picture for now. I fear you are not taking my point seriously. Can you deny that self-identified radicals played a key and effective role in social justice campaigns, including the antislavery movement, the feminist movements, civil rights, and women's suffrage? Can you imagine living today without enjoying the benefits of their struggles and achievements? Visionary radicals like Martin Luther King Jr. provide the tailwind and open new vistas by expanding the boundaries of the possible. Moderation never goes far enough. Our dysfunctional institutions cannot be reformed with moderation and the time for small ideas has run out.

For all these reasons, we should not discard too quickly the idea of living in a socialist system. For us, the word socialism does not carry the same stigma as for our predecessors. We must be angry and bold; if we

want to make any significant progress, we ought to be prepared to question and challenge everything. We should even be willing to rethink all forms of resistance, both the non-violent and the violent ones, and reflect on what they may or may not be able to achieve.

It's unclear what you mean by rethinking violence. Are you making a case for it?

Lauren: I only meant to say that it might be good to shatter some norms every now and then, and we should be prepared to do it without timidity when necessary. To change the existing power structures, a willingness to think the unthinkable may often be a source of real power.[10] *Shattering some norms can, in fact, help enhance democracy and promote equity and fairness, particularly when it comes to race, gender, and minority issues.*

That's why we need to support the Black Lives Matter movement (or Occupy Wall Street in the past) and endorse radical measures such as defunding the police or cancelling student debt. When our system becomes a ruthless oligarchy catering only to the interests of the very rich, then there is no middle ground to stand on. Our present situation calls for bold actions and uncompromising positions; a halfhearted or incomplete approach would be self-defeating. There is little or no value in conserving a rotten house about to fall apart. Do you disagree with that?

Let me make sure I understand your point of view. Are you prepared then to say that our current political problems admit of no partial reforms and justify violent forms of protest? Are you willing to defend the destruction of property and the plundering of stores as a reasonable and articulate expression of anger and disappointment in a regime that has not lived up to our expectations? Are you ready to say that "in light of the economic deprivation experienced by large portions of the population, the vandalizing of property and the theft of goods could just as easily be framed as the enforcement of a moral economy – the rightful reappropriation of stolen wealth and an acceptable way for people to intervene in and regulate unjust distribution"?[11]

Lauren: What we know for sure is that we are not going to get anywhere by embracing a politics of appeasement or timid reforms when fundamental issues of justice and rights are at stake. We must vigorously denounce the vocabulary of oppression omnipresent around us. Your moderation and prudence would not be able to help much in this regard. There are many issues on which no middle ground is possible: abortion, racism, climate change, gun reform, healthcare, criminal justice reform, immigration reform, or the bloated military budget that has made possible our endless wars.

Rob: On some of these points, we are again in partial agreement, even if we have different priorities. We fight against the dictatorship of relativism; in the realm of politics, we reject identity politics and globalism. A good illustration of what we oppose is the critical race theory that is more apt to divide than unite us. In the realm of culture and education, "the movement we are up against prizes autonomy above all."[12] *According to this view, the individual may be allowed to define what is true, good, and beautiful, against the authority of tradition.*[13] *That doesn't seem possible or desirable. That's why we don't believe there can be any middle ground or compromise on fundamental issues. We must either win big or be defeated.*

Let's reflect for a moment on the nature of the current radicalism. Lauren mentioned earlier the word *socialism* and I'd like to return to it for a moment. A November 2019 Gallup poll found that since 2010, near 50 percent of young adults have a positive image and rating of socialism. Almost 50 percent of millennials declared that they would be open to living in a socialist country. An October 2019 YouGov Internet survey found that "7 in 10 Millennials Say They'd Vote for a Socialist."[14] Most of the new forms of radicalism pay more attention to identity and culture than to social/economic issues.

I am sure you will agree with me that the consequences are not insignificant. Many among the young display a surprising loss of faith in democratic institutions and principles. Several decades ago, 71 percent of Europeans and Americans thought it is essential to live in a democratic system. Only 29 percent of those born in the 1980s believe that any longer. In the United States, a quarter of millennials think that representative democracy no longer offers a viable framework for governing the country. What is deeply concerning (at least for me) is that this is not a phenomenon limited to one aisle of the political spectrum. The declining faith in political institutions and norms is accompanied by the tendency to see conspiracies everywhere and the propensity to rely on fake news and "alternative" facts.

A surprisingly high number seem inclined to prefer a strong hand or military rule to the rule of law and parliamentary government.[15]

Lauren: So, what? The risks of doing nothing and watching the crisis unfold far exceed the risks of doing something and trying to end it. For the first time in our lives, there is a growing call for a firm and radical response that encourages us to go far beyond the constraints imposed by our economic system. Capitalism as we know it can no longer save us.[16] "We've amassed some of the largest amounts of wealth in American history, but we have never seen so many people struggling and living paycheck to paycheck in the way that we are today."[17] "When the survival of the planet is at stake, calls for moderation and compromise aren't a mark of adult politics – they're a threat to civilization."[18]

I get it. You believe that politics is all about having good or pure intentions and goals and being on the "right" side of history, that is, on the side of revolution. Anything that can trigger it – economic crises, pandemics, natural disasters, or even civil unrest – is deemed good and useful as long as it serves the right cause. Since moderation and compromise oppose revolutionary methods, they must be condemned.

But you know as well as I do that that radicalism, like moderation, comes in many flavors and nuances and manifests itself in various forms and venues.[19] Are you prepared to endorse all of them without making distinctions? Consider a few examples. I have already referred to calls for rejecting objectivity in journalism, in particular the claim that news organizations' core value may no longer be objectivity, an old and allegedly discredited concept, responsible for the failure of both-sides journalism. According to this radical view, the entire media industry must be rebuilt from scratch as one that "operates from a place of moral clarity"[20] in the pursuit of social justice. But can there really be effective journalism without objectivity?

Another type of radicalism challenges the core values and principles of Western civilization which, so the argument goes, are based on systematic racism, oppression, and white supremacy. This idea is at the heart of the controversial "1619 Project" that sees America first and foremost as a republic founded on slavery, racism, and imperialism. Moreover, left-wing radicals denounce the "repressive" tolerance of the capitalist order and see private property and the free market as the root of all our economic, social, and political problems.

Rob: Isn't it obvious that radicalism has come to define the agenda of the entire Left, not just the woke Left? Radical ideas like free college or cancelling all student debt are very popular on the entire Left today.

Maybe, but don't forget that there are also various forms of radicalism that can be found on the Right as well. They all share a similar dissatisfaction with moderation, seen as the opposite of toughness and manliness. This is visible in the initiatives proposed by the most zealous anti-government activists railing against the deep state; the extremist advocates of the Second Amendment; and the moral crusaders in the pro-life camp who see the world in black and white. They use litmus tests on issues such as abortion and taxes, attack the independence of judges who have different viewpoints, and reject new immigrants, same-sex marriage, and multiculturalism.

Lauren: Aren't these forms of radicalism different from each other? Don't they reflect separate agendas and distinct priorities? If so, why conflate them?

Granted, these forms of radicalism are different. They may be looking for meaning and purpose in different ways and places, but they share something important in common, namely, a propensity to hyperbole and a lack of nuance. This is manifested, among others, by the pathos and conviction behind their unmasking strategy, replete with debunking jargon, angry denunciation, and vituperation. The task is to constantly search for targets and scapegoats everywhere and expose a matrix of domination or oppression, along with those who make it possible.

Have you heard of the recent trend among university libraries to hire diversity-inclusion auditors entrusted with the task of conducting diversity audits of their print collections with the view to "decanonizing" the stacks? This sounds to me like a bad idea. It isn't as dangerous as targeting election officials for conducting fair democratic elections or forbidding teachers from teaching certain topics, but it is still an extreme idea unlikely to lead to any good outcomes.

Lauren: Let's leave all that aside for a moment, for I don't think we speak the same language. I still cannot understand why you find radicalism unjustified.

I didn't say unjustified, nor do I equate radicalism with extremism. What I disagree with is your belief that embracing moderation amounts to being a bystander or a form of cowardly surrender. That is not true. Those who hold this view think that moderation is nothing but a form of acquiescence to an unjust system and society, a moral and political capitulation to prejudice, domination, and injustice. The radical assumption based on this belief is that we must fight it with every tool we have to replace this unjust and unreformable system with another one in which equality and solidarity will coexist harmoniously with liberty and justice. The dominant idea is that we are running out of time and the fire is already consuming us. For those who embrace this view, moderation and piecemeal reforms cannot possibly offer a remedy to the ills of our age.

Rob: Don't the new social media and the big tech companies also have a key role and responsibility in this regard? If consumed in excess, the Internet, its many opportunities and temptations tend to make our thoughts and imagination increasingly immoderate. Many of us appear to be morally illiterate or immature, despite being able to operate the most developed technologies. There hardly seems to be any balance in our society, given the tendency to immoderation that pervades all aspects of our lives, both private and public. That is why we need to limit the power of the big tech companies over our lives, among other things.

It's no secret that many around us live disconnected from each other and in parallel universes made possible by the new social media. The Internet fosters radicalization and hyperbole and emboldens anonymous actors to constantly compete for attention and influence. Twitter, for example, puts everyone "on a massive stage, with the nastiest put-downs, insults, and provocations often receiving the most applause."[21] Thus, it offers powerful incentives to exaggerate with the aim of provoking a series of reactions through endless iterations of hyperbolic negativity. The media that thirsts for bold narratives and breaking news also encourages people to see themselves engaged in an all-or-nothing existential battle. Pundits call their friends to arms and denounce the weak or lukewarm sisters and brothers within their own ranks. You can understand now why it is so difficult to practice moderation under these circumstances.

Lauren: It's easy to blame social media for everything, but it can also be a force for the good. Because of social media we are aware of how dysfunctional our system is. "Too many lines have been crossed, too many innocent people murdered, too many communities over-policed and otherwise neglected to expect anyone to react 'reasonably'."[22] The new social media help us "stake out clear ideological terrain, marry it to an ambitious, transformative policy agenda, and build a mass movement to carry it through."[23] This is a momentous task. How can we achieve our goals then with moderation's half-measures and timid steps?

Rather than trying to answer your (rhetorical) question directly, I'd like to quote again Montaigne's words, if I may. "Our most glorious achievement," he once wrote, "is to live life fittingly."[24] I have always wondered what he meant by "fittingly" – the original French term is *à propos.* In rereading his essays, I have come to suspect that what Montaigne meant to say in his inimitable style is that our most glorious achievement is to live with . . . moderation.

Here is an idea for you derived from his essays: it is more difficult to be a moderate than make one's journey along the extremes, where the edges and borders serve as signposts and guides. Most of us cannot live without relying on such visible markers. In your case, it is belief that our system is rotten to the core and unreformable, or the idea that there is one single (and simple) cause and solution for our present discontents and turmoil. It is easy to believe all that. But, as Montaigne reminds us, it is much more difficult to take "the wide and unhedged middle way"[25] where there are few signposts, and you must rely on your judgment, knowledge, and intuition at all times. Do you see his point?

Rob: I have not read Montaigne and perhaps I should do it soon. But the problem as I see it is not that there are too few moderates, but far too many.

You might think that there are too many moderates out there, but in truth, there are very few real ones. If you don't believe Montaigne, listen to what Montesquieu had to say on this point. "By a misfortune attached to the human condition," he wrote, "great men who are moderate are rare; and, as it is always easier to follow one's strength than to check it, . . . it is easier to find extremely virtuous people than extremely wise men."[26] His contemporary Adam Smith agreed: "In a nation distracted by faction, there are, no doubt, always a few, though commonly but a very few, who preserve their judgment untainted by the general contagion." These are the moderates "held in contempt and derision, frequently in detestation, by the furious zealots of both parties."[27]

This is all more evident in our age of hyper-polarization when it is not what knowledgeable and experienced people think, say, and do that gains the attention and favor of the public. What carries the day instead is what drives the imagination of the extremists and fires up their dreams and those of their supporters.[28] But how can you be so sure that the language of moderation isn't still relevant? What if, appearances notwithstanding, prudential incremental changes rather than big transformative schemes still offer the best ways to improve our imperfect democratic institutions?

To answer these questions, the next letters will clarify what the spirit of moderation implies and how it relates to key virtues such as modesty, civility, prudence, common sense, realism, and pragmatism.

1

The Spirit of Moderation

What then is the spirit of liberty? I cannot define it . . . The spirit of liberty is the spirit which is not too sure that it is right; the spirit of liberty is the spirit which seeks to understand the minds of other men and women; the spirit of liberty is the spirit which weighs their interest alongside its own without bias.[1]

(Learned Hand)

EVER SINCE I READ THESE WORDS OF JUDGE Learned Hand (1872–1961), one of the most respected judges of his time, I have thought that one could easily replace liberty with moderation and keep the rest intact to describe the ethos of moderation. It is the spirit that is never sure it is right but seeks to understand the minds and hearts of others. Much like the spirit of liberty, the ethos of moderation cannot be defined with precision, but at least we can get a sense of it by examining a few concrete examples.

You might ask now: why is it so important to talk about the *spirit* of moderation? First and foremost, "moderation" and "moderate" are not just empty words that can be applied indiscriminately to many things. They share a distinctive ethos that allows people to cooperate and peacefully negotiate their differences and disagreements. It is not a mere accident that the attacks on democratic institutions and norms always begin with assaults on the spirit of moderation, closely linked to the democratic way of life. Second, when this ethos is under siege, as is the case today, democracy itself which is based on compromise is jeopardized as well. Then, the spirit of moderation is gradually replaced by hatred, enmity, and total war. When this happens, the corruption of democratic institutions is well underway and their future uncertain.

Now, we must recognize that there are several ways of being and acting like a moderate. One can be a moderate on purpose, out of the conviction that it is preferable to embrace moderation rather than radicalism or extremism. This does *not* exclude, however, the possibility of sometimes having immoderate instincts and desires, or occasionally engaging in immoderate enterprises. One can also be a moderate by temperament or nature; some are lucky to be born this way, but many are not.

One such example was the Dutch theologian and philosopher Desiderius Erasmus (1466–1536), the author of *In Praise of Folly*, a witty satire written in 1509 that I highly recommend to you for both its insights and humor.[2] Erasmus had an inborn aversion to dogmatism, cruelty, and bloodshed. He was aware that most princes are ignorant of the laws of their country and are often willing to pursue their own personal advantage, no matter what. The worst of them are always bellicose, while the truly great leaders do everything in their power to avoid war and destruction. Erasmus' critics mistook his moderation for a constitutional weakness and temperamental defect, but they were wrong to do so. He remains, in my view, one of the best examples of moderation as temperament, so make sure to read him at some point.

Finally, one can also be a moderate, as it were, by accident or forced by circumstances. This mode of being a moderate is, of course, different from the previous ones, but they all share a few things in common. One of them is the propensity to skepticism and doubt, which stems from moderates' recognition and acceptance of human imperfection and fallibility. Aware of their limited knowledge and understanding, they always operate with a reserve clause. Moderates understand that their points of view are always contingent, fallible, and incomplete, and must therefore be taken with a grain of salt.

You may wonder now what I mean by acting with a reserve clause; it is, I suppose, a fancier word for being skeptical, prudent, and patient. I hasten to add that this doesn't mean that moderates cannot be resolute after having carefully considered all the available options. They can be firm, yet their decisiveness never hardens into dogmatism. They are aware that mankind is made up of many inconsistencies and paradoxes; the wisest among us sometimes act foolishly, while those whom we see as foolish characters may sometimes act, well, . . . wisely, if I may use this term.

That is why moderates are reluctant to make absolute claims and categorical assertions about other people's motives and intentions. They are aware that as a rule, many conjectures about the motives and outcomes of human action are uncertain, and we are rarely able to see accurately through the labyrinth of our desires. Moderates know that many of our beliefs have at least "a penumbra of vagueness and error."[3] They are skeptical that the world can be made intelligible with the aid of our abstract theories or philosophical systems, no matter how brilliant they may be. They are particularly careful to draw inferences only from *real* facts and are extremely cautious about passing definitive judgments about things which they know only imperfectly. Because they regard the world as unfinished and incomplete, they are always ready to listen to and learn from others.

Does all this sound implausible or utopian to you? Do you perhaps find the bar impossibly high? I hope not. Why should it be so hard to embrace moderation after all? In some ways, the mere fact that we live in an immoderate world prone to excess should be enough to convince us of the virtue of moderation, modesty, and prudence. I have always been uncomfortable in the presence of those who have no hesitation and doubt, who have only certitudes and strong beliefs, especially on key controversial issues (such as pro-choice, pro-life, guns, or immigration) on which they are unwilling to compromise. These people are self-important and self-righteous to a fault. They tend to be intransigent and dogmatic and embrace a "politics of faith" grounded in absolute claims and categorical litmus tests meant to sort out the impure from the pure ones. For them, politics is always a zero-sum game, in which their interests are incompatible and irreconcilable with those of others. Their moral intransigence derives from their belief that they alone possess the truth and are called to enlighten the unfaithful.

It should be obvious to you by now that the true spirit of moderation is opposed to all that. The motto of all moderates is: no panaceas! They acknowledge that conflict and disagreement about the good life are not only inevitable and healthy, but also necessary and beneficial, if properly channeled through democratic institutions and norms. And they recognize that intractable political and moral conflicts can never be solved with the help of miraculous solutions, whether from science, religion, philosophy, or the bench of the Supreme Court.

The spirit of moderation also casts doubt on anyone who claims absolute authority or divine sanction for their views. It calls upon us to recognize the relativity of all human perspectives. Moderates know that the world can be seen through many windows, and each offers a unique perspective that adds to life's colors. That is why being a moderate requires and implies treating people with respect, recognizing their equal dignity, and embracing diversity and pluralism of ideas and viewpoints.

The ethos of moderation has nothing of the sententious and axiomatic style that uses a cascade of peremptory affirmations, negations, and commandments. When moderates come across conceited claims and platitudes, they do not shy away from calling them by their real name. They emphasize instead rational arguments, real facts, and logic. Moderates resist the temptation to draw up proscription lists of enemies or critics slated for punishment. The spirit of moderation requires that we endure the discomfort of adversarial and sometimes uncivil exchanges and controversies with our political opponents who share different visions of the good. It relies upon a judicious balance between robust partisanship and prudent self-restraint.

Equally important, those who share the ethos of moderation never throw in the towel but seek to build bridges across ideological divides. It is consistent with the spirit of moderation to hear all sides, gather all the relevant known facts, and assess them with the aid of rational criteria. This presupposes a readiness not only to discard all hypotheses that have been proven inaccurate but also to continue to search for the truth with an unbiased and open mind. As such, the spirit of moderation, which is incompatible with sectarianism, can help build trust because it is generous, graceful, and humorous, doesn't frown on others, and is never pretentious or self-righteous.

I hope you will take some inspiration from those who belong to the party of the eternally anxious and questioning and simultaneously think *for* themselves and *against* themselves. Of course, I don't expect you to join their ranks right away, just listen carefully to what they have to say. They do not want any further crusades to build a radiant future or create new and better human beings. Their spirit is relaxed and open-minded without ever being vulgar in expression. It delights in embracing irony and directs it against anyone who pretends to have ready-made answers or the final word in public debates.[4] While moderates believe that there is always room for progress, they distrust the zealous engineers of the human soul who pretend to have quick and infallible solutions for improving human beings.

I'd like to end on a lighter note by pointing out what may be the moderates' greatest advantage after all. They are equipped with what Carl Sagan once called a "baloney detection kit" that fortifies their spirit and the minds of others against fake news and half-truths.[5] "In addition to teaching us what to do when evaluating a claim to knowledge," Sagan wrote, "any good baloney detection kit must also teach us what *not* to do. It helps us recognize the most common and perilous fallacies of logic and rhetoric."[6] That is exactly what moderates do and that is no minor achievement, in my view. They identify and suggest precautionary measures that we may take against falsehood, and they point out tried methods we may use when pushing back against fake news and "alternative" facts.

In other words, moderates act as examples and teachers of intellectual hygiene in our society. This may not be a magnetic idea for those who are thirsting for bold stories and grand narratives, but it is certainly a salutary one for many others, including myself, who more modestly, seek first and foremost to avoid extreme forms of cruelty and chaos. I would be curious to learn your thoughts when you have a few spare seconds. Until then, my very best wishes! Yours, . . .

2

Modesty and Humility

It is deserting humanity to desert the middle way. The greatness of the human soul lies in knowing how to keep the course; greatness does not mean going outside of it, but rather keeping within it. . . . Nature has set us so exactly in the middle that if we alter one side of the scales, we alter the other as well.[1]

(Blaise Pascal)

I WOULD LIKE TO WRITE TO YOU TODAY about two virtues closely linked to moderation – modesty and humility – that I have previously mentioned. They should never be absent from our public and political life in our new age of anxiety, cynicism, and discontent. Along with courtesy and good manners, these are essential virtues that help us find the middle way described by Pascal. How often do you hear about them today in our society? And how often do you see our politicians practicing these virtues on social media or in their public appearances? Unfortunately, these seem to be rhetorical questions which should put us immediately on guard.

Let's begin by defining the terms. The word humility derives from humus, earth. Acting with humility (or meekness) means staying close to the ground, embracing earthbound values rather than shooting imprudently for the sky. It also entails staying close to others, listening to them, and talking to them rather than past them. To be humble (or meek) does *not* imply being excessively submissive and passive; it means showing respect for a world that is greater (and more important) than any of us. In other words, to be modest amounts to playing your role as best as you can and trying to actualize all your potentialities in full, without trying to be someone else or playing someone else's role.

Simply put, modesty and (epistemic) humility allow us to better understand our limits, who we are, and what our real place in the world is, as opposed to the imaginary one we often fancy to occupy. They are virtues of human beings who know that they are not superhuman and may not compete with their Creator.[2] The meek ones never pretend that God or history is on their side. Such a claim would be a sign of hubris, the antithesis of modesty and epistemic humility. Nothing is so conceited as ignorance combined with excessive ambition, pride, and delusion. It is a part of true knowledge as a form of "learned ignorance" to recognize that certain things are beyond our power to know. That is why along with moderation, humility may well be the crown jewel in the pearl-chain of all virtues.[3]

You might object that modesty and humility are most necessary in normal, peaceful times, but they are not made for exceptional circumstances like war, when courage, heroism, and the willingness to fight and defeat the enemy are needed. They are not the qualities of those who want to command or dominate over others. Yet, it would be difficult to deny that they are ordinary virtues that can be practiced virtually by everyone on a daily basis. Although adapted to the human scale, they require constant effort and determination. At the same time, there is a certain note of unsung heroism implied in these virtues. This is all the more important to point out since modesty and humility (or meekness) are often equated with being excessively compliant or submissive, being willing to go along with whatever other people want us to do.

This view, I believe, should not go unchallenged. Modesty and humility lack neither greatness nor boldness and are *not* virtues of the weak, as you might be inclined to believe. Consider, for example, Mahatma Gandhi's exceptional career that shows why these virtues can often be powerful and effective. As the antithesis of pride and arrogance, modesty and humility allow us to remain human and overcome all sorts of intoxication – with power, physical prowess, fame, and reputation. They teach us how to fight against the temptations of nihilism, resentment, and vanity. As faces of moderation, modesty and epistemic humility are grounded in a profound awareness of our limits and shortcomings as human beings. They leave little room for self-indulgence, self-righteousness, or hatred.

What I am trying to say is that moderates do not chase after power, positions, and status; instead, their priority is to strengthen the bonds that keep people together and sustain their free way of life. By being modest, humble, and forbearing, moderates oppose the inflationary logic of all bidders at political auctions of popularity in which the most extreme positions often prevail. They believe that non-violence is always superior to violence and forgiveness is preferable to punishment. Gandhi's embrace of non-violence and passive resistance is a proof of the power of humility. His entire life and martyrdom show that it takes a lot of courage and audacity to be modest and humble in worldly affairs, where so often might makes right and loud voices and strident headlines dominate the scene.[4]

As for me, I admire and respect those who are neither afraid nor ashamed to recognize that they do not possess any keys or definitive answers to life's countless dilemmas; those who have the courage to admit that the world is far too complicated and eclectic to fit into any single ideological framework or theory; those who are free from delusions of greatness or illusions about their power.[5] They do not try to predict the direction of history or the course of events and are skeptical about deterministic theories that deny free will and individual agency.

It is this principled reticence of moderates that distinguishes them from the self-righteous confidants of Providence or history who are ready to sacrifice almost everything to achieve their ambitious goals. Young people like you may be inclined to see this reserve as a weakness or liability in politics, while I believe it can be a major asset. When we act with humility, we learn to discover the otherness of "Thou." Listen to these beautiful words of a wise rabbi, the late Jonathan Sacks, who described humility better than I can do it here. "Humility, then, is more than just a virtue, it is a form of perception, a language in which the 'I' is silent so that I can hear the 'Thou,' the unspoken call beneath human speech, the Divine whisper within all that moves, the voice of otherness that calls me to redeem its loneliness with the touch of love. Humility is what opens us to the world."[6]

Being humble not only opens up the view from above, but also gives us the perspective from below, revealing how things are at the grassroots level, where real people live, animated by real passions, and fighting against real challenges. It is there, at this level, below, that the hidden side of life, most often invisible to our superficial and hurried eyes, is revealed in full. What makes the modest and humble ones often stand out is their generosity – the most unassuming people also tend to be the most charitable ones. The moderates I admire are simple and straightforward without being self-righteous or conceited. They are never hypocritical and go steadily their ways, being capable of forgetting themselves to serve others and the common good.

What do I want to say with all that? My point is simple: there is a close relationship between moderation, modesty, epistemic humility, meekness, and happiness that is not always properly recognized. Our ability to cherish the little joys of life, our openness to cheerfulness, the capacity to enjoy the beauty and poetry of life and experience true friendship, all this also depends, to some degree, on cultivating the virtue of moderation.[7] The latter is grounded in a philosophy of life that allows us to become content by getting to know our true place in the world, neither too high nor too low. Although the epigraph from Pascal's *Pensées* doesn't mention modesty, meekness, and humility directly, I believe that it implies them to a significant degree. For the true and only greatness of humanity depends on – and is linked to – finding the middle between extremes and knowing how to remain attached to it. Modesty, meekness, and humility play a key role in this respect.

This may sound like a truism to you, but it is not. Take, for example, the ancient Greeks. They knew a lot about balance, moderation, or lack thereof – you've certainly read some of their classic plays – but they did not think much of humility and modesty. The truth is that these self-effacing virtues did not loom large in their vocabulary.[8] Unlike the ancient Greeks, the Scandinavians are known to profess special appreciation for these unassuming virtues. The Swedes, for example, have a special word, *lagom,* which is sometimes seen as analogue to the Danish *hygge,* although linking it to *hygge* may be a bit farfetched. I don't presume you are familiar with any of these terms. Let's take a closer look and see what *lagom* might teach us about the style of moderation and its relationship with modesty and epistemic humility.

Lagom is very popular in Sweden where it has mostly positive connotations, although not everyone seems to love it (there's a hashtag *#NoMoreLagom* to express dissatisfaction with this form of moderation there). For some, it carries the connotation of mediocrity and conformity to what may appear as an unappealing austere way of life, that disapproves of expressions of strong individuality and personal success. On this view, *lagom* is an expression of a certain form of collectivism that breeds stinginess and doesn't allow individuals to be different or excel. Since *lagom* involves moderation in relation to what others are doing, it requires that you don't think you are different from anyone else.

Although finding a correct translation of *lagom* is not easy, its meaning is more or less clear: neither too little, nor too much, just the right amount. Living according to *lagom* means living a balanced and modest life, with humility. Etymologically, *lagom* is related to both law and team in Swedish. Its roots go back to the Viking time when *laget om* meant sitting around the team had a particular meaning. It referred to the habit of gathering around the fire after a long day of work when people used to talk to each other about their exploits and pass around horns filled with mead. The expectation was that everyone would sip neither too much nor too little, just the right amount so that others could have enough to drink in their turn. Over time, *laget om* has been shortened to *lagom*, the term the Swedes still use today.[9]

You can easily guess what I am hinting at. Moderation is grounded in a concrete philosophy and involves a daily routine that makes possible a sound way of life, lived in balance, with modesty and humility. "*Lagom*," writes an expert, "isn't about denying yourself life's pleasures; it's about enjoying everything in moderation."[10] The secret lies in achieving a judicious balance between individuals' needs, nature's resources, and society's requirements as well as between work and leisure. There should be neither too little nor too much of either of these elements in a well-adjusted and harmonious life.

Modesty and humility allow people to enjoy the good and natural things in life, while getting along reasonably well with others. Living according to the rules of modesty and humility is a salutary reaction to the tendency to extremes and recklessness in many aspects of our modern life, from language and dress codes to work and dietary habits. *Lagom* reminds us that we do not have to practice rigorous asceticism to enjoy the little joys of everyday life; neither do we have to repudiate our limits to live a full life. On the contrary, we must learn to embrace and live with them, as a useful form of intellectual and bodily discipline.[11] Moderation, modesty, and humility – which are all part of *lagom* – raise red flags, teaching us what to avoid and what to embrace. They promote a balanced lifestyle, based on limits, simplicity, and naturalness, away from luxury, frivolity, and arrogance.

Lagom implies a few unwritten rules as a form of hygiene for the body, mind, and soul. Here are a few guidelines that I hope you might find useful in your own life, even if they seem to go against the hyper-individualist mentality which we all share in America.[12] You're not to think you are anything special, regardless of your talents and skills. You're not to think you are smarter than *we* are; we are all equal in our dignity as human beings. You must not imagine yourself better than *we* are, nor should you ever think you know more than *we* do. You're not to think you are more important than *we* are.

As you easily guess, the language of these rules is not accidental. The emphasis falls not on you but on *we*, on what we all share and need to do to find common ground. You might not find all these rules particularly inspiring, but one thing would be difficult to dispute. They all describe an intriguing type of mental and intellectual discipline that seeks balance by tempering excessive individualism and promoting harmony, conviviality, and contentment. And this is no small matter.

Let us return finally to the subject of *lagom* as a face of moderation. I do not mean to reduce the entire meaning of this intriguing concept to modesty or humility, nor would I want to suggest that being modest and acting with humility amount to being servile, kneeling down or groveling. Ambition often has the merit of pushing us forward and stimulating our energies. The key point I want to emphasize is that the philosophy of *lagom* overlaps with the school of common sense. It is not obsessed with what is flashy and excessive, and is distrustful of the bravado of the supermen (like Nietzsche) who regard humility as the virtue of the weak or slaves. By embracing modesty and epistemic humility, we learn to live patiently and enjoy what we have without being excessively restless or longing for superficial rewards and distinctions. *Lagom* also affords freedom from pride and teaches the importance of limits that define who we are and what we may be. It is the quality of thinking that we all share in equal dignity as human beings, regardless of the position and honors we happen to enjoy in society.

Moderates are tolerant of others' shortcomings because they begin by recognizing their own fallibility that makes them, along with everyone else, prone to human errors and follies. In their universe, there is room neither for haughtiness, complacency, and snootiness, nor for the self-righteous moral posturing, aggressiveness, and condescending tone of the narcissistic types. Because moderates are aware of the role that folly, ignorance, and pride play in life and society at large, they lack the stubbornness and obstinacy that often perpetuate futile and prolonged quarrels over trifling matters and silly absurdities. They are usually self-restrained in promoting their views and hold them tentatively, with a grain of salt, being open to revising them when necessary.

Remember the words of an ancient Eastern sage? "The superior man accords with the course of the Mean. Though he may be all unknown, unregarded by the world, he feels no regret."[13] He reminds us that the aim of life is higher than the mere satisfaction of material wants. In politics, modesty and humility help us withstand the temptation of pride, anger, and cynicism. The two virtues can serve as antidotes to the *libido dominandi* of the wealthy and the powerful. In life, they warn us against becoming virtuosi of small wares or excelling in things that ultimately are of little importance in the true hierarchy of values. Moderates are not vindictive and do not bear grudges. They are never first to start the fire or begin a fight; when others start one, they refuse to let themselves be burnt by it. They are capable of enduring storms without becoming angry and they maintain their composure without seeking revenge.

As such, the moderates' attitude is an act of defiance of the prevailing partisan politics of our age. Yet, while challenging the rules of normal politics, they are not prepared to entirely repudiate them. They only seek to humanize them, by instilling a necessary dose of humility, modesty, skepticism, and restraint. Moderates do not engage in conflictual relations with others with the aim of conquering, destroying, or defeating them once and for all. Their perspective is not of the either–or type, and the winner-take-all mentality has no appeal to them. When they enter political battles and controversies, they do not consider conflicts as zero-sum games, but rather as opportunities that may be used to the profit of the majority.

Before I close, I'd like to return one last time to Pascal's words. Leaving the middle in which nature has wisely placed us would mean betraying our human nature and trying to usurp the place reserved only to gods. We can best realize our humanity and full potential by embracing our limits rather than ignoring or denying them. It is a true sign of wisdom to wear our ideas and illusions lightly and play the comedy of life as artfully and intelligently as we can, without seeking to overstep our boundaries.[14] Humility and modesty (as faces of moderation) are two virtues that can help us find the middle that nature itself has ordained for us. They might be the orphaned virtues of our age, but they are life-enhancing and healing ones that cannot be praised too much.

Farewell! Yours, . . .

3

Civility

We still live in the age of indignation. But if we maintain our sense of relativity, then come what may, all can be saved.[1]

(Albert Camus)

After reading my last letter, you wondered whether anyone could embrace humility and modesty and still expect to be successful in public life. In our personal lives, you wrote, these unassuming virtues might work, but in politics, the rules of the game are different. Anyone who chooses to be humble and modest is doomed to join the ranks of losers. I believe the picture is much more nuanced than you think. To succeed in public life – and let's remember that the word *success* itself is quite ambiguous – these virtues must be practiced in conjunction with others, such as civility. It is about the latter that I'd like to write to you today starting from Camus' words above.

He wrote them almost eight decades ago, toward the end of the war. At that time, the French people were exhausted, restless, and angry. The war had taken a heavy toll on a country that was trying to come to terms with the shameful collaboration with the enemy during the Vichy regime. A few years later, communism replaced Nazism as the greatest challenge to liberal democracy on the world stage. The moment was ripe for recrimination, condemnation, and outrage. Some, arrogantly attributing to themselves the superiority of those who never made mistakes and stopped listening to their critics or opponents. Cultivating a sense of the relativity of one's beliefs was a risk many were unprepared or unwilling to take.

In this regard, our age of anxiety and indignation has a lot in common with the postwar epoch in which Camus lived and wrote. We may be more knowledgeable today, but it is impossible not to be shocked by the coarsening and vulgarity of political life, with its overblown rhetoric, invectives, and ideological intransigence that often serve short-term sectarian agendas and interests. Our political world is seething with wrath and cries for revenge. Are you surprised then that the spirit of civility and earnestness which can temper political passions and raw selfishness is absent from our debates?

None of us should be astonished to see civility being one of the first victims when the deliberate spreading of confusion and vitriol accompanies the proliferation of fake news and "alternative" facts. That is where we are today, and it is not a good place. Why is it that civility is one of those virtues that many are willing to praise in principle, but so few are ready to practice in public life? On the radical Left, it is viewed as a conservative virtue and a tool of oppression that may, in fact, reinforce existing hierarchies and repressive norms. On the hard Right, civility is regarded as a derivative virtue only for suckers, a sign of softness and weakness, the opposite of "manliness." On this view, "civility and decency are secondary values. They regulate compliance with an established order and orthodoxy."[2] Rage and indignation seem to be the only logical reaction to our discontents.

Let me suggest that we might be able to understand better the importance of civility if we consider first what happens when it is stripped away. Then, everything becomes a vast arena for conflict and a pretext to use slander and invective. Our families and communities, our public debates, media, and institutions may fall prey to violence and the virus of coarseness. In the absence of civility, our society risks "hacking away" at its democratic core by succumbing to extremism, sectarianism, and fanaticism.[3]

Here is one of those truths that cannot be stressed enough. Civility is not only a core value of civilization, but also an indispensable virtue that makes possible the smooth functioning of democratic regimes and their representative institutions. It emphasizes good manners, courtesy, and reasonableness, virtues that ensure social cooperation between individuals holding diverse worldviews and pursuing different interests. I would be inclined to regard civility as the political equivalent of the epistemic humility discussed in a previous letter. It reminds us that nobody is the bearer of the absolute truth, and encourages us to be open-minded and prepared to learn from others.

But civility's critics do have a point: it is *not* always an unambiguously good thing, and we must learn to tell the difference. Sometimes, the invocation of civility is meant to silence and humiliate people and discourage them from asking tough and arguably "uncivil" questions. Then civility may become an impediment to social and political change, especially when the need for this virtue is rhetorically invoked to stifle free expression or individual creativity. That is what people mean by "repressive civility."[4]

No one can deny that in progressive eras and nations, many people are able to debate complex moral, religious, scientific, and political subjects without excessive acrimony, by carefully weighing evidence and critically considering the facts. Yet, we all know that open-mindedness and respect for truth never come naturally; they require many things, among them, civility, toleration of diversity, and freedom. Being civil relies on the existence of liberty and implies the exercise of judgment and toleration. As the Earl of Shaftesbury once put it, "All Politeness is owing to Liberty. We polish one another and rub off our Corners and rough Sides by a sort of amicable Collision."[5] Civility assumes that social, political, economic, moral, and cultural pluralism is an ineradicable aspect of our modern society that imposes a set of duties upon all of us, regardless of the station we occupy in the world. One of those duties is to listen and try to accommodate our differences in an amiable manner, while respecting the freedom of others to live and think as they please.

That is why civility requires self-restraint and self-control that temper excess and outrage and allow us to put up with the shortcomings of others while holding ourselves to higher standards. Sometimes, civility may even go hand in hand with a certain degree of hypocrisy, at other times with a form of outward honesty that consists in saying what we really think and feel and being ready to hear what others have to say in turn. While we cannot be frank all the time, we can at least try to be civil by doing our best to grant others the dignity and freedom they are entitled to, even when we disagree with their views.

You asked: can civility really help neutralize the effects of sectarianism, tribalism, and fanaticism? I gather that you are not ready to answer in the affirmative and, frankly, neither am I. We must recognize that civility is not the panacea that some may dream of. It is only safe to say that civility, reinforced by other virtues, can act as a restraint on the passion with which we pursue our interests, ideas, and beliefs. It helps temper the zeal with which we seek to achieve our individual goals, allowing us to affirm and negotiate our personal and political differences without hyperbole or violence.

Yet, there is something else that civility does for us: it demands that we refrain from suppressing facts or arguments and misstating the details in public debates. Misrepresenting the opposite opinions in an argument or discussion, for political advantage, is as unacceptable as stigmatizing those who hold contrary opinions as bad and immoral individuals. Furthermore, being civil requires that we do not infer any vices from the position a person takes. Civility demands that we always seek to understand (as best as we can) what our opponents stand for and give merited honor to everyone, regardless of their political opinions. That is why, in reality, being civil is not a sign of weakness, as is often believed, but of genuine confidence and real strength.

Hence, there is no reason why civility could not work as an effective antidote to a festering climate of fear, hatred, and rage, although it is not always easy to remain civil when others around us are aggressive and bellicose. As a virtue that instills in us a sense of the relativity of our ideas and actions, it may also be a cure for the arrogance of anyone who exercises power and is inclined to abuse it. Yet, to achieve its goals, civility must work in tandem with moderation, prudence, and polite manners. So, let's take a closer look at the relationship between them.

You have already heard me saying that civility, courtesy, and compromise are essential to the functioning of parliamentary regimes. Yet, there is much more to civility than polite manners. Civility presupposes that while we are free to pursue our private ends, we are also called on to abide by the requirements of the common good, never ignoring the interests of the communities whose members we are. Being civil is the opposite of self-righteousness and involves a healthy dose of skepticism, beginning with skepticism toward our *own* ideas. Confident claims to moral clarity and political purity should be tempered by an awareness not only of the relativity of our beliefs and our limitations but also of the virtues and merits of our opponents and critics.

Here is what we all can do to avoid being uncivil. We may begin by doing our best to reject the false clairvoyance of those who think they are always right. This implies that we must hold our views with a reserve clause – the sense of relativity invoked by Camus and others – and honor tacit, unwritten rules that govern social interaction. The survival of open regimes like ours requires that those who govern should be willing and able to regularly socialize with the members of the opposition and their critics. Civility demands that they shun the idea that one side must win at all costs and achieve a total and definitive victory. Its rules allow us to pursue certain things in common that are essential for the preservation of our free way of life, despite our personal disagreements and differences and without being able to eliminate them altogether. As such, civility is the antithesis of any type of scorched-earth politics that normalizes systematic norm-breaking in the pursuit of narrow short-term or sectional goals.

I hope you will agree with me, at least in part, that this virtue is particularly relevant today. Never in living memory has our country been so divided to the extent that there seems to be no room left for moderation, compromise, and civility. Listen, for example, to what a prominent representative of the national conservativism movement said not long ago: "To recognize that enmity is real is its own kind of moral duty."[6] The phrase may be short and crude, but it is instructive. This perspective appeals to those who share a crusading mentality and are convinced that "toughness" and "manliness" are preferable to civility, compromise, and dialogue in the pursuit of political goals. The manliness they prefer is that of "a man who is not afraid to say out loud what others only whisper and to incur the wrath of the ruling class for doing so."[7] He is ready to choose "trial by combat" and incivility as a means of fighting the culture wars with the aim of decisively crushing the enemy and enjoying the spoils.

The threat posed by incivility will become clearer if you consider a few other contemporary examples. I have previously written about the Flight 93 mentality that has come to dominate a good part of the hard Right. According to another radical voice, "the stakes are high and the time to fight is now – wielding whatever levers of power are available."[8] On this view, even the option of using violence should be on the table as long as it is in the service of allegedly good ends: the total crushing of the enemy. The choice is simple: fight back with whatever means are available, including uncivil ones, or face ignominious defeat. The justification is straightforward: since our enemies have declared war on us, we must fight back as if there were no tomorrow. The time to play nice is over, civility is futile at best; battles that are not ruthlessly fought are never won.

Alas, that seems to be the mentality that dominates our political and public life today. You may think that our present situation requires a stronger medicine than civility, but you should still be prepared to give the latter a second chance before dismissing it as a weak and ineffective virtue. Of course, you may still wonder whether we should really put civility first, given the uncompromising and sometimes unrelenting antagonism between opposing political positions and platforms. You are perfectly entitled to ask if civility can actually work among rival groups competing for power in our Twitter age, when the incentives for incivility provided by the social media seem endless.

Do not expect civility to entirely evacuate passion, anger, and disagreement from politics and public life. You cannot count on living among individuals who are always sincere, well-meaning, polite, and transparent. That would be utopian. But "mere civility"[9] may still go a long way to calm passions and lower the temperature of politics, when the political scene becomes dangerously overheated and campaigning and winning at all costs turn out to be more important than legislating and governing.

Make no mistake. Civility does *not* require that we abandon our most cherished beliefs for the sake of reaching a fragile or illusory consensus with our opponents. It does not imply giving up our principles and ideals in pursuit of a fictitious common ground. Nor is civility expected to lead to the disappearance of disagreement in open societies. We must never forget that principled disagreement is different from sheer hostility and hyper-partisanship that leave no room for compromise and negotiation. If moderation and civility may often lessen the ardor of ideological disputes by emphasizing what we share over what divides us, it may not always be possible to do that. Sometimes, any compromise seems an unacceptable betrayal of one's beliefs and a sacrifice of personal integrity.

One of the greatest benefits of civility is that it allows us to combine audacity and caution, emotion and dispassion, reserve and commitment in pursuing our goals. Being committed to civility requires that we resist the temptation of silencing those whose views we disagree with. There will always be hope when people accept that free speech and rational argument might bring everyone a little closer to the truth, even if the latter continues to elude us.

Remember that there will always be enticing voices that you must steer clear of, voices that seek to lure you away from reason and civility, raising your expectations and making you impatient. Yet, there can never be too much civility in our midst, and I will never tire of recommending it, although I do not believe that civility can ever be a panacea for achieving political harmony.

It is your chance now to practice this virtue in our age of indignation, while maintaining your sense of relativity, defending your principles, and embracing your limits. Do not hesitate to seize this opportunity and make good use of it. Yours, . . .

4

Prudence

Don't be overly clever. Better to be prudent. . . . Common sense is safer.[1]

(Baltasar Gracián)

IT IS GOOD EVERY NOW AND THEN to take some distance from contemporary events to gain a better perspective on them. This time, I propose to start from the words of a favorite author of mine – Baltasar Gracián (1601–1658) – before turning to a famous painting by Titian whose main theme is prudence, the subject of the present letter. I don't presume you are familiar with Gracián's work nor do I expect you to have seen Titian's painting which is in the National Gallery in London. If you haven't read Gracián yet, I strongly recommend his writings to you, because they have a lot to teach us about another important virtue – prudence – that is closely connected with the ethos of moderation.

But first, who was he? A Jesuit priest, Gracián was one of the most prominent representatives of the Spanish Baroque age and one of the greatest Spanish moralists. Posterity has been less gracious to Gracián than to Francisco de Quevedo, Calderón de la Barca, Lope de Vega, Miguel de Cervantes, or Luís de Góngora, to name only a few of his famous contemporaries. If Gracián is still remembered today, it is mostly for an enigmatic book titled *The Pocket Oracle and the Art of Prudence* (1647). Arthur Schopenhauer translated it into German and praised it as "one of the best books in the world" and a faithful companion for life. He read all of Gracián's writings and declared the Spaniard to be his favorite author. Friedrich Nietzsche, too, hailed Gracián in glowing terms. "Europe," he wrote, "has never produced anything finer or more complicated in matters of moral subtlety."[2] Why were these two tough philosophers so impressed by this short book about prudence, and what can the latter teach us about the style of moderation?

Gracián's *Oracle* consists of 300 aphorisms meant for constant use in life and expressed in an enigmatic style. The book offers a path to worldly success with the aid of several rules of prudence and discretion that must be adapted to varying circumstances and contexts. They begin with the call to self-knowledge and promise to provide "a compass for sailing toward excellence"[3] that requires a combination of discernment, sagacity, astuteness, discretion, common sense, and taste. The prudent person knows how to distinguish between human and divine orders, avoiding any confusion between the means appropriate to each of them. As Gracián explains in one of the most obscure and important aphorisms of his book (#251), "we must use human means as though divine ones didn't exist, and divine means as though there were no human ones."[4] This rule of a great master, he added, requires no comment. I should note in passing that the great master in question (whose name he did not mention) was St. Ignatius of Loyola, the founder of the order to which the Spaniard himself belonged. The Jesuits regarded Gracián's literary works with skepticism and he was obliged to publish almost all of works under pseudonyms to avoid censure.

In reality, Gracián's aphorism does require commentary, for it is quite difficult to understand. At first sight, one wonders whether it is connected at all with prudence. Gracián does not explicitly say, like Edmund Burke, that prudence is "the god of this lower world,"[5] nor does he imply that prudence is the first in rank of all political virtues. In fact, the book uses the word *prudence* rather sparingly, despite its title. Instead, Gracián comments on synonyms of prudence, and related concepts such as self-knowledge, sound judgment, caution, luck, appearances, and self-control. He also writes about the manifestations and effects of prudence such as maintaining one's reputation, dissimulating one's true intentions, keeping expectations alive and matters in suspense or knowing how to wait patiently for the ripe moment to act well.

If there is one conclusion I'd like to draw from all that, it is that the art of prudence cannot be taught in the abstract; its rules can be learned only from long practice and experience. For Gracián, life in society is constant warfare, swimming in shark-filled waters, a relentless competition and struggle in which we are constantly tested by the malice of others. We are challenged by the stratagems of those who try to outwit us or conspire against us. Because we can suffer a fall at any moment, we must always be vigilant and ready to strike first before it is too late. That is what Gracián (the Jesuit) teaches us.

Where does moderation come into play in all this, you might wonder? Among the important lessons of Gracián's book is that sharpness and clear-sightedness of judgment along with wit and attention are crucial components of discernment, a key concept related to moderation and prudence. The prudent and the moderate ones do not live by generalities but use their discernment to adapt themselves to shifting circumstances in keeping with their moral compass. The focus of their proposed reforms is always on remedying particular grievances rather than pursuing abstract goals, no matter how appealing the latter may be. They are aware that it is not enough to have the right principles and abstract ideals to succeed; one must also have discernment, discretion, and common sense to see around various corners and orient oneself in the labyrinth of life.

Now, moderates skilled in the art of prudence may appear as modest and simple, but they are never naïve. They know that judgment is necessary to dispel illusions and take stock of the real worth of things. Attention and wit are required to read others' thoughts and guess their intentions and guiles. To see through the many layers and veils of existence, moderates arm themselves with "heightened attention" and "with eyes from head to foot ... with huge eyes, wide awake ones."[6] Their eyes and ears help them detect falsehood, hear what others say, and interpret accurately what they really mean.

But what kind of prudence is that after all, you might ask? I grant that it is not easy to grasp its nature; we perceive it in a mirror, but it may not be possible to define it precisely. Yet, if words cannot take us too far, an image might help in this regard. Consider a famous painting attributed to Titian (1488/90–1576) and titled "Allegory of Prudence." This memorable painting

ILLUSTRATION # 2 Titian, "Allegory of Prudence," National Gallery, London

from the mid-sixteenth century is, in my view, one of the best images that one could choose to help us grasp the complexity of this virtue. While prudence had been described by many others before Titian, his visual representation was so original that it had neither predecessors nor followers in the history of modern painting.

To realize what this mysterious and fascinating painting has to do with prudence, I propose we take a close look at its main figures. The three heads in the painting describe the three main ages of human beings. The left profile is that of an old man looking backward, while the right profile depicts a young man looking forward. In the middle is a mature bearded man gazing straight at us. The three heads have corresponding images below them; they represent the heads of a wolf (for the old man), a lion (for the mature person), and a dog (for the youth). To understand the deeper meaning of this strange painting, we must also pay attention to the barely visible Latin inscription above and behind the three heads. In English translation, it reads as follows: "From the past, the present acts prudently, lest it spoil future action."[7] Does it make any sense to you now?

One thing that you can easily understand from Titian's painting is that prudence is a complex virtue with several faces. There is a false type of prudence that chooses unsavory means to achieve evil or morally dubious ends. This is a synonym of crude shrewdness and ruthless opportunism and has little to do with sound caution and circumspection. True prudence acts differently. It applies theoretical and practical knowledge to human action in the pursuit of good ends prescribed by reason. It enables us to identify and choose suitable means for proper ends, avoiding the confusion between profane (secular) and sacred realms. This type of prudence requires memory, understanding, and keen perception along with foresight and power. That is why genuine prudence should not be confused with astuteness or mere cunning. Its core is common sense, a gift from heaven (according to Gracián) that implies the inclination to do what most conforms to practical reason. Common sense draws on the lessons of experience, warns us against evil, and incites us to search for the good.

Let us return to Titian's painting and focus for a moment on its central, dominating figure. I am curious to know how you interpret it. For me, the mature face exudes power and expresses the exhilarating feeling of living in the present, something that many of us would like to be able to do, but so few do well. Young people tend to live in a hurry and easily give way to their emotions, in their anticipation of the future. Being rash, they often commit themselves to risky and dangerous enterprises that they come to regret later. The old ones tend to go in the opposite direction. They are overly cautious and prefer to delay, thus failing to seize opportunities when they appear. They do not live fully in the present. Instead, they are drifting between past and future, exchanging one hope and dream after another, when the thing that really matters – being here and now – is available everywhere and right under their eyes.

Also worth noting are the ways in which the three dimensions of time are linked to prudence in Titian's painting. The past is related to a key element of prudence, memory, that allows us to remember what has come before us. The present is linked to intelligence that enables us to draw appropriate lessons and make sensible decisions about the proper course of action. The future is connected to foresight that anticipates the course of events and makes necessary adjustments in due time. If we were to live only in the past, we would be lost in our recollections and would risk being overwhelmed by memory, much as the wolf devours its victims. Living in the present alone is the unmistakable sign of true force, the attribute of the lion, the king of all animals.

And this brings me to the supreme achievement of prudence: being able to live in the present and enjoy it in its fullness. The rest of our life is either past or not revealed yet; we have no control over it any longer. If we tried to live only in and for the future, we would resemble the dog that always searches for something and is never satisfied. What matters is having "a prudent sort of boldness that neither cringes nor cavils,"[8] that knows how far to look back into the past without losing sight of the present or the future.

Titian's visual message overlaps with Gracián's words in another interesting way: "The health of prudence lies in inner moderation."[9] True prudence derives from the ability to control and govern oneself, in other words, it is inseparable from the temperance of the mature person at the heart of Titian's painting. Think about that: no one should try to ignore this lesson, and nothing bad will happen to you if you follow it. And yet, how many born into this world turn away from prudence!

What about the political realm, you might wonder? Like moderation, prudence is related not only to the private good of individuals, but also to the common good of an entire community. Political prudence, directed toward governing other people, depends on (and presupposes) the ability to make quick decisions based on the quick estimation of all risks involved.[10] It implies the capacity to deliberate about things that happen both regularly and irregularly and requires the ability to judge when it may be necessary to depart from general laws and conventions and when they ought to be strictly followed.

Furthermore, those who embrace this virtue acknowledge the fallibility of all human beings and never expect to find perfection in the world at large. In their plans for reform, prudent moderates follow the rules of common sense and walk "under the midday sun of reason."[11] Given the intricate nature and utmost complexity of society and political life, they seek to combine and reconcile many diverse and variable interests. For that, there is neither a textbook of prudence nor an algorithm of civil wisdom. As a wise man once put it, "nothing universal can be rationally affirmed on any moral or any political subject. Pure metaphysical abstraction does not belong to these matters."[12] Justice, liberties, and rights vary with times and circumstances, and cannot be settled upon any abstract universal rule. Not only are their real effects not always visible or immediate, but human actions themselves have unintended consequences that can jeopardize even the best plans.

Here is a timely lesson for young people like you who are passionate about political affairs and committed to bringing about social change. The rules of politics and the lines of morality are different from the perfect lines of mathematics or logic. In politics, "we balance inconveniences; we give and take, we remit some rights, that we may enjoy others."[13] This is always best done according to the rules of prudence and moderation. You must simultaneously look backward and forward while never losing sight of the present. Never seeking to be excessively systematic, you should aspire to combine the wisdom of old age, the vigor of mature age, and the curiosity of youth, as recommended by Titian's painting. To do that, you can always apply Gracián's great and mysterious rule of prudence: use human means as though divine ones didn't exist, and divine means as though there were no human ones.

Does all this sound too obscure or complicated? In my next and final letter, I will try to explain how you might go about achieving this synthesis in practice. Farewell! Yours, …

5

Realism and Pragmatic Partisanship

When my convictions make me devoted to one faction, it is not with so violent a bond that my understanding is infected by it. . . . I want us to win, but I am not driven mad if we do not. I am firmly attached to the sanest of parties, but I do not desire to be particularly known as an enemy of others beyond what is generally reasonable.[1]

(Michel de Montaigne)

YOU ASKED: CAN MODERATES COMBINE REALISM, pragmatism, and partisanship? I was a little surprised by the tacit assumption underlying your question, that such a combination would be impossible to achieve in practice. Do you really believe that? If so, allow me to remind you of one of H. L. Mencken's famous quips: "Half the sorrows of the world, I suppose, are caused by making false assumptions."[2] The belief that moderates seek to eschew partisanship and abandon their principles in search of a flimsy consensus is one such false supposition. But it is hardly the only one. The idea that moderates are not brave enough to fight for their beliefs is another commonplace among critics of moderation. It is as far from the truth as the assertion that moderation amounts to always adopting easy, middle-of-the road positions. Let me explain.

It is true that if anyone wants to succeed in the political realm today, it does not seem worth formulating and advancing an agenda unless it is a crude one, painted in bright or stark colors and proclaimed as loudly as possible. How can anyone make headway in an environment in which dialogue, cooperation, and civility are slowly replaced by monologue, obstruction, and hyperbole? It's no secret that it would be extremely difficult to promote a pragmatic and realist agenda under these circumstances. Yet, moderates manage to do just that by performing a complex balancing act. They are pragmatic trimmers with a sound sense of proportion and self-command, ready to defend their view of the good society without ever going to extremes.

What distinguishes them from others is how they go about achieving their goals. In critical times, when public discontent is on the rise and the spirit of faction threatens to undermine the proper functioning of democratic institutions, moderates are prepared to endorse bold and wide-ranging measures to strengthen existing institutions and norms. They understand that half-measures would be counter-productive and self-defeating and are prepared to go farther. Yet, in normal times, their priorities may change. While moderates are willing to support institutional reforms with a view to improving (incrementally) the balance among various groups and interests in society, they tend to be skeptical about comprehensive plans for radical change. They seek instead to address concrete inconveniences and deal with problems for which remedies might not be found if more radical measures were used.

But aren't moderates partial like anyone else, you might reply? My answer would be yes, except that the partiality displayed by moderates, though it may sometimes be controversial, never turns into total enmity or fanatic partisanship. Even if moderates are passionate about their ideas, they always strive to build civic bridges and promote dialogue across the aisle. When they engage in battles, they do not view their actions as an excuse for ideological purification or score settling. Nor do the excesses of their opponents turn them into intransigent inquisitors. The real heroes are often not those who hold the strongest views and proclaim them loudly, but those who calmly defend their principles and are still able to find a basis for dialogue, negotiation, and reasonable compromises.

Do you see now better the difference between moderation and zealous partisanship? When moderates defend their ideas, their partiality is antithetical to the zealotry, arrogance, and conceit that mark the extreme spirit of faction. They do not seek to discredit or obtain total victory over their opponents, and their public interventions are not meant to create general panic for instant electoral advantage. More importantly, they do not see themselves as being members of a tribe under siege, one that requires unconditional obedience and conformism. As a result, they never treat political issues as religious matters concerning personal salvation. Politics remains for them a *limited* activity that does not occupy their entire lives.

Ponder these words carefully and you will understand how it may be possible to combine pragmatic partisanship with moderation and prudence. Here is a contemporary example that might intrigue you. Moderates are not anti-woke; they are simply *not woke.* What do I mean by that? They are not persuaded that the best answer to the rise of woke culture would be a counter-faith, equally fervent and militant, perhaps even more so. And they see no point in decisively defeating the other side if their own beliefs turn out to be simply the inverse of their opponents' ones in the end.[3] As pragmatic and realist spirits, moderates understand that political matters are never simply black or white; they have many shades of gray and allow for exceptions. They must be decided not by a litmus test that equates woke with good (or bad), and anti-woke with bad (or good), but by the rules of prudence that call for nuance and discernment.

In case you are still unconvinced, let me add another important trait that distinguishes moderates' partisanship from that of others. As realists, moderates combine passion and partisanship with a touch of humor and detachment about their commitments and battles. They do not fancy themselves as the wisest people in society, not do they ever regard their judgments as infallible or beyond reproach. If you asked moderates what they would recommend as a cure for our present discontents, their answer would be more enlightened skepticism and less messianic ardor or ardent faith. That is why, as trimmers, they tend to adhere firmly to the sanest of the existing parties at any moment without being overly hostile to the others.

Perhaps more importantly, moderates prefer to act and speak like citizens united by common civil bonds. They start from the assumption that living in an open and free society requires that people never view themselves as masters exercising power *over* others. Instead, they must educate and cultivate their instincts through patient deliberation and reflection so that they learn how to exercise power *with* their fellow citizens. That is why moderates are particularly careful not to view their own scale of values as the sole standard of right and wrong to be followed by everyone else.

Is that so different from how radicals proceed, you might ask? I think so, and here is why. Radicals are convinced that they must always carry the battle to their opponents rather than letting them bring it to them. They seek to put them on the defensive and don't feel the need to ever retract anything or admit they were wrong. For them, the stakes are always very high. They believe that opponents, if they win, will destroy them, which leaves them with no other option than to strike first. Listen, for example, to what one member of the hard Right had to say in this regard: "We are not having a policy debate with the Left and the ruling class. We're in the midst of an all-out bar brawl. We're fighting to preserve what's left of our country. And since the other side isn't hewing to the Marquess of Queensbury rules, neither should we."[4] Do I need to add more?

Moderates reject this maximalist and bellicose way of thinking grounded in a misleading interpretation of toughness. Their partisanship eschews any type of scorched-earth policy that turns the political game into a war of all against all. As I have already mentioned, there are tacit rules of civil politics that moderates are reluctant to break even when that might be to their advantage in the short run. When they fight and win, they do not seek to crush their opponents or eliminate them. They do their best to play hard but fair, even though they are always aware of the risks and concerned about the consequences that their actions might have for others.

When engaging in public debates and defending their ideas and principles against the objections made by opponents, moderates are careful how they present their views and values to others and how they describe the positions of those who disagree with them. They know that they must act with self-restraint and temper how they voice their feelings and thoughts. They never allow their passions to get the better of them to the point of turning them into blind zealots.

Notice how moderation can be a fighting creed rather than a passionless view from nowhere. How strange that so many still equate it with lukewarm neutrality, especially in conflictual situations! Moderates may be prudent but they also understand that there are moments when they must decisively take sides and may not remain indifferent between the warring factions of the day. They spare no word or deed in this regard, but they do it in a peculiar way. If they feel their attachments deeply, moderates always take them with a grain of salt. When their will inclines them to one party or cause, it should never be with such feverish passion that their understanding is compromised. Their ability to express themselves openly and frankly, without holding grudges, coexists with their capacity to hold partisan convictions and robustly defend their beliefs. Their example shows that it is possible to speak freely and passionately and display our emotions while moderating our tone and without losing our sense of proportion.

It is the moderates' detachment and inner reserve that gives them a sound perspective on the proper role of politics in society. Although passionate about their commitments, they refuse to politicize everything in their lives. They know that we all are wearing masks in the theater of the world, and we should not take our roles too seriously. We need to approach them with the appropriate lightness of touch so that we never become their powerless prisoners.

If you asked me for advice, here are a few suggestions derived from Montaigne's essay "The Art of Conversation" that I cannot recommend to you highly enough.[5] First, try to follow the example of moderates who never fly into a frenzy that blinds them to either the laudable qualities in their adversaries or the reproachable ones in the people they follow. Emulate those who try to modulate their faith and relativize their convictions by admitting that they can be reasonably rejected by others motivated by different interests and beliefs. Then your partisanship will allow you to get along comfortably and in good faith with most (if not all) parties and negotiate effectively with them, while simultaneously maintaining a prudent distance from them.

Second, if you wish to practice partisanship-*cum*-moderation, you might start by keeping your minds open and being ready to revise your positions and ideas according to experience and new facts. No argument ought to shock you in principle, no fact or belief should upset you, no matter how opposite to your own it may be. In political debates, you should feel free to criticize opposing viewpoints with clear arguments in plain language, but you must be neither irritated nor offended by what your critics and opponents have to say against you. When you are contradicted, that ought to arouse your attention rather than your wrath.

This brings me, finally, to the iconoclastic face of moderation, a point that I hope you will consider with utmost seriousness, whether you agree with me or not. You should cheerfully welcome the possibility of periodically revising your beliefs as a salutary and necessary corrective to dogmatism and crude partisanship. Consistency, Emerson once famously said (in his essay on "Self-Reliance"), is a hobgoblin of little minds. I am not sure he was entirely right, but I think he has a point worth thinking about. Sometimes it is necessary to claim the right to hesitate and admit without any feeling of guilt that you don't know the precise answers to most of the problems you face. You ought to be able to weigh, without bias, the pros and cons in each case and be ready to amend your views when necessary. While you should not be reluctant to openly challenge others' ideas, you must not be afraid of subverting your *own* ideas and beliefs, when appropriate.

Developing this capacity for self-correction and reevaluation doesn't come easy to anyone, but it is vital for your intellectual sanity and maturity. So what can you do in this regard? For a start, you can actively cultivate a "propensity to self-subversion"[6] as a means of self-correction and testing the validity of your ideas. This propensity is incompatible with dogmatism and ideological intransigence and goes hand in hand with modesty and humility. It requires open-mindedness and receptivity to criticism along with willingness to engage in rational debate. It implies readiness to reconsider your views, amend, or discard them altogether when proven incomplete or wrong.

Though the art of self-subversion may look difficult, do not suppose it is beyond you. I recommend it to you as a means of periodic self-renewal and a way to improve your arguments and learn new things. It can widen the limits of what you perceive as possible or desirable and give you a possibilist perspective that liberates you from the grip of deterministic theories. This way, your ideas never become rigid or dogmatic and you may continue to air your views freely and fight for them with passion and conviction without zealotry. You will never need to conceal your true convictions or self-censor out of fear of being wrong.

All this is possible and consistent with the flexible pragmatism of moderation, a fighting virtue for honorable and principled minds. It radiates openness toward others, avoids excessive bitterness and anger, and refuses to practice political vendettas for temporary electoral gain. This form of moderation is a strong, realistic, and "radical" virtue which must be clearly distinguished from pusillanimity and indecision.[7]

Are you prepared to test it? You should give this type of moderation a try and see how it goes. You might even come to enjoy the art of self-subversion. Yours, . . .

PART V

WHO NEEDS MODERATION TODAY?

Above all we need teachers, men who will bring to our youth the capacity for moderation and judgment and who, by their example, will instill a reverence for truth, obedience to the spirit and service to the word.[1]

Hermann Hesse

Interlude

MY YOUNGER INTERLOCUTORS WANTED to discuss one more time the prospects for moderation in America today. I was more than happy to honor their request since the topic – what place and role moderation might have in our contemporary culture and society – continues to intrigue me. What follows is our final exchange that gives voice to their dreams, concerns, hopes, and fears.

The Last Beacon of Hope?

[The Americans] are the hope of the world. They may become a model to it . . . . The Asylum they open to the oppressed of all nations should console the earth.[1]

(Jacques Turgot)

IT IS NO MERE ACCIDENT THAT SINCE its early days, America has fired the imagination of many people around the world who regarded it as an original political experiment, an exotic geographic space, and unique place of endless opportunities. In the eighteenth century, the French economist Turgot wrote that the Americans were "the hope of the world." Foreign visitors such as Alexis de Tocqueville often saw in America "more than America." In the New World, they contemplated "the shape of democracy itself, . . . its inclinations, character, prejudices, and passion."[2]

I thought we should start our final conversation with Turgot's striking claim before we go on to examine whether moderation might still serve as a remedy to some of our present political challenges. Given the contested reputation of America on the world stage today, Turgot's optimistic words may seem detached from the current reality. America might once have served as an asylum to those around the world who fought for freedom, but can it still be a beacon of hope for those living under tyrannical or authoritarian regimes?

Lauren: I wish that were the case, but I don't think so. The once vaunted asylum for the oppressed of all nations is not doing well today, and its future seems increasingly uncertain unless a radical change of direction occurs. Would it be possible to imagine anything more cacophonous and dispiriting than our political scene today? I defy you to find something similar anywhere else in the entire civilized world. In other countries, one can still find real ideas and well-meaning public

officials seeking to advance the common good of the planet. But not here.

You quoted Mencken earlier; here is another memorable line of his: "I hold that this elevation of politics to the plane of undiluted comedy is peculiarly American, that nowhere else . . . has the art of the sham-battle been developed to such fineness."[3] *How can this country still be a beacon of liberal democracy in a backsliding world? If America has any ideas left – a big if – they are mostly the dogmas of neoliberalism that have wrought so much havoc around the globe. Who would want them? Moreover, an unhealthy obsession with American greatness, particularly on the Right, has obscured the need for rethinking what "the land of the free" should stand for.*

I agree that the image of democracy in America is currently tarnished by the country's real and imaginary sins, and – let's recognize it – there are quite a few of them. For many on the radical Left, most problems in the world are the consequence of the imperialist actions and policies of the United States. Nonetheless, I want to warn you against jumping to conclusions too quickly. It is always tempting and easy to find a scapegoat for global problems and point the finger at America and its real problems. Nonetheless, on balance, and in spite of all its obvious faults, I believe that our country has been a force for the good in the world, given its stable Constitution, its robust political liberties, the important economic opportunity the country offers, and its unrivalled openness to economic invention and entrepreneurship.

Rob: I concur, but not everyone agrees with that. Not only is the wisdom of our Founding Fathers under intense scrutiny today, but the very idea of America has been called into question from various quarters and for many reasons. I'd like to ask: can America, with its culture and democratic institutions, be reduced to a "bastion of hatred, intolerance, and illiberalism – a deplorable, irredeemable project"? Can we legitimately frame everything in American history as a toxic expression of racism and bigotry? I am asking these questions because this is exactly what the controversial "1619 Project" does. By claiming that our nation is hypocritical and built on evil foundations, its authors call into question America's very legitimacy and essence.[4]

Can we then stand still and remain indifferent as the woke media slowly undermines our democracy? I don't think so.

The radical Left has created an obsession with identity politics and embraced subjects such as intersectionality, open borders, "defund the police," and critical race theory that are likely to divide us even further. That's where our greatest challenges and dangers come from in the long run.

Lauren: Wow! Do you really believe all that or are these talking points you feel the need to repeat here to convince yourself that you are on the right side of history?

Rob: Of course, I believe what I said. Since we talked earlier about Lincoln, allow me to quote his words from a famous speech given in 1858: "A house divided against itself cannot stand. I believe this government cannot endure, permanently half slave and half free."[5] *We seem to be in a similar situation today. Hence, we are entitled to ask ourselves whether a nation that is so divided and polarized as ours can stand and survive in the long run. The hyperbolic tone of this question reflects the uneasiness we all feel about the future of the American experiment in self-government. And let's face it: moderation will not be able to save us from the present predicament. Moderation is the problem rather than the solution.*

There is no doubt we are in a moment of change, but there is a deep irony here. You are making claims that are hardly new, even in our recent history. Remember the electoral cycle of 2012? Then, the GOP presidential candidate worked hard to defend himself against accusations of being moderate made by his own party members. Four years later, we saw Donald Trump mocking the three previous presidential nominees of his own political party and suggesting (wrongly) that they all lost because they were moderates lacking a strong vision for the country.

The sad truth is that many of our politicians running for office often espouse obstructionist and intransigent stances that fuel political sectarianism. They prefer gridlock and hyperbolic rhetoric to compromise and cooperation across the aisle. In so doing, they adopt a "permanent campaign" mentality and cynically exploit the rules of the democratic game to score political points in the service of short-term electoral goals. Should we be surprised then that their reckless behavior risks delegitimizing important democratic institutions and norms?

Lauren: This seems to be a rhetorical question. But do you really think that our politicians and the media are the only culprits in this regard?

Let's admit it openly: we are a divided (and pluralist) country, and the polls reflect it. The deepening of polarization mirrors not only the ways in which our democratic institutions and mass media function, but also the evolution of the electorate itself. There is Red America that votes Republican, and Blue America that votes Democrat. In Red America, people drink mass-produced domestic beer, and still work in manufacturing or agricultural jobs. Many drive pickup trucks and send their kids (if they can afford it) to community colleges. No such things happen in Blue America, sprinkled with "Latte Towns" and "super" zip codes,[6] where educated and affluent families do everything they can – hire expensive tutors, and are even prepared to make false claims on admission forms – to send their kids to selective Ivy League universities. In such places, the average house prices are around or above one million dollars, coffee comes in many sophisticated flavors, and savvy customers know the subtle differences between Bordeaux, Rhône, and Burgundy wines. We live in parallel realities. Are you surprised then that we argue about everything, including the origin of our country?

Yet, I wonder whether the increase in partisanship in America may have less to do with ideological disagreement, which is normal in any free society, than with a rise in factionalism and total identification with one's party, which is a form of tribalism. This trend should not be overlooked since it fuels a pernicious form of negative or affective partisanship. As a result, partisans are rallying less for a specific cause or party and more for fighting together against a collective enemy – real or imaginary – that, in their opinion, must be resisted and defeated at all costs.[7]

Rob: What do these "Latte Towns" and "super zips" have in common with the fly-over country where the "deplorables" like my family and friends live? I fear we inhabit different planets held together by tenuous links that might break at any moment. What can moderation mean for the two Americas then? How can it bring them together,

when emotional appeals, anger, and frustration have replaced politics understood as a search for the common good?

There is no reason to give up hope. Don't forget that the very idea of America was conceived from the outset as an open-ended experiment, susceptible to being improved over time. We seem to be at the end of a long political cycle – that happens roughly every fifty years or so – or, better said, at the beginning of a new one. The entire country is looking for a novel political framework, legitimate norms, and effective institutions to mediate our differences.

Now, it is true that we live in an era when parties and factions tend to be ideologically purer than ever before. The purity criteria are not only political, they also apply to education, occupation, religion, morality, sexuality, and lifestyle choices. They influence everything, including how we choose our leaders and representatives at all levels. The qualities we should prize in our leaders and representatives ought to include discernment, prudence, integrity, and moderation. Instead, we rank loyalty to one's tribe – sometimes even to one person – as the supreme criterion and we make it into a litmus test requiring unconditional obedience. Voters tend to reward inflexible politicians who claim to stand on principle even when they follow their own short-term interests; their mental universe consists of primary colors and sharp contrasts meant to make them electable. Not surprisingly, sectarian loyalty has become the only thing that matters these days for those who run for office and their supporters in the mass media.

Lauren: Because we are deeply divided, moderation is powerless to fix our broken home. Why not admit that radicals have a big advantage in this regard? They are prepared to go all the way, while moderates just go away and tend to withdraw from politics in the end.[8]

The sad truth is that moderate politicians are a dying species in need of urgent protection. History has shown us that the road to crisis and paralysis is to ignite rage at the moderates and expose them to the constant and ruthless crossfire of the extremes. This is the road we have traveled lately. There is little doubt that the current political climate with its structure and incentives does not favor moderates. Open primaries and redistricting tend to tip the scales against them and reward candidates closer to the political extremes who embrace litmus tests and Manichaean political views. As a result, those prepared to make necessary compromises across the aisle have seen their ranks thinning out at a worrying speed. Their willingness to work with the other side has slowly put them out of step with their own parties and decreased their chances of being (re)elected.

Lauren: You equate moderation with realism, common sense, and reasonableness, but are you sure that's right? The term itself is ambiguous – your letters have demonstrated it. Wouldn't we be better off refraining from using it altogether? It is possible to argue, after all, that the real obstacle to change has been the endorsement of a detestable type of moderation that finds injustice and inequalities acceptable and puts up with them. "A world of breathtaking poverty and injustice that may well be on the brink of a cataclysmic civilizational collapse is hardly one crying out for another round of centrist meliorism."[9] This type of moderation plays directly into the hands of those who want to maintain the status quo. Let's not forget that the Democratic Party itself has slowly been moving away from the label "moderate." Those rank-and-file members who still cling to it are acting as if we were living in the 1990s, not in the twenty-first century. By the way, Bernie Sanders never uses the term either.

So what? Should the reluctance of some radicals to use the term "moderate" prevent others from using the concept? I don't think so. Let's not forget the daunting challenges we are facing today. In our post-truth world, we are segregating ourselves into separate political realities, with a truth for the Left and another one for the Right. Strong feelings and emotions lead people to band together, as if they fight a mortal enemy in an existential, all-out war, in which the forces of good are locked in a deadly confrontation with the agents of evil. Blind party spirit prevails over compromise, and those who refuse to put their party above the country are regarded with disdain. Facts are suppressed, distorted, or fabricated, while invectives and character assassination replace dialogue. The beneficiaries of this aggressive style of politics are the anti-liberal populist movements and their leaders who claim that they are in possession of magical answers to our problems. They resemble those who say "I know the truth – give up all other truths! No need for people anywhere on earth to struggle."[10]

Lauren: You may lament the waning of moderation, but there is little evidence to suggest that moderation is an integral part of the American mind and ethos. Moderation may work, perhaps, in Scandinavia or some Asian countries – the example of lagom that you brought earlier was intriguing – but in a country like the United States, where the general philosophy is bigger is better, moderation is hard to come by. Just look at our rhetoric, the size of our portions, cars, houses, and . . . ourselves! Where is moderation in all that?

Not so fast! There is nothing wrong asking what role moderation has played in the development of the American political tradition. Our present political discourse may be hyper-polarized, but if history is to be trusted, permanent gridlock and destructive partisanship have *not* always been the norm in American politics. You may remember that I have previously argued that moderation had been a constant if discreet presence in the history of the American republic, from Washington and Adams onward. Brave moderates have displayed consistency of purpose and played key roles in times of crisis.

Now, it is true that not all of them may have called themselves moderates. Yet, whether they preferred to be known as Whigs, Federalists, early Republicans, Progressives, or, closer to us, members of the Rippon Society, moderates broadly speaking have constituted a "vital center" of American politics. Let's not forget that only four decades ago, in the 1980s, moderates accounted for almost 60 percent of the US Senate.[11] Forty years ago!

Lauren: Times have changed, and we must change as well. Aren't you too nostalgic and excessively wedded to the past?

I will gladly accept your challenge and try to convince you that although moderates may not be very visible on the national scene, they represent nonetheless a significant part of the electorate at the local or state level.

Let's take a close look at a study conducted by the think tank Third Way in 2010. If you read the findings, you'll see that 47 percent of moderates are independents while only 43 percent of independents are moderates.[12] Recent polls suggest that a sizable part of the electorate, a little over 40 percent, distrust labels and identify as moderate, either on the center-left or center-right. Another study, conducted in 2014, revealed that 37–39 percent of registered voters defined themselves as moderates. Among them, four in ten described themselves as Democrats and 21 percent as Republicans.

Moreover, a Gallup poll conducted in 2010 concluded that 70 percent of American moderates would like to see a third major party to counterbalance the two top parties that dominate our national political scene.[13] That has not happened yet, and nobody knows if it will ever happen in America, given the peculiar configuration of our political system. But you don't need too many moderates to trigger change after all. In fact, all you need is to have a relatively small number of moderate dissenters in each party ready to gain leverage and cross the aisle on essential issues to promote greater cross-party agenda-setting.[14] For that to happen, it would be necessary to find new donors and rely on the expertise of think tanks and organizations devoted to bridging the ideological divide such as the Niskanen Center, the Third Way, No Labels, Braver Angels, to name only a few that I am familiar with.

Rob: Are you implying that many who seem uncomfortable with their present political affiliations embrace moderation? If so, I don't see the logical connection between the two. People may very well be unhappy about their party and yet reject moderation when they go to the polls.

I don't dispute that. What I wanted to say is that there are many who hold mixed ideological positions and an eclectic assortment of views on various economic, political, social, and cultural issues. They also constitute a racially and ethnically diverse group, something that might come as a surprise to you. Recent polls put the number of self-declared "independents," who value their independence of mind and are not motivated by ideology, at 39 percent of the electorate.[15] In some ways, they are moderates, simultaneously hopeful and skeptical about government. They are concerned about both individual responsibility and government protection, about both privacy and safety, liberty and justice. In sum, I believe that there are enough encouraging signs for our future to make us (moderately) hopeful, for once.

Rob: ***Sorry! I see the Left and I see the Right. But I can't find the party of moderates. Where is it? I am afraid that the moderates you are talking about are mostly a statistical myth. "When you dig into their policy positions, the people who show up as moderates in polls are actually pretty damn extreme – and efforts to empower them may, accidentally, lead to the rise of more extreme candidates."***[16]

It is true that at the present moment, moderates are people without a country or in search of one; they form an invisible party without banners, so to speak. But that doesn't mean they are condemned to political powerlessness forever. Nor am I so sure that the prospects of moderation depend exclusively on the existence of a party of moderates in the proper sense of the term. As I said, the key is to find moderate dissenting voices within the two main parties and empower them, while enhancing their presence on the social media.[17] And don't rule out either the possibility of new parties or groups that might spring up in the future.

Lauren: ***May I press you further on this point? Do you really believe in the possibility of moderation in a country that has elected a narcissistic and egotistic billionaire as president who refused to hand over power when defeated at the polls? Do you think moderation is possible in a country that has an excessive celebrity culture, has been engaged in endless and costly wars for over half of a century, and which is characterized by permanent political gridlock and rising inequality? How can moderation be held in esteem in a nation where big money and super-wealthy donors dictate the rules of the political game? And what role can moderation play in a country where 52 percent of GOP voters and 41 percent of Democratic voters agree (in full or in part) that the situation in America is such that they would favor red and blue states seceding from the union to form their own separate country?***[18] ***Forgive me, but to believe in the chances of moderation in this context seems childish, if not utterly absurd. To suggest that moderation has any chance of tempering the excesses of the current toxic climate is puerile or disingenuous.***

Your remark reminds me again of Mencken's words: "We produce such mountebanks in greater number than any other country, and they climb to heights seldom equalled elsewhere."[19] True, mountebanks do not like moderation; they relish hyperbole and are often prone to violence. Fortunately, we are not surrounded only by mountebanks, narcissists, or psychopaths. There are still enough reasonable people around who understand that it is impossible to get the whole loaf and, as a result, the only realistic path ahead is to try to figure out how to divide the loaf in such a way that it satisfies a wide range of interests without violence, chaos or anarchy. The real question is whether we will be able to restore our civic unity in diversity in due course, or whether we have already crossed our own political Rubicon into a dark era of discord, enmity, and fake news.

Lauren: You may spin the facts, but they don't lie: moderates have been powerless to bring about meaningful change in America. They have made poor choices and concessions and engaged in rotten compromises. Why should we repeat their mistakes over and over again? "A new way to understand the forces at play is urgently needed. But it will come about only if we make a conscious attempt to interrogate and discard the formative influences of many thinkers over the age of forty."[20] At the beginning of the twenty-first century, the entire Left – not only its progressive wing – is compelled to reinvent itself, create new models, and discover a new revolutionary and utopian imagination.[21] This is the only viable option ahead of us, and we must have the audacity to dream big and entertain vast ambitions.

Rob: Of course, we must dream big, but your utopianism is the last thing we need now. Whether we like it or not, we are a "fractured republic"[22] that resembles a campsite of strangers more than a genuine community of citizens sharing meaningful bonds. Ours is a world of "elementary particles" mired in materialism and hedonism, moral relativism, and extreme individualism. What is wrong with us is that we no longer seem to have the courage to ask and do what is right. That's what we have forgotten to do. What is required now is a refounding of the idea (and ideal) of America, which now exists only in the hearts and minds of a minority of citizens, the real patriots. That refounding cannot be done with moderation, a weak virtue for feeble minds.

We must be honest and admit it: the old conservatism that worked during the Cold War has come to an end. It needs to be reinvented today, and moderation is not the virtue that will help us redefine it. We will not be able to take back our country with moderation, that is, with

weakness. I agree with the authors of a recent manifesto: "During the Cold War, this conservatism too often tracked the same lodestar liberalism did – namely, individual autonomy. The fetishizing of autonomy paradoxically yielded the very tyranny that consensus conservatives claim most to detest."[23] *We will be able to defeat the extreme Left only if we consolidate our power at the state level where we can best defend our freedoms in a concrete way.*

Today, we need a strong and muscular vision of conservatism that prioritizes not a vacuous form of free-market idolatry – that would certainly lead to more liberalism, individualism, and anomie – but an energetic political agenda dedicated to vigorously fighting our culture wars. The American Right can do this and win the war only if it regains power before it is too late and then wields it in a firm manner while pursuing its own version of the good. This requires that we properly reward our friends and work together to create a new public square "re-ordered to the common good and ultimately the Highest Good."[24]

These are bold and general statements, and I won't be able to address them here as thoroughly as I wish. Before we jump to any conclusions, it may be helpful to consider a few examples that could help answer your questions. You wondered earlier whether a party of moderates exists or might make sense. You will be surprised to learn that such a party exists in Sweden – the Moderates Party, also known as *Moderaterna.* It started out as a conservative and nationalist party in 1904 and today it espouses a liberal-conservative agenda emphasizing individual choice, lower taxes, and economic liberal principles. The Moderates were the second largest party in the 2014 elections and continue to be an influential player in Swedish politics today.[25]

But the example of Swedish moderates is not entirely singular. In Rhode Island, for example, the party which calls itself the Moderate Party defines itself as "a centrist political party dedicated to the idea that elected officials should serve the best interests of the state's residents."[26] In 2007, a Philadelphia-based activist founded "The New Moderate," a community for centrist thinkers exasperated by the dogmatism of our national politics. On its vigilance list for 2017, one finds a host of priorities from resisting "a rogue presidential administration" and America's excessive gun culture to combatting polarization and the hollowing of the center, the rampant identity politics and political correctness, and the rule of moneyed interests in American politics and society.

Lauren: I appreciate these examples, but they seem quite exotic and marginal and don't hold much promise for our future. Some seem utterly insignificant or may no longer be valid. "Small-bore solutions are a waste of time. Our only viable option is to have the courage to be ambitious."[27]

I realize I won't be able to change your mind and I don't intend to try it. I propose instead that we look for answers to your questions at the local level, in the sphere of civil society.[28] That's where you will find many green shoots and local roots of institutional change. Better Angels, recently renamed as Braver Angels, is one of the most successful grassroots initiatives to date seeking to bridge our ideological divide. It has many local chapters throughout the entire country, including in the college town where I live. Its mission is to organize workshops and debates that promote dialogue and the free and civil expression of ideas between members of both major parties with a view to restoring civic trust and healing the wounds created by hyper-polarization.

The members of Braver Angels along with those of other similar organizations like the American Exchange Project, More in Common, No Labels, and the Heterodox Academy believe that when we politicize everything, society splits into violent factions and risks succumbing to anger and chaos. We often rest our hopes far too much on parties, governmental institutions, and courts, while in reality, our liberties and rights are rooted, first and foremost, in the hearts of individuals and the bonds between them. Therefore, the main mission of these organizations – and frankly, our task as citizens as well – should be to build new civic bridges and open new venues for social dialogue.[29]

Rob: This all sounds promising but rebuilding civic bridges in a country dominated by hyper-individualism and excessive materialism won't be easy. It is not possible to achieve that without a profound change in our moral values and attitudes. That, I think, should be our priority.

I don't believe we should wait for a moral revolution to start our civic work. Instead, we need to create and empower new fora to encourage greater openness to alternative views so that we may be able to find practical solutions to seemingly intractable problems. Braver Angels' strategy for depolarizing, for example, rests on the assumption that people on both sides would be more amenable to compromise if given the opportunity to interact on concrete issues at the local level with citizens outside of their political tribe. It allows them to shift the focus away from the national scene to state and local settings, where face-to-face relations humanize politics and make the political scene less polarized.

My point is simple, and I hope you will agree with me on this. We need more Braver Angels workshops, more academic initiatives like those promoted by the Heterodox Academy, and more global initiatives such as those sponsored by More in Common. They all play a seminal role in restoring trust in democratic norms and institutions in America and across the world. Whether they seek to give local communities cutting-edge data and unbiased information on issues of election integrity or the new trends in climate change, they encourage people to join forces and resources to explore seminal and urgent issues of common interest.

Their successes to date, although not always sufficiently highlighted by the media, demonstrate that people can overcome their sense of powerlessness when given the opportunity to relate to one another and work toward resolving concrete problems in their daily lives. And nobody can deny that we have a lot of common ground and share many interests, from clean air and water or good and affordable education to decent healthcare and safe neighborhoods, to name only a few.

Lauren: I must admit I have not heard of these organizations thus far. But I fear their initiatives might be quite ineffective in dealing with our larger structural problems. People attend workshops where they get to talk to each other about concrete local problems, and then . . . what? How is that going to change the general picture, when one of the two main parties has become ideologically extreme, scornful of compromise

and scientific evidence, and unwilling to recognize the legitimacy of the outcome of democratic elections?

Don't underestimate the power of face-to-face dialogue. By appealing to common sense and giving people the opportunity to hear from all sides of the political spectrum, these initiatives mark a step in the right direction. We should applaud them and, whenever possible, support them. The good work of these organizations can bear fruit in the end. This is confirmed by various studies that focus on the causes of polarization.

Consider, for example, a recent comprehensive study examining concrete ways for limiting the effects of hyper-polarization in America. Starting from the assumption that our present polarization is neither simple nor insoluble, researchers associated with More in Common explore in detail the core beliefs that drive polarization. They distinguish between difference and tribalism and offer concrete proposals for communicating and working across ideological and racial divides. Their study points out that the exhausted majority may be less politically active and partisan than the wing segments, but it is still frustrated enough with the status quo of American politics and the tone of public debate to play an important political role.

The conclusion is a cautiously optimistic one: "Despite America's profound polarization, the middle is far larger than conventional wisdom suggests, and the strident wings of progressivism and conservatism are far smaller."[30] Empowering and giving voice to this exhausted majority is one of the keys to countering hyper-polarization.[31] Again, our disagreements are real and deep, but they are *not* so great that we cannot come together in the end to turn the tide of sectarianism and tribalism in public life.

Rob: It's still unclear to me how the moderates might be able to break the current cycle of distrust and enmity. Personally, I don't think they have the energy or power to do that.

Those who describe themselves as the new moderates and belong to the "exhausted majority" must have the ambition to form the "mod squad"[32] and take the lead. What does it take to do that, you ask? For one thing, they must stay focused on getting things done and should do whatever they can to create visible platforms for expressing moderate opinions and ideas.[33] Do you know of any moderate versions of *The Nation*, *The Jacobin*, the *New Criterion* or the *National Review* that would put moderates' ideas before the public and recruit talent from the moderate Right and Left? There are some encouraging signs in this regard – I am thinking, for example, of two new online outlets, *Persuasion* and *The American Purpose* that have embraced moderate agendas – but much more remains to be done.

Moderates should consider every idea and proposal and judge them for what they are worth and how they can contribute to their overall agenda. They ought to understand that rage alone should not be allowed to dictate their political priorities, nor may the obsession with past failures be allowed to affect the course of the future. Even if some political problems turn out to be insoluble, the good can only come from the continuing attempt to try and solve them step by step.

Lauren: Let's be honest: if we choose this path, we will never have real change in America. Never!

What I want to suggest (again) is that it is essential to distinguish between small and large-scale frameworks of governance whose effectiveness depends on scale and context. Sometimes, governments are too big to handle complex local issues, while at other times they may be too small to address issues that require a larger scale of cooperation. Some issues are often (though not always) best solved locally, while others are best addressed globally. A balancing act is needed, one grounded in the recognition that there are no one-size-fits-all solutions and no miraculous answers to our problems.

In other words, moderates believe that there is no single form of organization that can be declared good for all actors and in all contexts. Policy solutions and strategies need to be context-specific, sensitive to the limits of each jurisdiction of governance. The fact that we pay far too much attention to national politics and not enough to local and state politics, where moderates *can* often make a big difference, comes with a high cost. That is why I think that the Archimedean point of civic life needs to shift away from Washington DC to subsidiary institutions of governance to empower moderate voices at all levels. At the same time, moderates should not forget that local politics, too, can have its own pathologies that must be properly addressed.

Rob: So, in your view, do you really think that this is all it takes for moderates to rise and lead the exhausted majority into the promised land?

Well, I have a detailed answer to your question, but it is rather long. Do you really want to hear it?

Lauren: By all means, go ahead!

This is what I believe. So long as moderates remain vulnerable to getting primaried by extremist candidates, their influence will continue to shrink, and sectarianism will thrive. For moderates to have a chance to make their voices heard and counted, both major parties will need to reinstate mechanisms that weed out fringe candidates. That won't happen overnight. But merely redesigning the party rules will be insufficient. Of course, moderates and independents may try to form a new third party, but such initiatives have not been very successful in American politics in the past. It would be better, I think, and more realistic to try to find leverage *within* the two main parties, not outside of them, and focus on specific institutions, like the US Senate and local city councils.

It is not impossible to build over time moderate factions within the two major parties, even if it is true that the latter have become increasingly inhospitable to non-purists. This strategy may be the best investment of time, energy, and money if we want a more deliberative, entrepreneurial, and effective political system. Moderate politicians can organize as a coherent bloc by recruiting attractive candidates and mobilizing moderate voters in each party.[34] They will have to carefully choose their priorities and issues with a high degree of pragmatism, to avoid wasting precious political capital and time on futile battles.

If moderates want to influence their respective parties' centers of gravity, they will need to build a compelling political brand that is grounded in pragmatism but is bold enough to inspire the public at large. After all, let's not forget that the largest and arguably the fastest growing bloc of voters today consists of those who refuse to identify themselves as Democrats or Republicans.[35] Reaching out to these non-aligned voters who can tip elections one way or another is a realistic and promising strategy with good chances of success for moderates.

Rob: Assuming all this is true, what role could your moderates play in this regard?

True moderates value compromise and dialogue across the ideological divide and are not afraid of taking up controversial issues such as patriotism and religion, often considered exclusive topics of the Right. They tend to focus more on what is (or can be made) right rather than on what is wrong and evil in America.[36] By emphasizing civic bridges and solidarity across differences, radical moderates can motivate and empower others to do the same. Since they understand the importance of decentralization and polycentricity, they have the capacity to energize from below and show how to become more socially connected and less tribal or sectarian. These are no small matters, right?

Lauren: So, despite all the daunting challenges you have mentioned, do you still believe that moderates have a good chance to make their voices heard?

Yes, I do. And the main reason is that they do not coddle and do not seek to infantilize the electorate, nor do they want to reeducate it to see "the light." Moderates seek to build new capacities and work with people's existing resources, helping them maximize their own opportunities at the local level. They start from "seeing like a citizen" and want to empower people. That, I believe, is a genuinely democratic platform and may be a truly inspiring and magnetic idea that can help build civic bridges and revive the politics of moderation essential to democratic governance.[37]

But make no mistake. The road to success is a long one and will end neither with the first victory nor with the first setback. While the challenges ahead cannot be overestimated, they should be addressed with pragmatic realism, forbearance, and unbending determination. For that, moderates will need not only the innocence of the dove but also the wisdom of the serpent. In my final letter, I will try to outline a few rules for radical moderates that you might find useful and intriguing. Rest assured though that these rules are supposed not to close our conversation, but to enliven it and keep it open.

EPILOGUE

Rules for "Radical Moderates"

We suffocate among people who believe they are right.

(Albert Camus)[1]

THERE IS NO SECRET THAT THE UNITED STATES and the free world at large are facing a profound crisis of identity today. We find ourselves in the uncomfortable position of all those who have seen their old certainties challenged or proven wrong. Like Camus, we live in "a world of abstractions, bureaucracies and machines, absolute ideas, and crude messianism"[2] and gasp for air among people who believe they are absolutely right. We have been willing to give up things that are – and in my view, should remain – priceless values. Freedom of speech is one of them; the right to dissent, the peaceful transfer of power, and the rule of law are others. The danger is even greater when we exchange these precious things for limited gains that benefit short-term political agendas.

Let's not forget that we have recently had a former President, emboldened by fanatical supporters and zealous sycophants, who irresponsibly refused to accept the results of free and democratic elections. The legitimacy of our elections has been called into question simply because one candidate lost, and lost badly (by more than seven million votes). The outcome was the tragic day of January 6, 2021. There is little doubt then that our democratic norms and institutions are facing a moment of trial and reckoning, and we may be heading off a cliff unless we make necessary adjustments in due course.

The high stakes of the current controversies and their political implications were outlined in the hearings and documents released by the January 6 congressional committee that shed light on how perilously close our democracy came to an end on that fateful day. They were also highlighted in an important letter on justice and open debate published in July 2020 in *Harper's Magazine.* Signed by prominent American scholars, journalists, and public intellectuals from both sides of the aisle, the letter gave voice to what many think and fear for the future. "The restriction of debate, whether by a repressive government or an intolerant society," the signatories of the *Harper's* letter wrote, "invariably hurts those who lack power and makes everyone less capable of democratic participation. The way to defeat bad ideas is by exposure, argument, and persuasion, not by trying to silence or wish them away."[3] This concerns not only those who embrace cancel culture, but also those who deny the legitimacy of democratic elections and thus subvert the belief in democratic norms and procedures.

On what can we stake now our hopes for democracy's future? Before we can answer this question, we must acknowledge an undeniable fact. A great responsibility has fallen on those who still believe in the principles, norms, and values of liberal democracy, a responsibility that is greater today than that of previous generations. They see themselves as custodians of a precious heritage and cargo, engaged in a rescue mission at the eleventh hour. I include myself in this category as a committed observer who believes that our democracy has reached a critical point. Its "soft guardrails"[4] are under attack, sometimes paradoxically in the name of more democracy, at other times in the name of less. There is no miraculous cure for our ills, but we cannot go wrong if we pay more attention to moderation. Our politics and public life require balance and opposition to all forms of simplification and zealotry and moderation might be of help in that regard. At the very least, we should be prepared to give it a try.

Five decades ago, Saul Alinsky published a pragmatic primer for "realistic radicals."[5] It was a passionate counsel on how to bring about social change in a turbulent age. *Rules for Radicals* became an instant bestseller that influenced subsequent generations of community activists on the Left. The book is still in print today. Written with wit and verve, it raises important questions about how to go about promoting democratic reforms. You may perhaps not agree with all its conclusions – I, for one, don't – but cannot fail to be impressed by its style and passion. Can we do the same for moderation today? If so, what might be the rules for realistic and pragmatic moderates?

Although I am not a warmonger, I believe that if moderation is to have any chance to become relevant and succeed in our present climate, it must be a *fighting* creed and a *muscular* virtue. It cannot be otherwise since moderates are surrounded by enemies and opponents who are up for the fight and ready to attack from all sides. That's why moderates cannot afford the luxury of complacency or neutrality. They must fight back. But how?

It is therefore time to conclude our exchanges by focusing on what might appear to you as an oxymoron: the *radical moderate.* Although Alinsky was not a moderate in the common sense of the word, I believe we may use some of the qualities he regarded as necessary to community activists to sketch the portrait of radical moderates. The list of the traits I have in mind here begins with an open mind committed to freedom, civil equality, and justice for all and the courage to tell the truth. It includes curiosity, irreverence, imagination, eclecticism, a propensity to self-subversion, and a good sense of humor. All these traits are necessary to those willing to act like gadflies against apathy, conformism, and complacency. They must work with a blurred and ecumenical vision of a better world while avoiding the pitfalls of utopianism and sectarianism.

This is a task of high order that proves that moderation is a difficult virtue only for courageous minds. The ancients knew it quite well. "We let ourselves drift with every breeze," Seneca wrote; "we are frightened at uncertainties, just as if they were certain. We observe no moderation. The slightest thing turns the scales and throws us forthwith into a panic."[6] This should make us appreciate even more the courage of moderates, who bring to mind the daring tightrope walkers that we sometimes see in movies or documentaries, but rarely in real life. They must go forward but also maintain their balance against the prevailing winds. Sometimes they must lean a little to the left, at other times to the right to preserve their equipoise. Almost always, they need a bit of luck to stay alive.

Hence, far from being an uninspiring virtue for weak minds, moderation is a demanding virtue which requires a unique set of skills that not everyone possesses. It demands the ability to maintain one's balance, the willingness to engage in dialogue with adversaries and friends alike, and the wisdom and dexterity to combine the soundest attitudes and principles of all parties, without being a mere chameleon. Moderation may not always be able to prevent anarchy, but it can protect us against utopian expectations and cynical contempt for politics. Those who embrace this virtue are committed to rebuilding their societies from bottom up rather than top down. They resemble the true spiritual warriors that practice *satyagraha*, who are unafraid to fight without arms by preaching non-violence and self-sacrifice.[7]

I am not sure whether you will agree with my portrait of radical moderates. You may consider it implausible, exaggerated, or simply unacceptable. Rest assured that I am in no hurry to be proven right and only hope that my words might inspire you to think twice before dismissing moderation altogether. So, here are a few (tentative) rules that I would like to propose in the end as a Decalogue for radical moderates. They are *sui generis* and are to be taken, of course, with a minimal grain of salt.

One. Avoid speaking about moderation as if it had just one dimension. Remember that it is a complex and eclectic virtue to which there are many facets. It is "the knowledge of putting in their proper place things that one says or does"[8] and this implies many things at once (as explained below). Moderates always try to find in everything "those certain bounds, beyond and short of which rectitude has no place."[9] Discovering these boundaries is no easy task because they are marked by a very fine line that can only be found with discernment, common sense, and attention to nuance.

Two. Do not forget that moderation is much more than a simple trait of character, state of mind, or disposition, as is often argued. It also has important *institutional* dimensions that make representative government work. Moderates favor institutional complexity and intricate political systems and are skeptical of simple and uniform ones. They advocate for checks and balances, bicameralism, separation of powers, federalism, polycentricity, intermediary powers, and judicial review. All these rely on formal and informal structures of self-governance that remove impediments to collective action and facilitate cooperation between individuals and groups with heterogeneous perspectives, agendas, and resources.

Three. Do not confound moderation with indecisiveness and do not assume that moderation is to be equated with weakness, apathy, or appeasement. True moderation does not spring from exhaustion, fear, or indifference. If moderates claim the right to hesitate and weigh the pros and cons in each case, they never lack a compass when making their choices, nor are they wishy-washy in their commitments. They do have a moral and political compass given by their firm commitment to the principles of open society, among them, freedom, civil equality, toleration, pluralism, limited powers, and the rule of law.

Four. Resolve firmly to think politically rather than ideologically. If you do so, you will imitate the moderates who are pragmatic spirits, not perfectionists. Start working with the world as it is, not as it should be. Moderation is neither a fixed ideology nor a party platform that allows us to organize around it. Refuse to define a single best way and reject any form of monomania. Accept that most political and social issues have more than one side. Do not interpret events in light of any single value or principle. Instead, carefully examine the facts and be prepared to adjust your beliefs when facts change. Rely on critical reflection and scientific evidence, be prepared to assess all the arguments before voicing your opinion, and check all the known facts before making a decision.

Five. Keep open the lines of dialogue with your opponents, even when the conversation becomes uncomfortable and it is clear that they have different priorities than you. Make sure that your dislike of your opponents is never absolute to the point of making you blind to their potential virtues and valuable arguments. Whenever possible, do your best to build bridges across the ideological divide. If you think that we are on the brink of a civil war, then get off Twitter and Instagram right away and start talking to your neighbors, left and right.[10] Organize at the grassroots level to pursue modest but concrete goals to improve the life of your community. That's what moderates do. If you take inspiration from them, you will offer a much-needed example of civility in a time of heightened ideological intransigence.

Six. "Enter into the ruling principle of your neighbor's mind, and suffer him to enter into yours."[11] In other words, beware of echo chambers and bubbles. One way to avoid them is to read widely and ecumenically. Read the *New York Times,* the *Guardian,* and the *Washington Post* but also the *Wall Street Journal, Financial Times,* and the *Economist.* Also make sure you get your broadcast news from multiple sources, not just from one or a couple that suit your ideological proclivities. Social media makes grazing much easier than it used to be, even with paywalls. But as we know, too many people confine themselves to sources with which they are comfortable and forgo the rest. Don't do that!

We shall not be able to maintain our free way of life if we are not prepared to leave behind our bubbles and take seriously the ideas of our critics and opponents. Acting as a moderate is incompatible with living in echo chambers or with membership in a political cult or sect. Above all, you must be on alert and reject any blatant lies and misrepresentations of reality promoted by those who may happen to be in your bubble at a certain moment. You have the duty to denounce falsehood and refrain from telling untruths, even when it may be to your (and your party's) disadvantage. If you choose this path, you will put pressure on elected politicians and keep them accountable, forcing them to listen to the truth.

Seven. Don't be a snowflake, have a tough skin, and don't get offended too easily. Reject trigger warnings and the idea of micro-aggressions. Remember that most of our ideas and opinions are based on impressions and ideas borrowed from others, and that we rarely invest the necessary time and thought to become aware of the grounds of our beliefs. That is why no particular idea should hurt you, no matter how different from yours it may be, as long as it is expressed in a civil manner; it may contain a much-needed lesson from which you stand to benefit. Ask yourself whether and how your critics and opponents may yet be useful to you and what you may learn from them. Defend the right to question others' beliefs and invite them to do the same with yours. Subject others' ideas to a thorough cross-examination before you begin to sympathize with or criticize their cause. Do then the same with your own opinions. Remain vigilant and take necessary precautions against intellectual complacency and laziness, beginning with your own. Practice from time to time the art of self-subversion. That's what moderates like to do, and you will be wise to follow their example.

Eight. Do not think partisanship is always something bad and to be avoided. On the contrary, learn to live with – and benefit from – robust partisanship and principled disagreement; they can have positive effects if properly moderated and channeled by sound institutions and norms. Don't forget that there is always a market for moderation, even in tough times; it may be small, but it does exist. Great opportunities always accompany major crises. You can, in fact, benefit from tensions, conflict, and contradictions if you have enough courage and dexterity to handle them and do not allow yourself to be swept off your feet. Your exposure to the crossfire of your opponents may, in fact, stimulate your imagination and prompt you to develop original solutions and responses to complex social and political crises.

But do not be a zealot who imagines they are in possession of any final or revealed truth. You may think your cause is the right one and believe in it passionately, but you should remember that the conversation must remain open and there is always (more) room for disagreement and civil debate. Here is the main difference between a moderate and a zealot. The former regards all questions as open to discussion and refrains from saying "this is true and there is nothing more to discuss about it." Instead, a moderate says: "I am inclined to think that under present circumstances this opinion is probably the best."[12] Or "I would like nothing better than to be proven wrong." The zealot speaks only in categorical terms – "I am sure this is right," "I will prove you wrong" – and believes that some topics are off limits or are not to be discussed any further.

Nine. Do not espouse a black-and-white vision of the world. Be humble and learn to practice the art of doubt. In your actions let there be flexibility so that you are not entirely predictable. Follow the example of those who try to feel and understand the opposite sides of life. If you do so, you will never become obsessed with purity, axes of evil, or litmus tests, unlike those who think ideologically. Your universe will be made of many shades of gray (but rest assured, less than fifty!). And remember that gray, too, can often be beautiful.[13]

So, be prepared to make timely, reasonable, and necessary compromises and concessions when circumstances demand them. Fight against the inclination to make your radicalism a mere gesture of moral rectitude and virtue signaling. Be ready and willing to work across party lines to facilitate agreements for the common good. Remember that you may often "win justice quickest by rendering justice to the other party."[14] Your adjustments and actions may be small and unheroic, and they may rarely fit any party line. Yet, if they are not rotten compromises, they may be enough to save the country from ruin, and you will be honored for your courage to swim against the current.

Ten. Accustom yourself to think of moderation as a complex and courageous balancing act, not unlike that of a tightrope walker. It requires strong determination and constant effort to stand upright, think clearly, and act reasonably. It also presupposes foresight and non-conformism as well as a dose of lightness of touch and humor. "Gain the heart, or you gain nothing," Chesterfield said; "the eyes and the ears are the only roads to the heart."[15] Above all, don't be a bore. To make moderation a winning card, you must always gain the heart of your audience with a dash of spice and honey.

That is what I have been trying to do in our conversations. If I sometimes adopted a pedantic tone or lectured too much, giving the impression that I might have the right answers, I hope you will forgive me. Remember that I tried to understand your point of view and learn from your ideas, as much as I could. Our views differ, but I hope we all have gained something valuable from our exchanges. We shall be known by the fruit we bear, and the readers are the final judges to decide if we succeeded or not.

Thank you for this fascinating conversation. I wish you all the best in your future endeavors.

Ever yours,
A radical moderate

Acknowledgments

I have been privileged to receive good advice and encouragement from several friends and colleagues while writing *Why Not Moderation? Letters to Young Radicals.* The idea of publishing a short book about moderation for a large audience was first suggested by David G. Clarkson and Geoff Kabaservice. In a conversation we had at the Reagan National Airport in Washington D.C. several years ago, Geoff encouraged me to write a series of letters addressed to an imaginary interlocutor skeptical about the virtue of moderation. The imaginary interlocutor turned out to be not one person, but two young radicals from both sides of the political spectrum. Les Lenkowsky brought to my attention Leo Rosten's witty and provocative book *A Trumpet for Reason* and shared with me his suggestions for how to engage in an imaginary conversation with younger radical friends.

As always, Costica Bradatan has been a genuine partner of dialogue and cherished friend who has offered priceless advice and encouragement in our countless conversations over the past years. Binyan Li, Michael McGinnis, Dan Cole, Frank Hess, Tim Tilton, and Constantine Vassiliou read earlier drafts and generously offered useful comments and suggestions for improvement. I am indebted to all of them for taking time to do it.

I should like to express my gratitude to Robert Dreesen, Laura Simmons, and Sable Gravesandy at Cambridge University Press, and Subathra Manogaran at Integra for their expert assistance. Robert has been a great supporter of the idea of writing a trade book about moderation for a general audience. I appreciated his patience, trust, and advice in bringing this challenging project to completion. Thanks are also due to Ken

Moxham for his expert copy-editing work and to the three anonymous reviewers whose suggestions helped improve the original manuscript. Finally, a note of gratitude to Dr. Jeffrey D. Wagner, Jane Frankel, and their team in Indianapolis.

A sabbatical leave granted by my home institution, Indiana University, Bloomington, provided the necessary time and freedom to complete the book. I would also like to thank the Niskanen Center, the Institute for Humane Studies and the National Endowment for Humanities for their generous support given to my work on moderation over the past years. Being part of their intellectual communities has been a rewarding and enriching experience for me. In February 2019, the Niskanen Center (then led by Jerry Taylor), with the aid of the Madison Initiative (at the Hewlitt Foundation, then led by Daniel Stid), organized a major conference on moderation that brought long overdue public visibility to this topic and stimulated my own thinking on radical moderation.[1]

In the process of writing the *Why Not Moderation? Letters to Young Radicals,* I have relied and drawn upon the ideas and writings of many others who often managed to say the same things better than me. They are all acknowledged with gratitude in the endnotes. The present book also builds upon and develops some arguments I have previously presented elsewhere, most notably in *A Virtue for Courageous Minds: Moderation in French Political Thought, 1748–1830* (Princeton: Princeton University Press, 2012), *Faces of Moderation: The Art of Balance in an Age of Extremes* (Philadelphia: University of Pennsylvania Press, 2017), and *Elogiul moderației* [In Praise of Moderation] (2022; in Romanian) as well as articles and essays written for the general public and published on the Niskanen Center website, in the *Aeon Magazine,* the *Los Angeles Review of Books, The Daily Beast,* and *The Constitutionalist.*

This book is dedicated to the memory of my parents, Natalia and Adrian.

Notes

EPIGRAPH

1. Alexis de Tocqueville, *Democracy in America*, vol. I, ed. Eduardo Nolla, trans. James T. Schleifer, (Indianapolis: Liberty Fund, 2010), 32.

ABOUT THIS BOOK

2. Cornford's book is available online at https://gutenberg.ca/ebooks/cornfordfm-microcosmographia/cornfordfm-microcosmographia-00-h.html.

PROLOGUE

1. From George Orwell's review of Bertrand Russell's *Power: A New Social Analysis*, in *Adelphi* (January 1939). The full text of the review can be found at www.lehman.edu/faculty/rcarey/BRSQ/06may.orwell.htm.
2. David Brooks, "An Agenda for Moderates," *New York Times* (February 25, 2019), www.nytimes.com/2019/02/25/opinion/moderate-politics.html.
3. The phrase is borrowed from Joseph Hall, *Christian Moderation* (London: 1640), 5–6, https://quod.lib.umich.edu/e/eebo/A02520.0001.001?rgn=main;view=fulltext.
4. Montesquieu, *Persian Letters*, trans. Stuart D. Warner and Stéphane Douard (South Bend, IN: St. Augustine Press, 2019), 18–19.
5. Tocqueville, *Democracy in America*, vol. I, 32.
6. See Michael Walzer, "Should We Reclaim Political Utopianism?", *European Journal of Political Theory*, 12: 1 (2012), 24–30.
7. See Adam Zagajewski, *A Defense of Ardor*, trans. Clare Cavanagh (New York: Farrar, Straus, and Giroux, 2002), 21.
8. On the distinction between good and bad ardor, see ibid., 24.

INTERLUDE

1. Alain Finkielkraut, *The Defeat of the Mind*, trans. Judith Friedlander (New York: Columbia University Press, 1995), 135.

CAN LIBERAL DEMOCRACY BE SAVED?

1. José Ortega y Gasset, *The Revolt of the Masses* (New York: Norton, 1964), 76.
2. James Baldwin's words as quoted in Pankaj Mishra, "Grand Illusions," *New York Review of Books* (November 19, 2020), 31, www.nybooks.com/articles/2020/11/19/liberalism-grand-illusions.
3. Ibid., 31.
4. See a recent report by Freedom House on democracy in retreat: https://freedomhouse.org/report/freedom-world/2019/democracy-retreat.
5. Ze'ev Jabotinski, "Homo Homini Lupus," *Odesskie Novosti* (July 18, 1910), http://en.jabotinsky.org/media/9742/homo-homini-lupus.pdf.
6. See Lorna Finlayson as quoted in Mishra, "Grand Illusions," 32.
7. This part draws upon and develops some of the arguments originally presented in Aurelian Craiutu and Dan H. Cole, "The Many Deaths of Liberalism," *Aeon Magazine* (June 28, 2018), https://aeon.co/essays/reports-of-the-demise-of-liberalism-are-greatly-exaggerated. On liberalism's bold and complex agenda, see also Edmund Fawcett, *Liberalism: The History of an Idea* (Princeton: Princeton University Press, 2014; 2nd rev. ed., 2018); Adam Gopnik, *A Thousand Small Sanities: The Moral Adventure of Liberalism* (New York: Basic Books, 2019).
8. On this point, see also Fawcett, *Liberalism.*, 10.
9. Ibid.
10. "Successor ideology" (beyond diversity) is a term coined by Wesley Yang. See the debate on this issue organized by the Manhattan Institute in the summer of 2020 with Coleman Hughes, Roth Douthat, Reihan Salam, and Wesley Yang: www.manhattan-institute.org/the-successor-ideology.
11. Max Horkheimer and Theodor Adorno, *Dialectic of Enlightenment*, trans. John Cumming (New York: The Seabury Press, 1972), 38.

12. Donald J. Trump, *Inaugural Address*, Washington DC, January 20, 2017, www.whitehouse.gov/briefings-statements/the-inaugural-address.
13. Thomas E. Mann and Norman J. Orenstein, *It's Even Worse Than It Looks: How the American Constitutional System Collided with the New Politics of Extremism*, 2nd ed. (New York: Basic Books, 2013).
14. Seth Ackerman, "Failure Is an Option," *The Jacobin* (November 9, 2020), https://jacobinmag.com/2020/11/failure-is-an-option.
15. Patrick J. Deneen, *Why Liberalism Failed* (New Haven: Yale University Press, 2018), 3.
16. Yoram Hazony, "Conservative Democracy," *First Things* (January 2019), www.firstthings.com/article/2019/01/conservative-democracy.
17. Josh Hammer, "Yesterday's Man, Yesterday's Conservatism," *New Criterion* (January 2022), https://newcriterion.com/issues/2022/1/yesterdays-man-yesterdays-conservatism.
18. Deirdre Nansen McCloskey, *Why Liberalism Works: How True Liberal Values Produce a Freer, More Equal, Prosperous World for All* (New Haven: Yale University Press, 2019), xi.
19. Ibid., 175–76.
20. These are the words of Robin DiAngelo, author of *Nice Racism*, as quoted in *The Economist* (September 4, 2021), 16.
21. Ortega y Gasset, *The Revolt of the Masses*, 76.
22. McCloskey, *Why Liberalism Works*, 29–31.
23. Hammer, "Yesterday's Man, Yesterday's Conservatism."
24. Popper, "The History of Our Time: An Optimist's View," in *Conjectures and Refutations: The Growth of Scientific Knowledge* (New York: Harper & Row, 1968), 115.
25. See Deirdre McCloskey, *Bourgeois Virtues: Ethics for an Age of Commerce* (Chicago: University of Chicago Press, 2006).
26. Wilhelm Röpke, *The Humane Economy: The Social Framework of the Free Market* (Wilmington: Intercollegiate Studies Institute, 1998), 89.
27. Ryszard Legutko, *The Demon in Democracy: Totalitarian Temptations in Free Societies* (New York: Encounter Books, 2016), 177.
28. See ibid., 22.
29. For the interview with Vladimir Putin, see www.ft.com/content/2880c762-98c2-11e9-8cfb-30c211dcd229.

30. Wilhelm Röpke, "End of an Era?", in *Against the Tide*, trans. Elizabeth Henderson (Chicago: Henry Regnery, 1969), 89, https://vdoc.pub/documents/against-the-tide-405md31ucfn0.
31. Ibid., 83.
32. Leon Wieseltier, "The Radical Liberal," *White Rose* (March 20, 2021), https://whiterosemagazine.com/the-radical-liberal. Compare and contrast with Osita Nwanewu, "The Willful Blindness of Reactionary Liberalism," *New Republic* (July 6, 2020), https://newrepublic.com/article/158346/willful-blindness-reactionary-liberalism.

PART II WHAT KIND OF VIRTUE IS MODERATION?

1. Hall, *Christian Moderation*, 5–6.

INTERLUDE

1. Seneca, "On the Shortness of Life," in *Dialogues and Letters*, ed. C. D. N. Costa (London: Penguin, 1997), 76.

1 REDISCOVERING MODERATION IN OUR IMMODERATE AGE

1. *The Political Writings of John Adams*, ed. George A. Peek (Indianapolis: Bobbs-Merrill, 1954), 89.
2. Finkielkraut, *The Defeat of the Mind*, 135.
3. Stéphane Courtois et al., *The Black Book of Communism: Crimes, Terror, Repression*, trans. Jonathan Murphy (Cambridge: Harvard University Press, 1999).
4. Adam Michnik, *The Trouble with History*, ed. Irena Grudzinska Gross, trans. Elzbieta Matynia et al. (New Haven: Yale University Press, 2014), 98.
5. I borrow the phrase "animated moderation" from Walter Bagehot's *Physics and Politics* (New York: Alfred A. Knopf, 1948), 206. The combination between the spirit of rebellion and moderation (or measure) can be found in Camus' *The Rebel*.
6. Here is the full paragraph that explains what happens when moderation is replaced by cruelty: "Ill-considered boldness was counted as loyal manliness; prudent hesitation was held to be cowardice in disguise, and moderation merely the cloak of an unmanly nature. … Sudden fury was accepted as part of manly valor, while plotting for one's own

security was thought a reasonable excuse for delaying action. A man who started a quarrel was always to be trusted, while one who opposed him was under suspicion. A man who made a plot was intelligent if it happened to succeed, while one who could smell out a plot was deemed even more clever. . . . In brief, a man was praised if he could commit some evil action before anyone else did, or if he could cheer on another person who had never meant to do such a thing." (Thucydides, *On Power, Justice, and Human Nature*, ed. and trans. Paul Woodruff [Indianapolis: Hackett, 1993], 90–91).

2 THE SKEPTICISM TOWARD MODERATION AND WHAT ITS CRITICS MISS ABOUT IT

1. Will Wilkinson,"On the Saying that "Extremism in Defense of Liberty is No Vice,"" *Niskanen Center*, (January 5, 2016), https://www.niskanencenter.org/on-the-saying-that-extremism-in-defense-of-liberty-is-no-vice/.
2. William Lloyd Garrison, "To the Public," *The Liberator* (January 1, 1831), 1.
3. See Ezra Klein, "No One Is Less Moderate Than Moderates," *Vox* (February 26, 2015), www.vox.com/2014/7/8/5878293/lets-stop-using-the-word-moderate.
4. Albert Camus, *The Rebel*, trans. Anthony Bower (New York: Vintage, 1956), 303.
5. Martin Luther King Jr., "Letter from the Birmingham Jail," www.africa.upenn.edu/Articles_Gen/Letter_Birmingham.html. In 1964, King revised and included the letter as a chapter in his memoir of the Birmingham Campaign, *Why We Can't Wait*.
6. I borrow the phrase from Arnold S. Kaufman, *The Radical Liberal: New Man in American Politics* (New York: Atherton, 1968), 48.
7. See Edmund Burke, *Further Reflections on the Revolution in France*, ed. Daniel E. Ritchie (Indianapolis: Liberty Fund, 1992), 16.

3 THE ARCHIPELAGO OF MODERATION (I)

1. I have previously explored similar issues in *A Virtue for Courageous Minds: Moderation in French Political Thought, 1748–1830* (Princeton: Princeton University Press, 2012), 19–26.

2. Cicero, *On Duties*, ed. M. T. Griffin and E. M. Atkins (Cambridge: Cambridge University Press, 1991), 37.
3. See Plato, *Charmides*, 167a.
4. Aristotle, *Nicomachean Ethics*, trans. T. Irwin, 2nd ed. (Indianapolis: Hackett, 1999), 1106b6–7.
5. Ibid., 1106b17–34.
6. Ibid., 1109b24–27, 1109a25–30.
7. Cicero, *On Duties*, 55. Marcus Aurelius' *Meditations* also contain many valuable reflections on the relationship between moderation and the good life (see, for example, XI: 16, 18).
8. Ibid., 37; see also 98.
9. Cicero, *On the Commonwealth and On the Laws*, ed. James Zetzel (Cambridge: Cambridge University Press, 1999), 52.
10. Hall, *Christian Moderation*, 5–6; all emphases added. On the centrality of moderation in the hierarchy of virtues, see also ibid., 3–4.

4 THE ARCHIPELAGO OF MODERATION (II)

1. George Washington, letter to Thomas Jefferson (August 23, 1792), in *Something That Will Surprise the World: The Essential Writings of the Founding Fathers*, ed. Susan Dunn (New York: Basic Books, 2006), 68–69.
2. See Richard Hofstadter, *Anti-Intellectualism in American Life. The Paranoid Style in American Politics. Uncollected Essays, 1956–1965*, ed. Sean Wilentz (New York: The Library of America, 2020).
3. "By definition, moderates can't be brave – they don't have opinions! … Brave moderates? Great moderates in American History? Show me that book!" (Rush Limbaugh as quoted in Geoffrey Kabaservice, *Rule and Ruin: The Downfall of Moderation and the Destruction of the Republican Party, from Eisenhower to the Tea Party* [New York: Oxford University Press, 2012], 398).
4. See Arthur M. Schlesinger Jr., *The Vital Center: The Politics of Freedom* (Boston, Houghton Mifflin, 1962) (the original edition came out in 1949). See also David S. Brown, *Moderates: The Vital Center of American Politics from the Founding to Today* (Chapel Hill: University of North Carolina Press, 2017); Daniel Walker Howe, *The Political Culture of the American Whigs* (Chicago: University of Chicago Press, 1979).
5. George Washington, "Farewell Address" (1796), www.ourdocuments.gov/doc.php?flash=false&doc=15&page=transcript.

6. See Adam Smith, *Theory of Moral Sentiments,* eds. D. D. Raphael and A. L. Macfie (Indianapolis: Liberty Fund, 1982), 155–56; David Hume, *Essays: Moral, Political, and Literary,* ed. Eugene F. Miller (Indianapolis: Liberty Fund, 1985), 500.
7. George Washington, letter to Jefferson, July 6, 1796, in *Something That Will Surprise the World,* 79.
8. Ibid., 68–69. On Washington's political moderation, see also Paul O. Carrese, *Democracy in Moderation: Montesquieu, Tocqueville, and Sustainable Liberalism* (Cambridge: Cambridge University Press, 2016), 50–77.
9. Benjamin Franklin, *Autobiography,* in *A Benjamin Franklin Reader,* ed. Walter Isaacson (New York: Simon & Schuster, 2003), 469.
10. Benjamin Franklin's speech in *Notes of Debates in the Federal Convention of 1787 Reported by James Madison* (Athens, OH: Ohio University Press, 1966), 653–54.
11. Ibid., 654.
12. As quoted in ibid., 653.
13. Abraham Lincoln, "Eulogy on Henry Clay" (July 6, 1852), www.abrahamlincolnonline.org/lincoln/speeches/clay.htm.
14. See Greg Weiner, *Old Whigs: Burke, Lincoln, and the Politics of Prudence* (New York: Encounter Books, 2019), 48.
15. This philosophy was at the core of the political agenda of the American Whigs. See, for example, Walker Howe, *The Political Culture of the American Whigs,* 29–31.
16. Washington, "Farewell Address." See also John Avlon, *Washington's Farewell: The Founding Father's Warning to Future Generations* (New York: Simon and Schuster, 2017).
17. Lord Chesterfield, *Letters,* ed. David Roberts (Oxford: Oxford University Press, 1992), 171.

5 AN ALTERNATIVE TO IDEOLOGY

1. José Ortega y Gasset, *Toward a Philosophy of History,* trans. Helene Weyl (Urbana: University of Illinois Press, 2002), 70.
2. See Marylinne Robinson, *What Are We Doing Here?* (New York: Farrar, Straus, and Giroux, 2018).
3. See F. Scott Fitzgerald, *The Crack-Up with other Pieces and Stories* (New York: Penguin, 1965), 39. This is not the same as doublethink,

defined by George Orwell as the ability to hold two contradictory beliefs in one's mind simultaneously and accept both of them.

4. Michael Oakeshott, *Rationalism in Politics and Other Essays,* ed. Timothy Fuller (Indianapolis: Liberty Fund, 1991), 424.
5. Oakeshott, "On Being Conservative", in ibid., 432.
6. Russell Kirk, *The Conservative Mind: From Burke to Eliot* (Chicago: Regnery/Gateway, 1960), 7.
7. On this topic, see Jerry Taylor, "The Alternative to Ideology," *Niskanen Center* (October 29, 2018), www.niskanencenter.org/the-alternative-to-ideology.

6 AN ANTIDOTE TO FANATICISM

1. Eugène Ionesco, *Rhinoceros and Other Plays,* trans. Derek Prouse (New York: Grove Press, 1960), 64.
2. Amos Oz, *Dear Zealots: Letters from a Divided Land,* trans. Jessica Cohen (Boston: Houghton Mifflin Harcourt, 2018), 12.
3. Ibid., 24.
4. Ionesco, *Rhinoceros and Other Plays,* 19.
5. Ibid., 60–61.
6. Ibid., 84.
7. Ibid., 64.
8. Ibid., 67.
9. Ibid., 67.
10. Oz, *Dear Zealots,* 21. For a historical radiography of various types of fanaticism, see also Zachary R. Goldsmith, *Fanaticism: A Political Philosophical History* (Philadelphia: University of Pennsylvania Press, 2022). For a philosophical analysis of the extremist mindset, see Quassim Cassam, *Extremism: A Philosophical Analysis* (London: Routledge, 2021).
11. Oz, *Dear Zealots,* 6–7. Another insightful description of fanaticism was given by Vacláv Havel in a letter he sent from prison to his wife, Olga, on January 22, 1983. For more details, see Flagg Taylor, "Havel and the Ideological Temptation," *Law & Liberty* (July 30, 2020), https://lawliberty.org/book-review/havel-and-the-ideological-temptation/?utm_source=LAL+Updates&utm_campaign=ed5e27ba3c-LAL_Daily_Updates&utm_medium=email&utm_term=0_53ee3e1605-ed5e27ba3c-72437381.

12. For a contemporary perspective, see David Brooks, "How to Roll Back Fanaticism," *New York Times* (August 15, 2017), https://mobile.nytimes.com/2017/08/15/opinion/fanaticism-white-nationalists-charlottesville.html?smprod=nytcore-ipad&smid=nytcore-ipad-share&referer.
13. Ionesco, *Rhinoceros*, 19.
14. Ibid., 67.
15. Ibid., 79–80.
16. Ibid., 80.
17. Ibid., 32.
18. Oz, *Dear Zealots*, 35–36.

PART III DO MODERATES HAVE A POLITICAL VISION?

1. Burke, *Further Reflections on the Revolution in France*, 16.

INTERLUDE

1. The phrase belongs to progressive strategist Jonathan Tahini, as quoted in Hanna Trudo, "Progressive Democrats Seek to Purge the Term Moderate," *The Hill* (September 29, 2021), https://thehill.com/homenews/house/574399-progressive-democrats-seek-to-purge-the-term-moderate.

1 THE LIMITS OF MORAL CLARITY

1. Senator John McCain as quoted in William Safire, "Moral Clarity," *New York Times* (May 12, 2002), www.nytimes.com/2002/05/12/magazine/12ONLANGUAGE.html.
2. See Carlton Vogt, "'Moral Clarity' and You," *Infoworld* (January 13, 2003), www.infoworld.com/article/2680275/techology-business/-moral-clarity–and-you.html; Michael J. Boyle, "ISIS and the Perils of Moral Clarity," *The Federalist* (August 27, 2014), http://thefederalist.com/2014/08/27/isis-and-the-perils-of-moral-clarity.
3. Attorney General William Barr, "Remarks to the Law School and the de Nicola Center for Ethics and Culture at the University of Notre Dame," *The United States Department of Justice* (October 11, 2019), www.justice.gov/opa/speech/attorney-general-william-p-barr-delivers-

remarks-law-school-and-de-nicola-center-ethics. For a critique, see Laura K. Field, "Meet the Reocons", *Niskanen Center* (February 20, 2020), www.niskeanencenter.org/meet-the-reocons/?fbclid=IwAR3Ny8-WvIqx__Io_xm0Xu-jYocs4iIAoT2CyfCigFrgqwgFYL5Mnr0do0A.

4. See Wesley Lowery, "A Reckoning over Objectivity, Led by Black Journalists," *New York Times* (June 23, 2020), www.nytimes.com/2020/06/23/opinion/objectivity-black-journalists-coronavirus.html.
5. On the ambiguities surrounding the concept of moral clarity, see Andrew Sullivan, "Is There Still Room for Debate?," *Intelligencer* (June 12, 2020), https://nymag.com/intelligencer/2020/06/andrew-sullivan-is-there-still-room-for-debate.html?fbclid=IwAR38trXToeCOrgtfQStRx1mBoA2rSH0Cyv50U7fJiLjS1B1j-0e7wzytX4s and Matt Welch, "Journalists Abandoning 'Objectivity' for 'Moral Clarity' Just Want to Call People Immoral," Reason (June 24, 2020), https://reason.com/2 020/06/24/journalists-abandoning-objectivity-for-moral-clarity-really-just-want-to-call-people-immoral/.
6. On the politics of self-indulgence, see Kaufman, *The Radical Liberal*, 46–55.
7. See Gary Saul Morson and Morton Shapiro's *Minds Wide Shut* (Princeton: Princeton University Press, 2021). I have discussed the ideas of this book in "In Praise of Eclecticism and Viewpoint Diversity," *The Constitutionalist* (September 29, 2021), https://theconstitutionalist.org/2021/09/29/in-praise-of-eclecticism-and-viewpoint-diversity.
8. See Jean Birnbaum, *Le Courage de la nuance* (Paris: Seuil, 2021).

2 AGAINST THE POLITICS OF WARFARE

1. Publius Decius Mus (Michael J. Anton), "Flight 93 Election," *Claremont Review of Books* (September 5, 2016), https://claremontreviewofbooks.com/digital/the-flight-93-election.
2. C. Bradley Thompson, "The Rise and Fall of the Pajama-Boy Nietzscheans," *The American Mind* (May 13, 2020), https://americanmind.org/essays/the-rise-and-fall-of-the-pajama-boy-nietzscheans.
3. Carl Schmitt, *The Concept of the Political* (Chicago: University of Chicago Press, 1996), 26.

4. Michael Oakeshott, "Political Education," in *Rationalism in Politics and Other Essays*, 60.
5. Michael Oakeshott, *Notebooks, 1922–86*, ed. Luke O'Sullivan (Exeter: Imprint Academic, 2014), 390.
6. Eli J. Finkel et al., "Political Sectarianism in America," *Science*, 370: 6516 (October 30, 2020), 533.
7. Anton, "Flight 93 Election," https://claremontreviewofbooks.com/digital/the-flight-93-election.
8. See Jonathan Chait, "How Michael Anton's 'Flight 93' Essay Defined the Trump Era," *National Interest* (December 11, 2020). https://nymag.com/intelligencer/article/michael-antons-flight-93-election-trump-coup.html?fbclid=IwAR0m0hlJSUNmLJqTZsaAZ4dOh0ECqDXlpD1WnkUY0PyrmuDFTvaLXn1mOkg.
9. Ryan P. Williams, Arthur Milikh, et al., "The Fight is Now," *The American Mind* (November 5, 2020), https://americanmind.org/salvo/the-fight-is-now.
10. Glenn Ellmers, "'Conservatism' Is Not Enough," *The American Mind* (March 24, 2021), https://americanmind.org/salvo/why-the-claremont-institute-is-not-conservative-and-you-shouldnt-be-either.
11. See Hofstadter, *Anti-Intellectualism in American Life. The Paranoid Style in American Politics. Uncollected Essays*, 501–765.
12. The (redacted) text of the "1619 Project" can be found at https://pulitzercenter.org/sites/default/files/full_issue_of_the_1619_project.pdf. For a critique from the hard Right, see "The 1619 Project Exposed: A Special Edition of the *American Mind* Podcast" (April 27, 2020), https://americanmind.org/audio/the-1619-project-exposed-a-special-edition-of-the-american-mind-podcast.
13. Seth Moskowitz, "The Reactionary Trap," *Persuasion* (January 15, 2021), www.persuasion.community/p/the-reactionary-trap?fbclid=IwAR2MqKDFvRwrT3cioNb46x4fwahlFgoFm5zHPBiIdA5nIsfj9Cv945DaIDA.
14. Here is, for example, the Hungarian Prime Minister Viktor Orbán describing the new ubiquitous adversary, presumably cosmopolitan liberal democracy: "We are fighting an enemy that is different from us. Not open, but hiding; not straightforward but crafty; not honest but base; not national but international; does not believe in working but speculates with money; does not have its own homeland but feels it owns the whole world" (as quoted in Anne Applebaum,

"This Is How Reaganism and Thatcherism End," *The Atlantic* [February 2020], www.theatlantic.com/ideas/archive/2020/02/the-sad-path-from-reaganism-to-national-conservatism/606304).

15. Sohrab Ahmari as quoted in Laura K. Field, "Meet the Reocons."
16. On "partisan teamsmanship" in American politics and its perverse effects, see J. L. Martherus, A. G. Martinez, P. K. Piff, and A. Theodoridis, "Party Animals? Extreme Partisan Polarization and Dehumanization," *Political Behavior* 43 (2019), 517–40.
17. Michael Ignatieff, "Enemies vs. Adversaries," *New York Times* (October 16, 2013), www.nytimes.com/2013/10/17/opinion/enemies-vs-adversaries.html?mcubz=3.
18. See Peter Wehner, "Politics Is Not Total War," *New York Times* (June 1, 2019), www.nytimes.com/2019/06/01/opinion/sunday/politics-compromise-winner-take-all.html. For further evidence of the disconnect from reality fueled by this Manichaean type of politics, see Arlie Hochschild, "Think Republicans are Disconnected from Reality? It's even Worse among Liberals," *The Guardian* (July 21, 2019), www.theguardian.com/commentisfree/2019/jul/21/democrats-republicans-political-beliefs-national-survey-poll.

3 NO MANICHAEISM AND NO LITMUS TESTS

1. Robespierre as quoted in Alfred Cobban, *Aspects of the French Revolution* (New York: Norton, 1970), 187.
2. Robespierre as quoted in Ruth Scurr, *Fatal Purity: Robespierre and the French Revolution* (New York: Henry Holt & Co., 2006), 248. In turn, Saint-Just used to say: "Prove your virtue or go to prison" (as quoted in Camus, *The Rebel*, 125).
3. Robespierre as quoted in George Klosko, *Jacobins and Utopians* (Notre Dame: University of Notre Dame Press, 2003), 99–100. The full text of Robespierre's speech, "Report on the Principles of Political Morality" (February 5, 1794), is reprinted in *The Old Regime and the French Revolution*, ed. Keith M. Baker (Chicago: University of Chicago Press, 1987), 368–84.
4. Robespierre as quoted in Klosko, *Jacobins and Utopians*, 102.

5. Robespierre as quoted in David P. Jordan, *The Revolutionary Career of Maximilien Robespierre* (New York: The Free Press, 1985), 232.
6. Robespierre as quoted in Klosko, *Jacobins and Utopians*, 104.
7. Robespierre as quoted in Scurr, *Fatal Purity*, 247.
8. Saint-Just (December 17, 1792), as quoted in Michael Walzer ed., *Regicide and Revolution: Speeches at the Trial of Louis XVI* (New York: Columbia University Press, 1974), 175.
9. Ibid., 177.
10. Saint-Just as quoted in Klosko, *Jacobins and Utopians*, 105.
11. Ibid., 111.
12. See Peter Wehner, "Are Trump's Critics Demonically Possessed?", *The Atlantic* (November 25, 2019), www.theatlantic.com/ideas/archive/2019/11/to-trumps-evangelicals-everyone-else-is-a-sinner/602569.
13. This is a paraphrase of one of Baltasar Gracián's memorable lessons from *The Art of Worldly Wisdom: A Pocket Oracle*, trans. Christopher Maurer (New York: Doubleday, 1992).
14. See Angelo M. Codevilla, "The Cold Civil War: Statecraft in a Divided Country," *Claremont Review of Books* (Spring 2017), https://claremontreviewofbooks.com/the-cold-civil-war.
15. See Josh Hammer, "After Virginia, Fight the Culture War with the Aim of Victory," *Newsweek* (November 5, 2021), www.newsweek.com/after-virginia-fight-culture-war-aim-victory-opinion-1646206; also Hammer, "Why the Right Needs a More 'Muscular' and 'Masculine' Conservatism," *Newsweek* (December 3, 2021), www.newsweek.com/why-right-needs-more-muscular-masculine-conservatism-opinion-1655672. For a critique, see David French, "The New Right's Strange and Dangerous Cult of Toughness," *The Atlantic* (December 2021), www.theatlantic.com/ideas/archive/2021/12/the-new-rights-strange-and-dangerous-cult-of-toughness/620861.
16. Thomas Klingenstein as quoted in Cameron Joseph, "Meet the Obscure Think Tank Powering Trump's Big Lies," *The Vice* (November 4, 2021), www.vice.com/en/article/qjb4y3/john-eastman-claremont-institute-supporting-jan-6-trumpism. For more details on Klingenstein's positions and rhetoric, see https://tomklingenstein.com.
17. Barr, "Remarks to the Law School and the de Nicola Center for Ethics and Culture at the University of Notre Dame"; all emphases added.

18. Statement from Democratic Socialists of America's National Political Committee, "Beyond Bernie" (May 12, 2020; all emphases added), www.dsausa.org/statements/beyond-bernie-a-statement-from-the-dsa-national-political-committee.

4 COMPROMISE

1. T. B. Macaulay, "Speech on the Reform Bill of 1832" (March 2, 1832), https://sourcebooks.fordham.edu/mod/1832macaulay-reform.asp.
2. Bill McInturff, as quoted in Thomas B. Edsall, "We See the Left. We See the Right. Can Anyone See the 'Exhausted Majority'?", *New York Times* (March 24, 2021), www.nytimes.com/2021/03/24/opinion/Democrats-Republicans-left-right-center-html?campaign_id=39&emc=edit_ty_20210324&instance_id=28416&nl=opinion-today®i_id74916964&segment_id=54077&te=1&user_id=58b05ad34dcf93812b4b475992a91a8f.
3. See Amy Guttman and Dennis C. Thompson, *The Spirit of Compromise* (Princeton: Princeton University Press, 2012), 63.
4. See Edsall, "We See the Left. We See the Right."
5. Ibid.
6. Garry Kasparov, "America's Mission," *Persuasion* (July 23, 2020), www.persuasion.community/p/americas-mission?token=eyJ1c2VyX2lkIjoxMjQzNjI5NywicG9zdF9pZCI6NzUxNjQ4LCJfIjoid3AvWmMiLCJpYXQiOjE2MDYxNzAwNDksImV4cCI6MTYwNjE3MzY0OSwiaXNzIjoicHViLTYxNTc5Iiwic3ViIjoicG9zdC1yZWFjdGlvbiJ9.fnY2Shuzw-fEHCHnZfJsaERNuLEheDNx4hMceDSQtZ8.

5 TRIMMING AND BALANCE

1. Halifax, *Complete Works*, ed. J. P. Kenyon (London: Penguin, 1969), 50.
2. Ibid.
3. Ibid., 209.
4. See Macaulay's description of Halifax in Macaulay, *Critical and Historical Essays*, vol. II (London: Longman, Brown, Green, and Longmans), 37–38.
5. On the relationship between trimming and moderation, see Aurelian Craiutu, *Faces of Moderation: The Art of Balance in an Age of*

Extremes (Philadelphia: University of Pennsylvania Press, 2017), 25–33; Michael Oakeshott, *The Politics of Faith and the Politics of Skepticism*, ed. Timothy Fuller (New Haven: Yale University Press, 1996), 121–29; Eugene Goodheart, *Holding the Center: In Defense of Political Trimming* (New Brunswick, NJ: Transactions Publishers, 2013).

6. See Joseph Hamburger, *Macaulay and the Whig Tradition* (New Haven: Yale University Press, 1976), 188.
7. Oakeshott, *The Politics of Faith and the Politics of Skepticism*, 120.
8. The phrase belongs to Macaulay and is taken from his speech on copyright (February 5, 1841) in the UK's House of Commons (*Speeches of the Right Honorable T.B. Macaulay*, vol. I [Leipzig: Bernhard Tauchnitz, 1853], 276).
9. See Albert Camus, *The Plague*, trans. Stuart Gilbert (New York: Vintage, 1948), 219.
10. David Brooks, "What Moderation Means," *New York Times* (October 25, 2012), www.nytimes.com/2012/10/26/opinion/brooks-what-moderation-means.html?nl=todaysheadlines&emc=edit_th_20121026&_r=0. See also Brooks, "In Praise of Equipoise," *New York Times* (September 1, 2017), www.nytimes.com/2017/09/01/opinion/in-praise-of-equipoise.html.
11. Halifax, *Complete Works*, 54.
12. See Martin Luther King Jr.'s sermon with this title in *Strength to Love* (Minneapolis: Fortress Press, 2010), 1–10.
13. Halifax, *Complete Works*, 86.

6 CENTRISM

1. W. B. Yeats, *Selected Poetry* (London: Macmillan, 1962), 99–100; Brink Lindsey et al., "The Center Can Hold: Public Policy for an Age of Extremes," *Niskanen Center* (2018), www.niskanencenter.org/the-center-can-hold-public-policy-for-an-age-of-extremes.
2. Here are Yeats' words: "Turning and turning in the widening gyre/ The falcon cannot hear the falconer;/Things fall apart; the centre cannot hold;/ Mere anarchy is loosed upon the world,/The blood-dimmed tide is loosed, and everywhere/ The ceremony of innocence

is drowned;/ The best lack all conviction, while the worst/ Are full of passionate intensity" (Yeats, *Selected Poetry*, 99–100).

3. John Patrick Leary, "The Third Way is a Death Trap," *The Jacobin* (August 3, 2018), https://jacobinmag.com/2018/08/centrism-democratic-party-lieberman-ocasio-cortez.
4. Ibid.
5. Alexander Hamilton, "The Examination XI" (February 3, 1802), in *The Papers of Alexander Hamilton*, vol. XXV, ed. Harold C. Syrett (New York: Columbia University Press, 1977), 514. Thanks to Bradford Wilson for bringing this passage to my attention.
6. Hume, *Essays*, 46.
7. See Charles Wheelan, *The Centrist Manifesto* (New York: W. W. Norton, 2013); his centrist strategy built around the US Senate is outlined on pp. 121–33. For a different position, see Ben Zhang, "Beyond Moderate," *Duke Chronicle* (January 12, 2017), www.dukechronicle.com/article/2017/01/beyond-moderate. See also Michelle Diggles and Lanae Erikson, "The State of the Center" (*Third Way*, May 15, 2014), www.thirdway.org/report/the-state-of-the-center.
8. This is the title of Arthur Schlesinger Jr.'s book originally published in 1949.
9. See, for example, Leary, "The Third Way is a Death Trap"; Luke Savage, "Centrists Aren't Political Realists. Leftists Are," *The Jacobin* (November 21, 2019), www.jacobinmag.com/2019/11/realism-pragmatism-barack-obama-centrist-democrats-green-new-deal-medicare-for-all; Osita Nwanevu, "Centrism is Dead," *Slate* (July 25, 2018), https://slate.com/news-and-politics/2018/07/third-ways-centrism-is-dead-the-left-has-already-won-the-debate-over-the-democratic-party.html; David Adler May, "Centrists Are the Most Hostile to Democracy, Not Extremists," *New York Times* (May 23, 2018), www.nytimes.com/interactive/2018/05/23/opinion/international-world/centrists-democracy.html?mtrref=www.google.com&assetType=PAYWALL&fbclid=IwAR0m3HvKhZ4h02QwNo65XtBcehKHxxdy9PCNw6mNrY5JbPRdWA5Sr0WsT9Y; Aaron Bastani, "Centrists Are Pining for a Golden Age That Never Was," *The Jacobin* (September 8, 2020), www.jacobinmag.com/2020/09/centrism-clinton-bush-party-politics?fbclid=IwAR0LZZYl4V2ubo08SokkGF-X9-wxgyH3PM0I-_Xu-5A-ltPaTxQtCtWBLzk.

10. See the recent studies of Morris Fiorina and John Shattuck as reported in Edsall, “We See the Left. We See the Right.”
11. Todd Gitlin, *Letters to a Young Activist* (New York: Basic Books, 2003), 147.
12. See Robinson, *What Are We Doing Here?* For a review of the book, see Aurelian Craiutu, “Marilynne Robinson and the Spirituality of Centrism,” *Daily Beast* (March 9, 2018), www.thedailybeast.com/marilynne-robinson-and-the-spirituality-of-centrism.
13. For a moderate defense of such an agenda, see Dan Edelstein, “In the Ruins of Western Civilization. Preserve – and Add to – the Mosaic of the Past,” *Hedgehog Review* (July 28, 2022), https://hedgehogreview.com/web-features/thr/posts/in-the-ruins-of-western-civilization?fbclid=IwAR2YtSNZVDrm7rOagg90AFUSYDX__FixMH4zLhzOPel1fjLJaksqVY95ph4.
14. See Lindsey et al., “The Center Can Hold,” 4ff.
15. Ibid., 7.
16. Beverly Gage, “The Political Center Isn’t Gone, Just Disputed,” *New York Times* (February 7, 2019), www.nytimes.com/2019/02/07/magazine/the-political-center-isnt-gone-just-disputed.html.
17. On this issue, see Karol Soltan, “Liberal Conservative Socialism and the Politics of a Complex Center,” *The Good Society*, 11:1 (2002), 19–22.
18. For a thoughtful conservative perspective that emphasizes similar things, see Roger Scruton, *Conservatism: An Invitation to the Great Tradition* (New York: St. Martin’s Press, 2018).

7 ECLECTICISM AND PLURALISM

1. Chesterfield, *Letters*, 260.
2. Montaigne, *The Complete Essays*, trans. M. A. Screech (London: Penguin, 1991), 380.
3. Amoz Oz, *How to Cure a Fanatic?* (Princeton: Princeton University Press, 2006), 54.
4. Wieseltier, “The Radical Liberal.” See also Daniel Bell, *The Cultural Contradictions of Capitalism* (New York: Basic Books, 1976), 259; Brooks, “In Praise of Equipoise.” For a concise and witty defense of eclecticism, see Leszek Kołakowski, “How to Be a Conservative-Liberal-Socialist: A Credo,” in *Modernity on Endless Trial* (Chicago: University of Chicago Press, 1990), 225–27.

5. See Daniel Bell, "The Revolt against Modernity," *National Affairs* (Fall 1985), https://www.nationalaffairs.com/public_interest/detail/the-revolt-against-modernity. See also Bell's statement in Benli M. Schechter, "Why Bell Matters," *Society*, 48 (2011) https://link.springer.com/article/10.1007/s12115-011-9461-4).
6. Bell, *The Cultural Contradictions of Capitalism*, 10.
7. See Scruton, *Conservatism*, 6.
8. See Josh Hammer, "Why the Right Needs More 'Muscular' and 'Masculine' Conservatism," www.newsweek.com/why-right-needs-more-muscular-masculine-conservatism-opinion-1655672. For a recent reassessment of fusionism in America, see the symposium "Liberty and Virtue: Frank Meyer's Fusionism," *Liberty Fund* (June 2021) https://oll.libertyfund.org/page/liberty-matters-frank-meyer-fusionism-stephanie-slade.
9. This was one of the leading ideas at the core of Elinor and Vincent Ostrom's writings. For more details, see Aurelian Craiutu, "In Praise of Eclecticism: Why Elinor and Vincent Ostrom's Works Matter," in *Ostrom's Tensions: Reexamining the Political Economy and Public Policy of Elinor C. Ostrom*, ed. Roberta Q. Herzberg, Paul Dragos Aligica, and Peter J. Boettke (Arlington, VA: Mercatus Center, George Mason University, 2019), 211–46.
10. This idea is at the core of the concept of polycentricity as developed by Vincent Ostrom in his seminal essay "Polycentricity: The Structural Basis of Self-Governing Systems," reprinted in *Choice, Rules, and Collective Action: The Ostroms on the Study of Institutions and Governance*, ed. Filippo Sabetti and Paul Dragos Aligica (Colchester: ECPR Press, 2014), 45–60.
11. See Vincent Ostrom, *The Meaning of Democracy and the Vulnerabilities of Democracies: A Response to Tocqueville's Challenge* (Ann Arbor, MI: University of Michigan Press, 1997).
12. Bell, *The Cultural Contradictions of Capitalism*, 277.

8 DIALOGUE

1. J. S. Mill, *On Liberty*, in *Utilitarianism, On Liberty, and Considerations on Representative Government*, ed. H. B. Acton (London; J. M. Dent & Sons, 1972), 97.

2. See Jonathan Rauch, *The Constitution of Knowledge* (Washington DC: Brookings Institution, 2021), 199.
3. Mill, *On Liberty*, 112–13.
4. Montaigne, *Complete Essays*, 1045–46.
5. Mill, *On Liberty*, 111.
6. See C. Thi Nguyen, "Escape the Echo Chamber," *Aeon* (April 9, 2018), https://aeon.co/essays/why-its-as-hard-to-escape-an-echo-chamber-as-it-is-to-flee-a-cult. He defines an "epistemic bubble" as "an informational network from which relevant voices have been excluded by omission."
7. Mill, *On Liberty*, 97–98.
8. Ibid., 107.
9. David Bohm as quoted in Maria Popova, "Legendary Physicist David Bohm on the Paradox of Communication, the Crucial Difference between Discussion and Dialogue, and What Is Keeping Us from Listening to One Another," *The Marginalian* (December 5, 2016), www.themarginalian.org/2016/12/05/david-bohm-on-dialogue.
10. See Rauch, *The Constitution of Knowledge*, 200–209; Gitlin, *Letters to a Young Activist*, 121–22.
11. Plutarch, *Selected Essays and Dialogues*, trans. Donald Russell (Oxford: Oxford University Press, 1993), 183, 187.
12. See Isaiah Berlin in conversation with Steven Lukes, *Salmagundi*, 120 (Fall 1998), 90.
13. This is the point made by Mill in *On Liberty*, ch. 2. See also Janan Ganesh, "The Lost Art of Doubt," *Financial Times* (August 14, 2020), www.ft.com/content/de843f6e-0be1-4667-8a9f-f397cf840e72?accessToken=zwAAAXQreVzAkdPehD9uC-FGZ9OKn_OXz4QOcg.MEUCIGDgcnd7PCjgrPyLKlnqUueKdiGhp2UNDpoaqt5HK6XqAiEApjduQGa4uztDhsqJON2tIl4L1eHbskcBT4l4pB8GKwo&sharetype=gift?token=af7b2545-a8a9-438f-864e-6509f3a9bd64.
14. Montaigne, *Complete Essays*, 1046.
15. See Vacláv Havel, *Summer Meditations* (New York: Vintage, 1992), 11.
16. Gitlin, *Letters to a Young Activist*, 134.

PART IV THE ETHOS OF MODERATION

1. Frédéric Bastiat, *Œuvres Complètes*, II (Paris: Guillemin, 1854), 348.

INTERMEZZO

1. Thomas Paine, Appendix to *Common Sense*, https://oll.libertyfund.org/title/paine-the-writings-of-thomas-paine-vol-i-1774-1779#lf0548-01_label_080.
2. See Albert Camus, *Camus at Combat: Writing 1944–1947*, ed. Jacqueline Lévi-Valensi, trans. Arthur Goldhammer (Princeton: Princeton University Press, 2006), 153.
3. Ibid., 155.
4. Ibid., 301.
5. Thomas Paine, *Collected Writings* (New York: The Library of America, 1995), 9.
6. See Theodore Roszak, *The Making of a Counter-culture: Reflections on the Technocratic Society and Its Youthful Opposition* (Garden City, NY: Doubleday, 1969), 22.
7. The words are attributed to Tom Hayden, whom Leo Rosten once described as "an early messiah" of the New Left in the 1960s. See Rosten, *A Trumpet for Reason* (New York: Doubleday, 1970), 21.
8. See James Aroosi, "Are You a Moderate? Think Again," *New York Times* (October 30, 2019), www.nytimes.com/2019/10/30/opinion/ethics-moderation-politics.html?action=click&module=Opinion&pgtype=Homepage&fbclid=IwAR02Cg-GDZ7Ocz3Hiq4ePfvP3WZ6PtsjO36Sf_iap1bNoP46gTm1iMvNdpw.
9. The first use of the term "radicalism" was recorded in 1819 in England, where the group of the Philosophic Radicals upheld the doctrine called philosophic radicalism. Later, the term came to also mean unconventional and difficult to control. For more information, see www.etymonline.com/word/radical.
10. See Rob Goodman, "Hey, Democrats, Fighting Fair Is for Suckers," *Politico* (July 4, 2018), www.politico.com/magazine/story/2018/07/04/democrats-majority-rules-norms-trump-2020-218947.
11. R. H. Lossin, "In Defense of Destroying Property," *The Nation* (June 10, 2020), www.thenation.com/article/activism/blm-looting-protest-vandalism.
12. Sohrab Ahmari, "Against David French-ism," *First Things* (May 29, 2019), www.firstthings.com/web-exclusives/2019/05/against-david-french-ism.

13. Ibid.
14. P. J. O'Rourke, "This Is Why Millennials Adore Socialism," *NY Post* (September 12, 2020), https://nypost.com/2020/09/12/pj-orourke-this-is-why-millennials-adore-socialism.
15. See David Brooks, "The Chaos after Trump," *New York Times* (March 5, 2018), www.nytimes.com/2018/03/05/opinion/the-chaos-after-trump.html.
16. See Ibram Kendi's claim quoted in "Out of the Academy," *The Economist* (September 4, 2021), 16.
17. Alexandra Ocasio-Cortez as quoted in Miles Kampf-Lassin, "Bernie Sanders and Alexandria Ocasio-Cortez Are Pushing a Bold New Plan to Tackle Climate Change," *In These Times* (December 4, 2018), http://inthesetimes.com/article/21615/bernie-sanders-alexandria-ocasio-cortez-climate-town-hall-green-new-deal.
18. Luke Savage, "The Nihilism of Moderation," *The Jacobin* (December 6, 2018), https://jacobinmag.com/2018/12/the-nihilism-of-moderation-climate-change-beltway-centrism.
19. See Kaufman, *The Radical Liberal*.
20. Wesley Lowery as quoted in "Inside the Revolts Erupting in America's Big Newsrooms," *New York Times* (June 7, 2020), www.nytimes.com/2020/06/07/business/media/new-york-times-washington-post-protests.html.
21. See Damon Linker, "How Twitter Can Be the Death of Liberal Democracy," *The Week* (January 22, 2019), https://theweek.com/articles/818951/how-twitter-could-death-liberal-democracy; and "Our Dangerous Addiction to Political Hyperbole, *The Week* (February 19, 2019), https://theweek.com/articles/824408/dangerous-addiction-political-hyperbole?fbclid=IwAR381juUOGr1NCZOUCEHlD_1-HiuU5fwUuhHRXzM2IfznVTfoU-xsl8q1f4). See also Rauch, *The Constitution of Knowledge*, chs. 5–6.
22. Lossin, "In Defense of Destroying Property.". See also Savage, "Centrists Aren't Political Realists. Leftists Are."
23. Savage, "Centrists Aren't Political Realists. Leftists Are."
24. Montaigne, *Complete Essays*, 1258–59.
25. Ibid., 1261.
26. Montesquieu, *The Spirit of the Laws*, trans. Anne M. Cohler et al. (Cambridge: Cambridge University Press, 1989), 595.

27. Adam Smith, *Theory of Moral Sentiments*, eds. D. D. Raphael and A. L. Macfie (Indianapolis: Liberty Fund, 1982), 155.
28. For a similar point, see Alexis de Tocqueville, *The Old Regime and the Revolution*, trans. Alan S. Kahan, vol. II (Chicago: University of Chicago Press, 2001), 30.

1 THE SPIRIT OF MODERATION

1. *The Spirit of Liberty, Papers, and Addresses of Learned Hand*, ed. Irving Dilliard (New York: Vintage, 1959), 144.
2. See also Erasmus–Luther, *Discourse on Free Will*, trans. Ernst F. Winter (New York: Continuum, 1996).
3. Bertrand Russell as quoted in Maria Popova, "The Will to Doubt," *The Marginalian* (May 18, 2016), www.brainpickings.org/2016/05/18/bertrand-russell-free-thought-propaganda-doubt. See also Peter L. Berger and Anton C. Zijderveld, *In Praise of Doubt: How to Have Convictions without Becoming a Fanatic* (New York: HarperOne, 2009).
4. The way in which I understand the spirit of liberalism is akin to Andrew Sullivan's perspective in "Is There Still Room for Debate?."
5. See Carl Sagan, *The Demon-Haunted World: Science As a Candle in the Dark* (1996), as quoted in Maria Popova, "The Baloney Detection Kit," *The Marginalian* (January 3, 2014), https://getpocket.com/explore/item/the-baloney-detection-kit-carl-sagan-s-rules-for-bullshit-busting-and-critical-thinking?utm_source=pocket-newtab.
6. Ibid.

2 MODESTY AND HUMILITY

1. Pascal, *Pensées*, trans. A. J. Krailsheimer (London: Penguin, 1995), 184–85.
2. See André Comte-Sponville, *A Small Treatise on the Great Virtues: The Uses of Philosophy in Everyday Life*, trans. Catherine Temerson (New York: Henry Holt & Co./Metropolitan, 2002), 141.
3. See Desiderius Erasmus, *Praise of Folly and Letter to Martin Dorp*, trans. Betty Radice (Harmondsworth: Penguin, 1971), 231. See also the definition of humility given by Iris Murdoch in *The Sovereignty of the Good* (1970), as quoted in Costica Bradatan, "Everyone Fails, but Only

the Wise Find Humility," *Aeon* (August 18, 2016), https://aeon.co/ideas/everyone-fails-but-only-the-wise-find-humility. On the connection between humility and simplicity, see Comte-Sponville, *A Small Treatise on the Great Virtues*, 149–56.

4. Here is what Gandhi wrote: "What do you think? Wherein is courage required – in blowing others to pieces from behind a cannon, or with a smiling face to approach a cannon and be blown to pieces? Who is the true warrior – he who keeps death always as a bosom-friend, or he who controls the death of others? Believe me that a man devoid of courage and manhood can never be a passive resister" (Mahatma Gandhi, *Hind Swaraj or Indian Home Rule*, www.mkgandhi.org, p. 72).
5. See Jonathan Sacks, "On Humility," www.chabad.org/library/article_cdo/aid/83807/jewish/On-Humility.htm.
6. Ibid.
7. Here is what a great novelist (Hermann Hesse) wrote about this: "Moderate enjoyment is double enjoyment. . . . The ability to cherish 'the little joy' is intimately connected with the habit of moderation. For this ability, originally natural to every man, presupposed certain things which in modern daily life have largely become obscured or lost, mainly a measure of cheerfulness, of love, and of poesy" (Hermann Hesse, "On Little Joys" [1905], in *My Belief: Essays on Life and Art*, trans. Denver Lindley and Ralph Manheim [New York: Farrar, Straus, and Giroux, 1974], 899).
8. See Vladimir Jankelevitch, *Traité des vertus*, vol. II (Paris: Champs-Flammarion, 1986), 289.
9. See www.bbc.com/travel/article/20170818-the-swedish-word-thats-displacing-hygge.
10. Niki Brantmark, *Lagom: The Swedish Art of Living a Balanced, Happy Life* (New York: Harper Design, 2017), 281.
11. See David McPherson, *The Virtue of Limits* (Oxford: Oxford University Press, 2022), 119–25.
12. These guidelines are connected to the law of Jante or *Jantelag*, a term coined by the Swedish writer Aksel Sandemose, in his 1933 novel *A Fugitive Crosses His Tracks*, from which I adapted them for the present purpose.

13. *The Doctrine of the Mean*, in *Confucian Analects, The Great Learning, and the Doctrine of the Mean*, trans. James Legge (New York: Dover, 1971), 390.
14. See Erasmus, *Praise of Folly and Letter to Martin Dorp*, 105.

3 CIVILITY

1. Albert Camus, *Between Hell and Reason: Essays from the Resistance Newspaper Combat, 1944–1947*, trans. Alexandre de Gramont (Hanover, NH: Wesleyan University Press, 1991).
2. Ahmari, "Against David French-ism."
3. See Michael Gerson, "America Is Hacking away at Its Own Democratic Limb," *Washington Post* (June 29, 2017), www.washingtonpost.com/opinions/america-is-hacking-away-at-its-own-democratic-limb/2017/06/29/d5210204-5cea-11e7-9fc6-c7ef4bc58d13_story.html.
4. See Peter H. Schuck, *Meditations of a Militant Moderate: Cool Views on a Hot Topic* (Lanham, MD: Rowman & Littlefield, 2006), 209–13.
5. Earl of Shaftesbury, *Characteristicks of Men, Manners, Opinions, Times*, ed. Douglas den Uyl, vol. I (Indianapolis: Liberty Fund, 2001), 42.
6. Ahmari, "Against David French-ism."
7. David Azerrad, "Trump's Manliness," *The American Mind* (November 7, 2018), https://americanmind.org/features/thinking-about-thinking-about-trump/trumps-manliness.
8. Ryan Williams, "Power and Principle," *The American Mind* (April 6, 2021), https://americanmind.substack.com/p/power-and-principle.
9. See Teresa Bejan, *Mere Civility* (Cambridge, MA: Harvard University Press, 2016), Susan Herbst, *Rude Democracy: Civility and Incivility in American Politics* (Philadelphia: Temple University Press, 2010), 6–10; Stephen L. Carter, *Civility: Manners, Morals, and the Etiquette of Democracy* (New York: HarperCollins, 1999).

4 PRUDENCE

1. Gracián, *The Art of Worldly Wisdom*, 135.

2. From a letter of Nietzsche to Peter Gast (1884), as quoted in Christopher Maurer's "Introduction" to Baltasar Gracián, *The Art of Worldly Wisdom: A Pocket Oracle*, vi.
3. See Baltasar Gracián, *A Pocket Mirror for Heroes*, trans. Christopher Maurer (New York: Doubleday, 1996), 3.
4. Gracián, *The Art of Worldly Wisdom*, 141–42.
5. Edmund Burke, *Selected Writings and Speeches*, ed. Peter Stanlis (New York: Doubleday Anchor, 1963), 201.
6. This idea appears in Gracián's *El Criticón*. See also Gracián, *A Pocket Mirror for Heroes*, ix.
7. For more information, see www.titian.org/an-allegory-of-prudence.jsp; www.artinsociety.com/titian-prudence-and-the-three-headed-beast.html.
8. Gracián, *A Pocket Mirror for Heroes*, 107.
9. Gracián, *The Art of Worldly Wisdom*, 101.
10. See Thomas Aquinas, *The Cardinal Virtues: Prudence, Justice, Fortitude, and Temperance*, trans. Richard J. Regan (Indianapolis: Hackett, 2005), 10–11.
11. See Gracián, *The Art of Worldly Wisdom*, 51.
12. Burke, *Further Reflections on the Revolution in France*, 91.
13. Burke, "Conciliation with America," in Edmund Burke, *Pre-revolutionary Writings*, ed. Ian Harris (Cambridge: Cambridge University Press, 1993), 257. See also ibid., 148–49.

5 REALISM AND PRAGMATIC PARTISANSHIP

1. Montaigne, *Complete Essays*, 1144.
2. H. L. Mencken, *Prejudices. A Selection*, ed. James T. Farrell (New York: Vintage, 1958), 169.
3. See the interview with Thomas Chatterton Williams, *Financial Times* (October 1, 2021), www.ft.com/content/1bf6a540-0a7c-427f-9eea-b756acb81813.

4. David Azerrad, "Trump's Manliness," *The American Mind* (November 7, 2018), https://americanmind.org/features/thinking-about-thinking-about-trump/trumps-manliness.
5. See Montaigne, *Complete Essays*, 1040–69.
6. See Albert O. Hirschman, *A Propensity to Self-Subversion* (Cambridge, MA: Harvard University Press, 1998). See also Cyrille Ferraton and Ludovic Frobert, "A Self-Subversive Temperament: A Portrait of Albert Hirschman," *Books and Ideas* (July 23, 2014), https://booksandideas.net/A-Self-Subversive-Temperament.html.
7. Burke, *Further Reflections on the Revolution in France*, 16.

PART V: WHO NEEDS MODERATION TODAY?

1. Hermann Hesse, *Magister Ludi*, trans. Meryn Savill (New York: Frederick Ungar, 1949), 327.

THE LAST BEACON OF HOPE?

1. Turgot to Richard Price, in Price, *Observations on the Importance of the American Revolution and the Means of Making It a Benefit to the World* (Dublin: White, Whitestone, Bryne, & Co. 1785), 123.
2. Tocqueville, *Democracy in America*, I: 28.
3. H. L. Mencken, "On Being an American," in Mencken, *Prejudices. A Selection*, 123.
4. "The 1619 Project Exposed."
5. Lincoln, "House Divided Speech" (June 16, 1858), www.abrahamlincolnonline.org/lincoln/speeches/house.htm.
6. For the meaning of these terms, see David Brooks, *Bobos in Paradise: The New Upper Class and How They Got There* (New York; Simon & Schuster, 2000) and Charles Murray, *Breaking Apart: The State of White America* (New York: Crown Forum, 2012). See also Aurelian Craiutu, "Against Identity Politics," *The Modern Age* (January 2018), https://isi.org/modern-age/against-identity-politics.
7. See Jonathan Rauch, "Rethinking Polarization," *National Affairs*, 41 (Fall 2019), www.nationalaffairs.com/publications/detail/rethinking-polarization.

8. See Thomas Friedman, "Wanted: Fanatical Moderates," *New York Times* (November 16, 2003), www.google.com/url?sa=t&rct=j&q=&esrc=s&source=web&cd=&cad=rja&uact=8&ved=2ahUKEwjRhcjQ4ar1AhWvq3IEHX_oC2EQFnoECAYQAQ&url=https%3A%2F%2Fwww.nytimes.com%2F2003%2F11%2F16%2Fopinion%2Fwanted-fanatical-moderates.html&usg=AOvVaw2pIVYtT5KL1jpq8mekmKYZ.
9. Savage, "Centrists Aren't Political Realists. Leftists Are."
10. Marina Tsvetayeva, "I Know the Truth," www.rjgeib.com/thoughts/tsvetayeva/tsvetayeva.html.
11. See Brown, *Moderates: The Vital Center of American Politics from the Founding to Today*; Michael A. Smerconish, *Clowns to the Left of Me, Jokers to the Right: American Life in Columns* (Philadelphia: Temple University Press, 2018), esp. 204–207; and Kabaservice, *Rule and Ruin.*
12. See William Galston and Elaine C. Kamarck, "The Still-Vital Center: Moderates, Democrats, and the Renewal of American Politics," *Third Way* (February 23, 2011), www.thirdway.org/report/the-still-vital-center-moderates-democrats-and-the-renewal-of-american-politics.
13. See ibid.
14. Steven Teles and Robert Saldin, "The Future is Faction," *Niskanen Center* (November 25, 2019), www.niskanencenter.org/the-future-is-faction.
15. Smerconish, *Clowns to the Left of Me, Jokers to the Right*, 205–206.
16. Klein, "No One Is Less Moderate Than Moderates."
17. On the radicalization of the mass media, see Martin Gurri, "The Fall and Rise of Mediators," *Discourse Magazine* (November 8, 2021), www.discoursemagazine.com/culture-and-society/2021/11/08/the-fall-and-rise-of-the-mediators.
18. https://centerforpolitics.org/crystalball/articles/new-initiative-explores-deep-persistent-divides-between-biden-and-trump-voters.
19. *A Mencken Chrestomathy*, edited and annotated by the author (New York: Vintage Books, 1982), vii.
20. Mishra, "Grand Illusions."
21. Enzo Traverso, "We Can Only Go Beyond Communism by Coming to Terms With Its History," *The Jacobin* (December 26, 2021), https://jacobinmag.com/2021/12/communism-history-october-revolution-soviet-union-anti-colonialism-social-democracy?fbclid=IwA

R3ItB-wK5XCzYU13vj2h1WOWXDU0BtCx7HQ4L9pvvORnlG60erwyi7xRm4.

22. See Yuval Levin, *The Fractured Republic: Renewing America's Social Contract in an Age of Individualism* (New York: Basic Books, 2017).
23. Various authors, "Against the Dead Consensus," *First Things* (March 21, 2019), www.firstthings.com/web-exclusives/2019/03/against-the-dead-consensus. See also R. R. Reno, "Policies Are Not Principles," *New Criterion* (January 2022), https://newcriterion.com/issues/2022/1/policies-are-not-principles.
24. Josh Hammer, "The Only Path Forward Is National Conservatism," *The American Conservative* (November 5, 2021), www.theamericanconservative.com/articles/the-only-path-forward-is-national-conservatism; Ahmari, "Against David French-ism."
25. For more information about the Moderate Party in Sweden, see https://web.archive.org/web/20070209182955/www.riksdagen.se/templates/R_SubStartPage_12076.aspx.
26. See https://ballotpedia.org/Moderate_Party.
27. Martin O'Neill, "Against Incrementalism," *Boston Review* (August 18, 2021), https://bostonreview.net/articles/against-incrementalism.
28. This section draws upon and develops a few arguments presented in Aurelian Craiutu and Constantine Vassiliou, "In Search of a New Balance," *Niskanen Center* (February 3, 2021), www.niskanencenter.org/in-search-of-a-new-balance. The ideas developed and reformulated here reflect my own views and I am solely responsible for them.
29. For more information about these organizations, see https://braverangels.org/what-we-do/#red-blue; https://braverangels.org/what-we-do/red-blue-pairs; https://braverangels.org/our-story/; https://americanexchangeproject.org; https://heterodoxacademy.org; www.nolabels.org; www.moreincommon.com. For a recent book outlining a strategy of depolarization that draws on the examples of these organizations, see Peter T. Coleman, *The Way Out: How to Overcome Toxic Polarization* (New York: Columbia University Press, 2021).
30. Ibid., 138. For more information about "Hidden Tribes," see https://hiddentribes.us.

31. For more details, see Stephen Hawkins et al., "Hidden Tribes: A Study of America's Polarized Landscape" (2018), https://hiddentribes.us/media/qfpekz4g/hidden_tribes_report.pdf; ch. 6 describes the "exhausted majority" and the moderates.
32. See Daniel Neuhauser, "The Mod Squad," *Persuasion* (March 22, 2021), www.persuasion.community/p/the-mod-squad.
33. See, for example, Rick Bayan's "The New Moderate Action Plan," http://newmoderate.com/manifesto. See also www.usamoderateparty.org/platform.html.
34. See Teles and Saldin, "The Future is Faction." As Jonathan Rauch pointed out, as "parties weaken as institutions, whose members are united by loyalty to their organization . . . they strengthen as tribes, whose members are united by hostility to their enemy" (Rauch, "Rethinking Polarization").
35. Wheelan, *The Centrist Manifesto,* 126. For another concrete political agenda, see Schuck, *Meditations of a Militant Moderate,* 214–19.
36. For two examples of moderate agendas along similar lines, see Kasparov, "America's Mission"; Ronald W. Dworkin, "A Moderate's Manifesto," *The American Purpose* (November 11, 2020), www.americanpurpose.com/articles/a-moderates-manifesto/?fbclid=IwAR29GTimwNTiCEtOCyJY_GWqHGyoyqhsV2bvHaKMw18FE5m9g3vGFzIoF58.
37. Brooks, "Moderates Have the Better Story," *New York Times,* July 1, 2019, www.nytimes.com/2019/07/01/opinion/moderates-progressives-warren.html?smid=nytcore-ios-share&referringSource=articleShare. See also Jonathan Haidt and Greg Lukianoff, "The Polarization Spiral," *Persuasion* (October 29, 2021), www.persuasion.community/p/haidt-and-lukianoff-the-polarization.

EPILOGUE

1. Camus, *Between Hell and Reason:* 118.
2. Ibid.
3. "A Letter on Justice and Open Debate," *Harper's Magazine* (July 7, 2020), https://harpers.org/a-letter-on-justice-and-open-debate. On this issue, see also Anne Applebaum, "The New Puritans," *The*

Atlantic (October 2021), www.theatlantic.com/magazine/archive/2021/10/new-puritans-mob-justice-canceled/619818.

4. See Steven Levitsky and Daniel Ziblatt, *How Democracies Die* (New York: Crown, 2018).
5. Saul D. Alinsky, *Rules for Radicals: A Pragmatic Primer for Realistic Radicals* (New York: Vintage, 1971).
6. Seneca, *Epistles 1–65*, trans. Richard M. Gummere (Cambridge: Harvard University Press, 2002), 81.
7. On *satyagraha*, see Mohandas K. Gandhi, *Autobiography: The Story of My Experiments with Truth*, trans. Mahadev Desai (New York: Dover, 1983), 242, 284–88, 293–97, 298, 306–8.
8. Cicero, *On Duties*, 55.
9. Chesterfield, *Letters*, 133.
10. See Damon Linker, "If You Think Another Civil War Is Imminent, Get Off Twitter," *The Week* (September 26, 2018), https://theweek.com/articles/798002/think-another-civil-war-imminent-twitter.
11. Marcus Aurelius, *Meditations*, trans. Maxwell Staniforth (London: The Folio Society, 2002), 122.
12. See Bertrand Russell, "Philosophy and Politics," in *Unpopular Essays* (New York: Simon and Schuster, 1969), 15.
13. See Adam Michnik, "Gray Is Beautiful: A Letter to Ira Katznelson," in Michnik, *Letters from Freedom: Post-Cold War Realities and Perspectives*, ed. Irena Grudzińska Gross (Princeton: Princeton University Press, 1998), 317–27.
14. Gandhi, *Autobiography*, 160.
15. Chesterfield, *Letters*, 179.

ACKNOWLEDGMENTS

1. For more details, see www.niskanencenter.org/beyond-left-and-right-reviving-moderation-in-an-era-of-crisis-and-extremism.

Index

Note: Several concepts such as America, democracy, dialogue, equality, ideology, justice, liberty, moderates, moderation, politics, radical, and radicalism appear frequently in the text and are indexed only in connection with the main themes of the book. Most sources cited in the endnotes are not indexed, unless specific references are made to them that are relevant to the arguments of the present volume.